The K

Cookery

and

Household Guide

The Kenya Cookery Book

and
Household Guide

COMPILED BY
MEMBERS OF ST. ANDREW'S
CHURCH WOMAN'S GUILD
NAIROBI

HEINEMANN KENYA
NAIROBI

Published by
Heinemann Kenya Ltd.,
Brick Court
Mpaka Road/Woodvale Grove
Westlands
P.O. Box 45314
Nairobi.

ISBN 9966 46 108 6

First published 1928
Twelfth edition 1958
Thirteenth edition, published by
Heinemann Kenya Ltd. 1970

Reprinted 1972/75/79/83/87/89/91

Printed by Kenya Litho Ltd., P.O. Box 40775,Changamwe Road, Nairobi, Kenya.

CONTENTS

ACKNOWLEDGEMENTS

Unga Ltd.

Shell Afrigas.

Kenya Dairy Board.

Low and Bonar (E.A.) Ltd.

Public Health Dept., Nairobi City Council.

K.S.P.C.A.

APPRECIATION

The publishers wish to record their appreciation of the help and advice given by Mrs. E. S. Logie, Chairman of the Woman's Guild Cookery Book Committee, and her two colleagues in preparing this edition.

PREFACE

Members of a small committee of St. Andrew's Church Woman's Guild, Nairobi, have completely revised and brought up to date the old *Kenya Settlers' Cookery Book* and now present it as *The Kenya Cookery Book and Household Guide.*

The first edition was published in 1928 by St. Andrew's Woman's Guild in response to many requests from up-country housewives and in 1958 the 12th edition was published. Last year serious thought was given to the discontinuation of its publication but owing to a great demand, the Woman's Guild has prepared this 13th edition, the first to be published by Heinemann Educational Books.

It is sincerely hoped that this new and revised form of the old cookery book will prove even more useful and popular with all cooks and housewives in Kenya and in other parts of the world.

Many members of St. Andrew's Church, Nairobi, past and present, have given their well-tried recipes and assistance in compiling the book and have helped in distributing previous editions. To all of them (too many to mention by name) the Guild's grateful thanks and sincere appreciation is now recorded.

TERMS USED IN THIS BOOK

Bake   To cook in dry heat in the oven.

Baste   To cover food with liquid or melted fat at intervals in order to flavour and moisten.

Beat   To mix vigorously with a wooden spoon or egg whisk.

Bind   To use a small quantity of liquid to make the dry ingredients stick together firmly.

Blanch   To put an article in cold water, bring to boil, strain (skin if necessary) then use as directed.

Blend   To mix together slowly.

Boil   To cook in a liquid. Boiling point is reached when bubbles rise and break over the surface.

Braise   To stew.

Cayenne   Red pepper.

Cream   To beat a mixture until it is of the consistency of cream.

Croûtons or Croûtes   Small pieces of fried or toasted bread cut into dice shapes.

Dice   To cut into small cubes.

D'oyley   A fancy paper or plastic mat placed on a plate.

Dough   A mass of moistened flour or maize meal.

Fillet   A special cut of meat or fish.

Fillet   To remove skin and bones of fish and cut lengthwise.

Flake   To break up with a fork into shreds.

Fry   To cook in oil or fat.

Garnish   To decorate.

Grate   To make into small shreds on a grater.

Knead   To press with the knuckles to form a dough.

Mash   To beat or crush to pulp.

Mince   To cut into small pieces with a knife or mincer.

Paprika   Hungarian red pepper.

Parboil   To boil for only part of the necessary time.

Sauté   To fry in fat without browning, covering pan with a lid.

Scald   To pour boiling water over, or, to heat a liquid such as milk to just under boiling point.

Simmer   To cook slowly, just below boiling point.

Singe   To burn over the surface.

Whip   To beat to a froth.

Whisk   To beat quickly.

WEIGHTS AND MEASUREMENTS

Metric Units

In this book quantities are given in both metric and Imperial units. In converting from one system to the other attention has been paid to the convenience of the housewife in purchasing and measuring. For example, where 500 grams are likely to be bought instead of 1 lb. (453.59 grams), other weights have been adjusted in proportion.

Where weights have been adjusted in this way, liquid measures have been increased in the proportion that 1 pint (568 ml.) becomes 600 ml. Alternatively, if a liquid such as cream is likely to be bought in, say, 250 millilitre cartons rather than as ½ pint, then weights have been generally reduced. As far as seems reasonable, without affecting the recipes, quantities have been rounded off for convenience of measurement. For example, the cook will not be required to measure 28.3 grams for one ounce but either 30 g. or 25 g.

The use of two bases (solid and liquid) mentioned above leads to the apparent inconsistency that a particular weight in the Imperial system is not always given the same equivalent in metric measure. This of course does not matter where the cook is using only the metric units.

Usually other quantities such as tablespoonfuls, numbers of eggs or pinches have remained the same for both systems since the difference in quantities does not justify any alteration. However, where the weights have been increased in the metric quantities the cook should be slightly more generous in the spoonfuls of other ingredients and use large sooner than small eggs or fruits.

Abbreviations

C.	Centigrade	l.	litre
cm.	centimetre	lb.	pound
F.	Fahrenheit	ml.	millilitre
g.	gram.	mm.	millimetre
		oz.	ounce

Approximate Weights and Measures

It is advisable to have a set of accurate scales in every kitchen but if this is not possible then the table below is a useful guide.

Use the *same* cup and spoons for all the ingredients which go into one recipe.

1 saltspoon	= ¼ teaspoon
4 teaspoons	= 1 tablespoon
5 tablespoons	= 1 teacup of fluid = ¼ pint = 150 ml.
10 tablespoons	= 1 breakfastcup of fluid = ½ pint = 300 ml.
1 teacup of flour	= ¼ lb. = 125 g.
1 tablespoon of flour	= 1 oz. = 30 g.
1 tablespoon of butter	= 2.5 cm. (1 inch) cube = 1 oz. = 30 g.
2 tablespoons of butter (size of medium egg)	= 2 oz. = 60 g.
1 tablespoon of syrup, treacle or jam	= 2 oz. = 60 g.

For heavy ingredients such as sugar, use a little less.
For lighter ingredients such as coconut or breadcrumbs use a little more.
A rounded spoonful means as much above as below.
A level spoonful means scraping off excess with a knife.

OVEN CHART FOR BAKING

	Electric °C.	Electric °F.	Gas with Thermostatic control	Gas without Thermostatic control
Very hot oven	230-260	450-500	Nos. 10-11 ⎫	Tap full on
Hot oven	200-230	400-450	Nos. 9-10 ⎪ Tap	Tap ¾ on
Fairly hot oven	175-200	350-400	Nos. 8 ⎬ full	Tap between ½-¾ on
Moderately hot oven	150-175	300-350	Nos. 6-7 ⎪ on	Tap ½ on
Slow oven	120-150	250-300	Nos. 3-5 ⎭	

Simple Test for Temperature for Other Types of Ovens

1. Heat the oven.
2. Place a piece of white kitchen paper in the oven for 3 minutes.
3. If the paper is
   - (a) Black—the oven is too hot.
   - (b) Deep brown—the oven is very hot.
   - (c) Golden brown—the oven is hot.
   - (d) Light brown—the oven is moderately hot.
   - (e) Light biscuit—the oven is slow.

HINTS ON ELECTRIC COOKERS

General

1. Use heavy type saucepans with ground-flat bases on the enclosed boiling plate.

2. Use broad-based utensils for speed which will cover the whole of the surface of the boiling plate.

3. Two or three pans, according to size, can be kept simmering on one plate. Specially shaped pans are available.

4. Place the utensils on the boiling plate **before** switching on the heat.

5. Always use a boiling plate in preference to a grill boiler unless grill is in use or is hot from previous use.

6. Save electricity. The normal enclosed boiling plate will continue boiling operations for 10 minutes after switching off.

7. Watch the thermometer and the clock. Do not overheat the oven or cook at too high a temperature.

8. Use an electric iron. It is inadvisable to heat non-electric irons on a boiling plate.

9. Use an electric kettle for boiling small quantities of water.

Oven

1. Arrange oven shelves according to the type of food to be cooked.

2. Switch on FULL heat.

3. Leave on FULL heat until required temperature is obtained.

4. Place food in oven and turn switch to LOW position for cooking. Do **not** leave switch at HIGH for any length of time after the food is put into the oven.

5. Watch the thermometer and the clock and do not open the oven door frequently.

6. Turn oven switch OFF **for the last 20-30 minutes**.

7. Fill oven to capacity whenever possible.

8. A fully loaded oven should be given 50 degrees higher initial temperature to allow for the temperature drop caused by heat absorbed by the larger quantity of food put into the oven. But do not subsequently maintain this temperature during cooking.

Use of Boiling Plates

1. Bring liquid to boiling point with switch at FULL heat.

2. Turn switch to LOW to keep liquid boiling.

3. To simmer turn switch to LOW before liquid reaches boiling point.

4. Use a small amount of water for cooking vegetables and keep the saucepans covered.

Use of Grill Boiler

1. This is a double-purpose plate. The top surface resembles the enclosed type of boiling plate and the element which is encased below gives even heat downwards for grilling and upwards for boiling at the same time.
2. Place deflector plate under grill when using the top of the plate for boiling or cooking girdle scones.
3. When the food on the top of the plate is nearly cooked remove deflector plate. Turn switch to FULL to heat grill for 2–3 minutes before toasting or grilling.
4. Place food in grill pan underneath grill and use fat sparingly so that the food does not become dry.
5. Brown food on each side and then turn switch to LOW to cook
6. Turn switch OFF as soon as food is cooked.
7. Replace deflector plate and if necessary continue cooking on top of the grill boiler with switch at MEDIUM or LOW as required.

Care of Cooker after use

1. Always switch off the Main Control Switch.
2. Wipe over all enamel or paint with a damp (not wet) cloth.
3. Clean underneath hob and under hot cupboard.
4. Wipe inside of oven whilst still hot.
5. Clean and polish deflector plate.
6. Rub a very little grease over hotplates to prevent rusting.
7. Remove oven shelves for cleaning when necessary.

Pressure Cookery

Pressure cookery is cookery by steam pressure in a heavy saucepan with an airtight lid and safety valve.

Today there is an extensive range of Pressure Cookers in designs and sizes for large or small families.

The modern, compact, streamlined saucepan is easy to handle and to clean.

Pressure cooking saves time and labour and fuel costs are cut by 70%. It is specially useful for foods which take a long time, such as beetroot, tongue or ham.

When buying any type of Pressure Cooker always ask for a Booklet of Instructions and Recipes which will help you to get the best results from your particular type.

Gas Cookery

Gas provides a clean and reliable form of heat for cooking and there is a wide range of appliances available ranging from small table top models to large cookers.

The housewife should take the following precautions to ensure safety in the home:—

1. Fusable plugs and bursting discs should not be fitted to cylinders.

2. (a) Containers should be handled in the vertical position always.

(b) The containers must not be installed below ground level, nor should they be installed near any source of heat such as boilers or furnaces.

(c) When connecting up your new cylinders, a new washer must be fitted. Ensure that the regulator nut is properly tightened. The thread is anti-clockwise.

(d) Containers must not be changed near naked flames.

(e) Should the installation not be in use for any length of time, the gas should be turned off at the container valve.

(f) Since an empty cylinder is still full of gas vapours, it is essential, after the cylinder has been disconnected, that the valve be turned to the "off" position and the safety cap replaced before storing the cylinder away.

(g) If gas is smelled, turn the cylinder's valve to the "off" position and open windows and doors to allow circulation of air to drive out the gas. Gas is heavier than air and consequently will sink to floor level. A current of air must be created which will be quite sufficient to disperse the gas.

3. When lighting a burner have the lighted match ready before turning on the tap.

4. When containers are stored outside, care should be taken to:

(a) provide them with clear dry standing

(b) prevent access by unauthorised persons

(c) prevent accidental damage by vehicles.

Cooking at High Altitudes

Boiling point of water is 100°C. at sea level
212°F. at sea level

Boiling point is reduced by one degree centigrade for every 1,000 feet altitude:

e.g. At 5,000 ft. boiling point is 95°C.

At 5,000 ft. boiling point is 203°F.

Baking at High Altitudes

As the air is lighter the pressure inside a cake should be decreased by slightly reducing the amount of baking powder. If the same amount of baking powder is used then slightly more binding material such as flour and eggs should be used to keep the gas in after it has been formed.

FOODS REQUIRED BY THE BODY

Name of Food Substance	*Food in which found*
Protein (To build the body, to repair tissue, to give heat and energy.)	
(a) Animal protein	Meat, poultry, game, fish, cheese, eggs and milk.
(b) Vegetable protein	Pulse foods, nuts, unpolished cereals, brown flour, potatoes.
Carbohydrates (To give heat and energy, to help utilise the fat.)	
(a) Starch	Cereals, grain, some root vegetables, especially potatoes.
(b) Sugar	Sugar, treacle, syrup, honey, beetroot, fruit, milk.
Fats (To give heat and energy, to provide for future use by storing it.)	
(a) Animal fat	Butter, cream, cheese, lard, dripping, fat of meat, fat of oily fish.
(b) Vegetable fat	Nut oils, vegetable oils, olive oil.
Mineral Matter	
(a) Sodium (To assist the fluid of the body in its work.)	Common salt.
(b) Potassium (To assist the cells of the body in their work.)	Vegetables and fruit.
(c) Calcium (To strengthen tissues and bones.)	Milk, cheese, eggs, greens, nuts.
(d) Phosphorus (To strengthen nerves and bones.)	Milk, cheese, eggs, fish, liver, sweet-bread and wholemeal flour.

(e) Iron (To assist the red colouring in the blood.)

Liver, meat, pulse food, greens, raisins, prunes, oatmeal, wholemeal flour, parsley.

(f) Iodine (To help in the work of the thyroid gland.)

Fish, watercress, iodised salt.

Water (To purify the blood, to carry away waste matter, to form tissue.)

All foods.

Roughage (To prevent constipation, to protect the body from ill-health.)

Vegetables, fruit, oatmeal, wholemeal flour.

Vitamins

Vitamin A (To prevent eye disease, to promote growth, to help in resisting disease.)

Dairy produce, animal fats, green vegetables, carrots, tomatoes, halibut and cod-liver oils.

Vitamin B_1 (To strengthen the nervous system, to protect from neuritis, to prevent constipation, to prevent beri-beri.)

Yeast, germ of wheat, egg, pulse foods, wholemeal flour, liver.

Vitamin B_2 (To promote growth in the young, to aid the health of the skin, to prevent pellagra.)

Lean meat, fish, egg yolk, milk, tomatoes, liver.

Vitamin C (To prevent lowered resistance to infection, to prevent scurvy.)

Fruit, vegetables (especially raw), tomatoes, oranges, lemons, grapefruit, germinated pulses.

Vitamin D (To prevent rickets, to prevent decay of teeth.)

Animal fat, halibut and cod-liver oils.

Vitamin E (To aid reproduction and lactation.)

Meat, eggs, green vegetables, wheat germs.

Vitamin K (To assist normal clotting of the blood.)

Spinach, kale, liver, egg yolk, tomatoes.

7

FOODS REQUIRED FOR DIFFERENT AGES

Children.—Require a balanced diet with comparatively larger amounts of energy foods, especially animal protein, calcium, iron and vitamins. Body-building foods are used up at a greater rate in growing, physically active children.

Middle-age.—When the tempo of life begins to slow down. If the intake of food continues as before and physical activity is reduced the energy foods are not used up but are retained and stored as fat in the body causing "Middle-age spread". Therefore less sugars, starches and fats are required in the diet.

Old age.—The amount of food required decreases but the food must be well cooked, nourishing and easily digested. A balanced diet containing all essential foods, especially milk, should be given.

CHILDREN'S DIETS AND MENUS

POINTS IN PLANNING CHILDREN'S MEALS

In planning meals for children it should be realised that they require more body-building food than adults, even manual workers. Children require protein foods not only for the daily upkeep of the body, as in the case of adults, but also for growth and continuous activity.

Young children can take only small quantities at each meal, so the food value must be high.

Protective foods are vital necessities to growing children. Fruit, vegetables and salads should take an important place in their diet.

Fruit juices (orange or tomato juice) should be given daily, first thing in the morning.

Cod liver oil or halibut liver oil should be included.

The children's meals set out in the dietary given below are guides which should be studied in connection with the chart "Foods Required by the Body". It will be seen that all essentials are included.

SPECIMEN MEALS

1 to 2 years of age

Breakfast	*Dinner*	*Tea*
1 to 2 teaspoons porridge and milk ½ boiled egg wholemeal bread and butter cup of milk	chopped roast or boiled mutton, sieved cabbage, jacket potatoes, fruit and rusk	parsley sandwich rusk and seedless jam milk or milky cocoa
cereal steamed or baked fresh herring wholemeal bread and butter, syrup cup of milk	stewed tripe, mashed swedes and mashed potatoes baked custard	wholemeal bread and butter with tomatoes or fruit plain cake milk
rusks with milk ½ scrambled egg on toast cup of milk	Shepherd's pie made with fresh meat, mashed carrots and swedes mixed blancmange and seedless jam or jelly	dripping toast stewed or fresh fruit milky cocoa or milk
porridge ½ rasher of bacon wholemeal bread and butter cup of milk	baked white fish, tomatoes (skinned), mashed potatoes fruit and custard	wholemeal bread and butter, watercress, honey milk
cereal with milk ½ boiled egg wholemeal toast or rusk cup of milk	minced liver, mashed cabbage or sprouts, boiled or mashed potatoes stewed apple	Marmite and parsley sandwiches plain cake milk or milky cocoa
oatmeal porridge with milk crisp bacon toast cup of milk	cheese pudding, baked jacket potatoes, greens baked apples and honey	wholemeal bread and butter, watercress seedless jam or jelly cake milk
cereal with milk ½ scrambled egg with toast cup of milk	steamed or stewed roes on toast mashed swedes trifle with rusks	junket and fruit wholemeal bread plain cake milky cocoa

9

2 to 5 years of age

Breakfast	Dinner	Tea
porridge and milk scrambled egg toast and butter or margarine cup of milk	minced lamb or mutton, mashed potatoes, mashed carrots stewed mashed prunes and egg custard	watercress or Marmite sandwich wholemeal bread and butter, honey milk
cereal with milk bacon and tomatoes wholemeal bread and butter cup of milk	fish baked in milk, mashed potatoes, greens cornflour mould and stewed fruit	salad of watercress, chopped parsley, green raw cabbage, grated cheese wholemeal bread and butter, jam milky cocoa
stewed mashed prunes or figs bacon and crisply fried bread cup of milk	stewed rabbit, spinach, potatoes fruit blancmange	baked custard wholemeal bread and butter, honey or syrup cake milk
cereal with milk steamed fish wholemeal toast cup of milk	cheese pudding, jacket potatoes, baked tomatoes steamed apple pudding	stewed fruit and custard wholemeal or brown bread and butter madeira cake milky cocoa
stewed fruit bacon and crisply fried bread wholemeal bread and butter cup of milk	stewed tripe, potatoes, greens fruit blancmange	sardine salad wholemeal bread and butter seedless jam milky cocoa
cereal and milk creamed fish wholemeal bread and butter, honey cup of milk	minced meat, potatoes, mashed carrots and swedes mixed fresh fruit jelly or bread and butter pudding	egg and parsley sandwiches wholemeal bread and butter, syrup cake milk or cocoa

5 to 12 years of age

Breakfast	Dinner	Tea
porridge and milk poached egg on toast wholemeal bread and butter, honey milk or cocoa	Shepherd's pie, baked potatoes, cabbage chocolate mould and jam	raw salad and grated cheese wholemeal bread and butter jam and cake milk or cocoa
cornflakes bacon and tomatoes toast marmalade, cocoa or milk	stewed or braised liver, mashed potatoes, mashed swedes baked apple and honey or syrup	parsley or watercress sandwich cornflour or prune mould brown bread and butter milk or cocoa
stewed prunes boiled egg toast honey cocoa or milk	roast meat (cut up), roast potatoes, greens (raw or cooked) milk pudding	cereal and stewed fruit wholemeal bread and butter milk or cocoa
cereal bacon and potatoes rusk and brown bread, butter weak tea or cocoa	sausage toad-in-the-hole, jacket potatoes, stewed celery baked jam roll	sardine salad wholemeal bread and butter jam milk or cocoa
stewed fruit scrambled egg on toast brown toast weak tea	Irish stew with carrots and onions Eve's pudding	vegetables with cheese wholemeal bread and butter or jacket potatoes cocoa or milk
cereal fish wholemeal bread and butter, marmalade milk or cocoa	stewed meat and dumplings, potatoes and carrots and turnips	lentil soup with chopped parsley toast cocoa or milk
porridge bacon and fried bread brown bread and butter milk or weak tea	fish pie or mould, mashed potatoes, sprouts or cauliflower currant pudding and white sauce	stuffed tomato or other vegetable brown bread and butter cocoa or milk

Rusks

Use stale wholemeal bread 1 to 2 cm. (½ to ¾ inch) thick. Cut into squares or small oblongs. Put on a baking sheet and bake in a very slow oven until crisp and golden-brown. Store in an airtight tin. They may be served with milk and sugar.

CHEESES

There is a great variety of cheeses to be obtained in Kenya and the following list gives a guide to the housewife in finding the most suitable to her needs and taste.

Blue Highland
A fine blue-veined cheese which develops a strong flavour when allowed to mature.

Blue Valley
Easily recognised by its blue-green pattern of veins. Quickly ripening and enjoyed by those who prefer a stronger flavour.

Caerphilly
A semi-soft white cheese with a mildly acid flavour.

Cheddar
Close textured with a full, clean, slightly nutty flavour, it is creamy yellow in colour. An excellent cooking cheese but best of all at table with beer or red wine.

Gouda
A small round cheese. It is sweet-flavoured and patterned by little cavities. Melts well and is ideal for toasted cheese sandwiches and soufflés.

Gruyère
A mild close-textured cheese with a unique sweet flavour. The method of manufacture produces large holes in the texture of the cheese. It is excellent for making cheese dip or when served in thick slices with bread.

Highland El Roma
A sage-flavoured cheese suitable for cheese and wine parties and cold buffet meals.

Highland Red Leicester
A rindless cheese, russet in colour and crumbly in texture. Ideal for cooking or table use.

Home-Made Cream Cheese	Made by putting a piece of thick sour milk into a piece of butter muslin or a hair sieve over a bowl. Tie the muslin and hang up, putting the bowl underneath to catch the drips. After 24 hours take it down and fork a little salt into it according to taste and quantity. Put the curd into a clean piece of muslin, make into a round shape and press between 2 plates, putting a heavy weight on the top plate. The cheese will be ready for use in 2 days. (*See* also page 32.)
Jabiru Creamed Cheese	A soft white cheese which travels well and retains its quality for a considerable time in cold storage.
Lamuria Processed	This type of cheese is prepared from selected brands of Cheddar to which are added special emulsifying salts. It has excellent storage qualities and its smooth texture and sweet flavour make it ideal for sandwiches. It has a special appeal to children.
Limburger	This is a low-fat, semi-soft surface-ripened cheese with a characteristic strong flavour usually containing small irregular openings. It is made at Mariakani near Mombasa.
Pont L'évêque	Made from whole, fresh Kenya milk. When ripe it is pliant and yielding to the touch.
Protamu	A cheese spread which has excellent keeping qualities. Cold storage is not required. Ideal for sandwiches.
Provolone	This cheese is light in colour, mellow and smooth, cuts without crumbling and has an attractive flavour.
Red Highland	A semi-hard Dutch-type cheese of sweet flavour.
Rindless Cheddar	Creamy-yellow in colour, bland in taste, the whole cheese is edible.
Stilton	A blue cheese with a rich savoury flavour and loose, open texture. Serve with port, nuts and raisins after dinner.
Tavern and Bellevue	Cheddar cheeses which have been matured for longer than usual in order to produce a cheese of stronger flavour and "bite".

Tinned Cheese Processed Cheddar	A smooth, well-flavoured cheese, excellent for safaris and in hot climates.
Tilsiter and Highland Tilsiter	A soft, moist cheese with a sharp "bite".
Tybo	From Mariakani, Mombasa, this is a soft, pliable low-fat cheese with a mildish flavour.
Wensleydale	A white cheese, slightly acid and crumbly. Excellent for picnic lunches and sandwiches.
White Highland	Soft but firm, rich and delicately flavoured. It is delicious with fruit, keeps well, sharpening with age.
White Stilton	A quick ripening mild cheese with a delicate flavour. It is a creamy cheese with a crumbly texture.

To keep cheese fresh, even in hot weather, wrap it in a cloth which has been soaked in salt water and keep it cool in a well-ventilated place. In a refrigerator it is advisable to wrap it loosely in a piece of polythene and leave both ends open. Avoid placing cheese close to fish and other strong aromatic foods which may taint its flavour.

Cheese contains in concentrated form almost all the protein and most of the fat, minerals, vitamins and other nutrients of milk.

NOTE:—Great care must be taken in cooking cheese dishes so that the cheese is only melted and not boiled or overcooked in the oven. Nothing is more indigestible than overcooked cheese. Always bake cheese dishes in a moderately hot oven.

BREAKFAST AND LIGHT LUNCH DISHES

Porridge
2 tablespoons medium oatmeal   600 ml. (1 pint) of water
salt to taste

Bring fresh water to boiling point in a deep pan and add the salt, sprinkle in the oatmeal, stirring carefully with a wooden spoon to prevent lumps. Boil and stir for the first 5 minutes till the meal is swollen, then put on the lid and simmer for at least $\frac{1}{2}$ hour, stirring frequently. If necessary add more boiling water, as porridge should be of a good pouring consistency.

NOTE:—Some people find porridge more digestible if the oatmeal is soaked overnight in cold water.

Maize Meal Porridge—made as previous recipe.

Bacon and Eggs
Prepare your rashers by cutting off the rind neatly. If bacon should be salty and dry, scald in boiling water a few seconds before cooking.

Put the rashers in a cold frying pan and cook over gentle heat, turning continually with fork till crisp but not hard. Remove bacon on to a hot dish and keep warm in oven (not so hot as to continue cooking) until eggs are ready. Break each egg into a cup singly and slip into hot fat. There should be enough fat in the pan to allow the eggs to be well basted on the top until the white is set. Remove from pan on a slice into the dish of rashers and serve very hot.

Baked Eggs with Cheese

4 eggs	1 cup soft breadcrumbs
½ cup grated cheese	cayenne pepper (a few grains)

Break eggs into buttered pie-dish or ramekins. Cover with crumbs, cheese and seasoning and brown in very hot oven.

Baked Eggs and Gravy

4 to 6 tablespoons gravy	breadcrumbs
6 eggs	5 rounds buttered toast or French
pepper and salt	toast.
a little cream	

Put gravy into a frying pan. Break the eggs carefully into this, pepper and salt them and sprinkle a handful of breadcrumbs over them. Bake for 5 minutes in a quick oven. Prepare rounds of buttered toast or French toast and arrange on a hot, flat dish. As soon as the eggs are set, take them up carefully one by one, using a flat ladle or slice, and put them on the toast. Add cream and if liked add some finely chopped parsley and onion to the gravy left in the frying pan. Boil up quickly and pour over eggs. If parsley and onions are not at hand, add any other flavouring or sauce which may be liked.

For French toast use rounds of stale bread dipped in beaten egg and fried quickly in butter or dripping to a golden brown. Poultry gravy is particularly nice for this dish but any other kind will do.

Birds' Nests

4 medium potatoes	1 egg yolk
salt and pepper	2 eggs
30 g. (1 oz.) butter	watercress

Filling:—

2 tablespoons milk	30 g. (1 oz.) butter
2 small pickled onions	salt and pepper

Cook the potatoes and mash whilst hot. Season, add the butter and bind with the egg yolk. Shape into small neat cakes, making a nest in the centre of each. Beat up the two eggs, brush the cakes with a little of this and brown quickly in a hot oven. Add seasonings and finely chopped onions to the remaining egg. Melt the butter; add the milk and the egg mixture; stir over a gentle heat until lightly set. Pile quickly in the centre of the potato "nests". Dust alternate piles with cayenne pepper. Serve hot and garnish with watercress. The successful appearance of the dish depends on neat shaping and filling.

Boiled Eggs

The higher the altitude, the lower the boiling point. This has to be taken into consideration when boiling eggs. A new-laid egg will be sufficiently cooked if boiled from $3\frac{1}{2}$ minutes to 4 minutes at sea level but at a higher altitude will take $\frac{1}{2}$ to 1 minute longer. Only experience can give the right number of minutes required. Naturally a large egg requires longer boiling than a small one and a turkey egg about 6 minutes.

(*a*) Have ready a pan of boiling water, into which plunge the number of eggs required as nearly as possible simultaneously. When cooking eggs for any number over half a dozen, the eggs should either be placed in a wire basket or a muslin cloth so as to give an equal number of minutes to each egg. Salt added to the boiling water prevents the white oozing out should an egg by chance have a crack in the shell.

An egg to be hard-boiled for the table should boil $5\frac{1}{2}$ minutes. To be sufficiently hard-boiled for a savoury, give from 10 to $12\frac{1}{2}$ minutes. When boiling eggs for a savoury it is a good plan to stir them occasionally so as to keep the yolks in the centre. To cool eggs, have a bowl with absolutely cold water ready, chip the shells slightly and plunge eggs into the cold water, leaving them until quite cold before shelling. Thus treated, eggs will not turn black.

(*b*) Another satisfactory way of boiling eggs is to put them in a pan of cold water and bring to boil. Allow the water to boil briskly for 1 minute, put lid on pan and simmer. Allow to stand from 8 to 10 minutes. By this method the white of the egg is more creamy and more easily digested.

Cheese Croquettes

some puff or short pastry
2 tablespoons grated cheese
1 tablespoon cream
salt and pepper
1 beaten egg
breadcrumbs

Roll pastry very thin and cut into small rounds. Mix grated cheese with cream; season and put a teaspoonful on each round. Wet the edges with beaten egg and fold over. Dip in beaten egg and then in breadcrumbs. Fry in smoking-hot fat and serve very hot.

Cheese Eggs

2 eggs
a little milk
$1\frac{1}{2}$ tablespoons butter
3 dessertspoons grated cheese
salt and pepper
hot buttered toast

Heat butter and milk, stir in beaten eggs, cheese and seasoning. Cook until thick and creamy. Serve on toast.

Cheese Potatoes

500 g. (1 lb.) of hot, fluffy, mashed potatoes
$\frac{1}{2}$ cup grated cheese
1 tablespoon grated onion
yolks and whites of 2 eggs well beaten
seasoning to taste

16

Add to potatoes the cheese, onion, yolks of eggs and seasoning. Beat until creamy. Carefully fold in the beaten whites of eggs. Turn into buttered baking dish and brown in oven.

Cheese Pudding

1 cup grated cheese	1 heaped teaspoon butter
1½ cups milk	2 eggs
1 cup breadcrumbs	salt and red pepper to taste

Melt butter in the milk; remove from stove and add cheese, breadcrumbs and seasonings. Beat up the eggs and add them. Pour into a buttered fireproof dish and bake till nicely browned on top.

Cheese Soufflé

(a)

1 tablespoon butter	1 teacup grated cheese
1 dessertspoon flour	salt and pepper
1 teacup warm milk	½ teacup fresh breadcrumbs
2 eggs	

Heat butter in a small saucepan; stir in flour; add warm milk and grated cheese, breadcrumbs, salt and pepper. Let it cool. Beat yolks and whites of eggs separately, stir all together gently and pour into buttered dish and bake. Serve at once.

(b)

125 g. (4 oz.) butter	95 g. (3 oz.) grated cheese
30 g. (1 oz.) flour	3 yolks of large eggs
160 ml. (1 gill) milk	4 whites of large eggs
½ teaspoon salt and a little white and cayenne pepper	

In a small saucepan melt the butter, mix in the flour, then add the milk. Stir till it boils and thickens. Cool and add the seasonings. Mix well, add yolks one by one, then the cheese. Beat the whites stiff and stir them in gently. Pour all into a buttered soufflé tin or pie dish and bake for 20 minutes in a quick oven. Serve at once.

(c)

1 l. (1½ pints) milk	200 g. (6 oz.) grated cheese
100 g. (3 oz.) butter	6 (5) eggs
135 g. (4 oz.) flour	pepper, salt

Melt butter in a saucepan, stir in flour until smooth, add boiling milk and cook until the mixture will leave the sides of the saucepan. Stir in cheese and seasoning and egg yolks. Beat the whites to a stiff froth and stir lightly into the cool mixture. Turn into a buttered dish and bake in a moderate oven for 40 to 45 minutes. Serve at once. The cheese cut into tiny dice can be used instead of grated cheese.

Cheese Tartlets

60 g. (2 oz.) flour
30 g. (1 oz.) butter
yolks of 3 eggs
a little water
salt

60 g. (2 oz.) finely grated cheese
salt and cayenne pepper to taste
3 tablespoons cream
pastry

Make a paste with the flour, butter, yolk of 1 egg, little water and salt. Line some patty pans with this pastry (rolled out thin). Take grated cheese, beat it up in a bowl with the yolks of 2 eggs. Add salt and cayenne to taste, then work in the cream thoroughly. Fill each patty pan with this mixture and bake until brown.

Economical Rarebit

30 g. (1 oz.) butter
45 g. (1½ oz.) flour
300 ml. (½ pint) milk
100 g. (3 oz.) grated cheese

cayenne pepper
salt
1 teaspoon made mustard
toast

Prepare some rounds of toast. Make a thick white sauce with the butter, flour and milk. Add the seasoning. Cool slightly and stir in the grated cheese. Allow it to melt and pour this sauce on to the slices of toast, which may be buttered or not as preferred. Serve hot. Sufficient for four to six persons.

Eggs à la Bonne Femme

2 or 3 slices of beetroot
1 or 2 slices of cold chicken
   or any cold meat

3 heads of lettuce
3 new-laid eggs
mayonnaise sauce

Boil eggs for 10 minutes. Roll them to break their shells. Shell them and cut them in halves, cutting off a little of the white to make them stand. Take out yolks and fill them as follows:
two with beetroot already boiled and cut into dice, two with cold chicken or meat, and two with the yolks cut up into dice. Cut up lettuce, place on dish, put the eggs on it and serve with mayonnaise sauce.

Eggs à la Florentine

6 hard-boiled eggs
1 tablespoon thyme
1 tablespoon vinegar
½ teaspoon cinnamon
1 tablespoon milk
1 tablespoon white vinegar

1 tablespoon chopped parsley
3 tablespoons breadcrumbs
1 teaspoon castor sugar
salt and pepper
lettuce
a pinch of dry mustard

Soak the breadcrumbs in vinegar. Cut the eggs in half; remove the yolks and pound well in a mortar or sieve them. Add the herbs, cinnamon, sugar and seasoning, together with the breadcrumbs and milk. Cut a piece off the bottom of the whites and fill them with the stuffing. Arrange on a bed of lettuce. Add the white vinegar and mustard to the remaining stuffing and pour this over the eggs.

Eggs a la Macaroni

125 g. (4 oz.) macaroni	pepper and salt
60 g. (2 oz.) butter	300 ml. ($\frac{1}{2}$ pint) thick brown gravy
milk (enough to cover	some poached eggs
macaroni thoroughly)	grated cheese

Break up some macaroni into 2.5 cm. (1 inch) pieces; rinse it well. Put the butter into a saucepan, put the macaroni in and pour enough milk over it to cover it thoroughly, stirring it now and then. When it has cooked for 15 minutes take it out and put it into another dish, seasoning it well with pepper and salt. Pour over it the brown gravy; then put it into the oven and leave it till cooked. When ready lay some poached eggs on it, sprinkle liberally with grated cheese and serve at once. If preferred, a thick white sauce instead of brown gravy may be used.

Eggs au Gratin

6 hard-boiled eggs	small pieces of fried bread
2 tablespoons grated cheese	

Divide eggs into halves lengthwise and place in a circle round dish. Have a sauce prepared as follows:

1 tablespoon butter	4 tablespoons stock or water
1 tablespoon flour	$\frac{1}{2}$ cup of milk
a pinch of salt	1 tablespoon grated cheese
pepper and red pepper	2 raw yolks of eggs

Melt butter, add flour, salt, pepper, red pepper, stock or water, milk and grated cheese. Boil for 5 minutes; then add the 2 raw yolks of eggs. Mix well and pour at once over the hard-boiled eggs. Sprinkle grated cheese on the top and brown in the oven. Garnish with small pieces of fried bread and serve hot.

Eggs au Riz

boiled rice	eggs
salt and pepper	sauce or sliced tomato
a little butter	breadcrumbs

Put rice into buttered Pyrex dish. Season with pepper and salt and a little butter. Make a hole in centre of rice and drop in raw eggs. Cover with sauce or sliced tomato, sprinkle breadcrumbs on top and bake in a moderately hot oven.

Egg Croquettes and Spinach

4 eggs	$\frac{1}{4}$ teaspoon chopped parsley
3 tablespoons butter	1 cup of milk
3 tablespoons flour	breadcrumbs
$\frac{1}{4}$ teaspoon salt	1 beaten egg diluted with 3
$\frac{1}{4}$ teaspoon pepper	tablespoons milk
$\frac{1}{4}$ teaspoon scraped onion	spinach (cooked)

Boil the eggs hard. Cover with cold water and remove shell. Cut the eggs into 1 cm. ($\frac{1}{2}$-inch) cubes. Melt the butter; into it put the flour, salt, pepper, scraped onion and chopped parsley. Add milk and stir until boiling. Add the cubes of eggs. Turn on to buttered plate and

(Continued)

when cold shape into balls. Roll in sifted breadcrumbs; dip in beaten egg diluted with milk and again roll in breadcrumbs. Fry in deep boiling fat and serve on spinach. Grated cheese may be added to the croquette mixture if desired.

Daisy Eggs

4 or 6 eggs	salt and pepper
4 or 6 rounds toast	a little milk

Butter toast and place in oven. Separate white and yolks of eggs and beat up whites until very light and stiff. Pile them on the slices of toast, which should be previously dipped in milk. Make a hollow in the white and drop in the yolk of the egg. Bake in quick oven till yolks are set and whites a light brown, dust with pepper and salt. Serve very hot.

Golden Eggs

6 eggs	1 tablespoon flour
2 tablespoons butter	milk
salt and pepper	grated cheese
1 tablespoon grated cheese	1 teaspoon chopped parsley
or 1 tablespoon Worcester sauce	

Boil eggs hard; plunge into cold water to remove the shells easily, then cut lengthways. Carefully remove the yolks, place in a basin and beat into a smooth paste with a tablespoon of butter, a little salt, pepper, grated cheese or Worcester sauce, or both mixed together. If liked, add a dash of cayenne pepper to give sharpness. Refill egg cases, leaving a little of the paste for the sauce. Heat rest of butter in a saucepan, mix with flour, salt and milk sufficient to make a nice sauce; stir until it boils and let simmer 5 minutes. Remove from the stove; add the remainder of the paste and a little grated cheese to taste, also finely chopped parsley. Pour this sauce carefully over the eggs previously placed on an entrée dish. Set in a cool place and serve when quite cold or chilled.

Poached Eggs

a shallow pan of boiling water	1 tablespoon vinegar or lemon juice
rounds of hot buttered toast	$\frac{1}{2}$ teaspoon salt
eggs	

Add vinegar and salt to boiling water. Break eggs required, one at a time, into a cup and slip into boiling water. See that the eggs are all quite covered with water and that it keeps boiling all the time. As soon as the white is set (about 2 minutes) remove from pan in an open spoon or perforated slice and, when water has entirely run away, slip on to rounds of hot buttered toast. Both skill and care are required to place the egg on the toast without breaking.

Egg Pom-Poms

6 new-laid eggs	1 tablespoon mushroom ketchup
60 g. (2 oz.) butter	300 ml. ($\frac{1}{2}$ pint) aspic jelly
seasoning	

Boil the eggs for 12 minutes; crack shells and place in a bowl of cold water. Remove the shells, cut each egg in half and take out the yolk. Cut a small piece off the rounded end of each egg, then stand them on a dish and fill the cavity with aspic jelly and allow to set. In the meantime, cream the butter and yolk of eggs well together, beat in the mushroom ketchup and seasoning and then rub through a sieve or pointed strainer. Turn the eggs up the other way and force this mixture on the top of each in the form of a rosette. Garnish with chopped aspic and parsley.

Egg and Spinach

spinach
salt
poached egg

25/30 g. (1 oz.) butter
3 tablespoons cream or ½ teacup white sauce

Pick the spinach carefully and wash very thoroughly two or three times in cold water, then put into a pan with a little salt. Cover closely and boil for 25 minutes. Pour the water off and beat the spinach smooth with a wooden spoon; add the butter and cream or sauce. Mix all well together and reheat. Serve with a poached egg on top.

Scalloped Eggs and Cheese

3 eggs
45 g. (1½ oz.) butter
150 ml. (1 gill) milk

pepper and salt
95 g. (3 oz.) cheese

Grease some scallop shells or ramekin cases. Grate the cheese. Melt the butter in a saucepan with the milk. Beat the eggs slightly and add to the milk in the pan, then add half the grated cheese and season well. Stir over a gentle heat until the mixture is of a creamy consistency, taking care to remove from the heat before it becomes quite thick. Pour some of the mixture into each scallop shell and cover with grated cheese. Brown under a hot grill or in a hot oven. Garnish with parsley and serve hot with toast fingers.

Scotch Eggs

4 hard-boiled eggs
300 ml. (½ pint) rich brown gravy
250 g. (½ lb.) sausage meat or vegetarian forcemeat

1 egg (raw)
breadcrumbs

Beat the raw egg and bind the sausage meat or vegetarian forcemeat with half of it. While doing this, let the 4 eggs boil for 10 minutes. Warm the gravy. Take out the eggs; remove their shells and encase them thickly in the sausage meat or forcemeat. Coat them with the other half of the beaten raw egg and crumbs and fry them in smoking-hot fat. Cut in halves and stand nicely on a dish, with the egg showing in the centre of the rissole. Serve hot with the gravy poured over them. They may be served cold with salad.

VEGETARIAN FORCEMEAT:—

125 g. (4 oz.) lentils
30 g. (1 oz.) breadcrumbs
grated rind of ½ lemon

1 teaspoon chopped parsley
pepper and salt

Soak the lentils overnight. Put in a pan with water to cover, add salt and simmer till tender. Strain and sieve. Mix in the other ingredients and proceed as directed above.

Scrambled Eggs

When scrambling eggs, a double boiler is always preferable as then there is no danger of over-cooking.

(a) Allow 1 egg for each person and 1 over and a dessertspoon of milk or cream for each egg. Put milk in pan with a little butter, 5 g. per egg (½ oz. for 3 eggs), pepper and salt. Break the eggs required into the milk and stir so as to break the yolks but do not beat. Place on a gentle heat and allow to thicken but not boil, continually stirring from the bottom where the egg thickens first and occasionally lifting away from the heat so as to prevent boiling. When eggs are the consistency of thick cream, dish on to rounds of hot buttered toast prepared beforehand. Serve very hot.

(b) eggs (no milk)   rounds of hot buttered toast
    butter (size of a walnut   pepper and salt
       for each egg)

Proceed as above, first melting the butter before breaking in eggs.

(c) eggs (yolks and whites   milk
       separately)   pepper and salt
    butter

Proceed as in (a) but dropping in yolks only. While yolks are setting in pan, beat up whites till stiff and stir into cooking yolks before serving.

Scrambled Eggs and Tomato

1 large tomato   butter
2 slices of onion (optional)   salt and pepper
4 well-beaten eggs

Take tomato and free it from skin and pips. Mince it finely with the slices of onion, add a generous portion of butter and salt and pepper to taste. Stir together in a saucepan till onion is cooked but not coloured. Add eggs, stir till set. Heap on a hot dish and encircle with fried snippets of bread.

Stuffed Eggs

as many eggs as required   pepper
cheese   a little butter
anchovy   buttered toast

Boil eggs hard, cut in halves and remove yolks. Mash yolks with cheese and anchovy, pepper and a little butter and refill whites. Serve halves on buttered toast. Or place together, making whole eggs. Dip in egg and breadcrumbs and fry in hot fat. Serve on mashed potatoes, with tomato sauce.

Eggs Valentia

4 eggs   4 tablespoons grated cheese
1 teacup strained tomatoes   a little pepper, salt and
   (or tomato sauce)   nutmeg (if liked)
1 teacup boiled rice   chopped parsley

Put tomatoes into saucepan; add rice and, when quite hot, the cheese. Stir well together; add salt, pepper and nutmeg. Brush a pie dish with a little melted butter, pour in this mixture to form a border and drop eggs into the centre. Cook in a quick oven 4 to 5 minutes until eggs are set. Sprinkle with chopped parsley and serve hot.

Italian Macaroni

175 g. (6 oz.) macaroni or spaghetti
250 g. (½ lb.) tomatoes
a little butter
a little flour
a little grated cheese
some finely chopped onions

Fry the tomatoes in a little butter till soft. Add some water and put it all through a sieve. Next add the finely chopped onion and thicken with flour. Cook the macaroni or spaghetti in boiling salted water. Strain it and mix it with the tomato and onion. Put the mixture in a pie dish, grate a little cheese on top and bake in a good oven.

Macaroni Cheese

60 g. (2 oz.) macaroni
60 g. (2 oz.) cheese
salt and cayenne pepper
¼ teaspoon mustard

Sauce:—
15 g. (½ oz.) butter   15 g. (½ oz.) flour   300 ml. (½ pint) milk

Break up the macaroni into small pieces and boil in salted water. Make the sauce and mix into it half the cheese. Strain the macaroni and put it in a pie dish. Pour the sauce over it and sprinkle the rest of the cheese on top. Bake in a good oven.

Macaroni Cheese with Custard

60 g. (2 oz.) macaroni
2 eggs
1 cup milk
breadcrumbs
salt, pepper and a little mustard
60 g. (2 oz.) grated cheese

Boil the macaroni in water or milk. When it is tender, put it in a buttered pie dish. Make a custard with the eggs, salt, pepper, mustard and milk. Pour this over the macaroni and sprinkle the top with grated cheese and breadcrumbs. Bake in a slow oven.

Macaroni and Tomato Pie

125 g. (¼ lb.) macaroni
250 g. (½ lb.) tomatoes
125 g. (¼ lb.) onion
30 g. (1 oz.) butter
150 ml. (¼ pint) milk
60 g. (2 oz.) flour
2 hard-boiled eggs
pastry or breadcrumbs for the top

Put macaroni into enough boiling water to cover and cook till tender. Fry onions in half the butter, scald and peel tomatoes and add to onions and cook well. Put remainder of butter in pan; add flour and milk to make sauce. Add sauce to macaroni. Put macaroni and tomatoes in alternate layers in pie dish. Sprinkle with salt and pepper. Put eggs cut in slices on top. Cover with 250 g. (8 oz.) flaky pastry or with breadcrumbs. Bake in oven till brown.

Melba Toast

Slice stale bread as thinly as possible (3 mm. or $\frac{1}{8}''$). Remove crusts. Bake in slow oven. Turn several times till crisp and evenly browned (20 to 30 minutes).

Mushroom Omelette

4 eggs	sprig of parsley, chopped
2 dessertspoons milk	a few mushrooms
2 dessertspoons butter	pepper and salt

Slice the mushrooms and cook them in a little butter. Beat the eggs with the milk; add parsley, mushrooms, pepper and salt. Heat the butter in a pan. When melted without browning, pour in the mixture and cook for a few minutes. Serve doubled over.

Omelette with Flour

1 tablespoon flour	a pinch of salt
1 tablespoon sugar	1 teacup milk
2 eggs	a few drops essence of lemon
jam	

Put flour, sugar and salt into a basin and mix well together. Then put yolks of eggs into a bowl and stir until light and add the milk to them. Pour very slowly over flour, etc., stirring all the time to prevent lumps. Beat the whites to snow and add gently with the lemon essence to the rest of the mixture. Melt a piece of butter the size of a walnut in a frying pan and then pour in all the mixture and hold it over a very gentle heat till set and well risen (about $\frac{1}{4}$ hour). Next put the pan into a hot oven until the top is golden brown. Spread jam on one half and fold and dish on a hot plate. This omelette is delicious with grated cheese instead of sugar, as a savoury, when lemon should be omitted.

NOTE:—One teaspoon water added makes an omelette lighter.

Plain Omelette (for 2 persons)

3 eggs	1 tablespoon milk or cream
1 dessertspoon butter	pepper and salt

Melt butter in a small frying pan. Beat eggs and add milk and seasoning. Pour mixture into melted butter and stir till it begins to look creamy all over. Loosen edges with a knife and, while still creamy, roll up and serve immediately on hot dish.

To this add herbs, chopped bacon, flakes of cold fish, grated cheese or any other ingredient one has at hand to make a savoury omelette. For a sweet omelette add sugar and fold in jam when rolling.

Omelette Soufflé

4 eggs	salt and pepper
3 tablespoons milk	

Beat yolks of eggs and whites separately. Add to the yolks milk, pepper and salt and lastly stir in whites very lightly. Pour into hot buttered pan and cook slowly till brown on under-side. Place in oven to set the top. Fold and serve hot. Garnish with sliced lemon.

Parmesan Potatoes

some large potatoes
butter

grated Parmesan or Tavern cheese
pepper and salt

Bake potatoes in their skins. When done, cut off a round from the top of each. Scoop out the potato and well mash into it some butter, grated Parmesan or Tavern cheese and a little pepper and salt. Refill the skins with the mixture and reheat in the oven.

Ravioli

Paste:—

175 g. (6 oz.) flour
1 egg
a little water

2 dessertspoons olive oil (or melted fat)

Sauce:—

30 g. (1 oz.) margarine
475 ml. (¾ pint) water
a little onion
a soup cube
4 teaspoons sugar

30 g. (1 oz.) flour
1 small tin tomato pulp (or fresh tomato puree)
a few bacon rinds
pepper and salt

Fry bacon rinds in pan. Add margarine and chopped onion and flour to make a roux. Add tomato pulp to taste. Melt the meat cube in the water and add a little at a time. Stir well and allow to thicken. Add sugar and seasoning.

Filling:—

(1) Minced cooked meat or fish mixed with gravy or beaten egg and milk and seasoning;

or (2) Cooked spinach and cheese.

Make paste and knead till smooth and firm. Leave ½ hour.

Roll out paste thinly and cut 5 cm. to 6 cm. (2 to 2½″) rounds or squares. Fill with meat mixture, damp edges and pinch together. Plunge into boiling water for 8 to 10 minutes. Serve in hot dish with tomato sauce poured over the top. Hand grated cheese separately in small dish.

Rice and Tomato Pie

500 g. (1 lb.) firm tomatoes
½ teacup rice
325 ml. (2 gills) of stock
1 medium-sized onion

60 g. (2 oz.) butter
4 tablespoons fresh crumbs
salt and pepper

Mince the onion and fry in part of the butter. Add the rice and stock and cook till tender. When cooked, put in layers, in a thickly buttered pie dish, with the peeled and sliced tomatoes. Sprinkle each layer lightly with salt and pepper. Cover the top with a thick layer of crumbs and put on the butter, broken into small bits. Bake in a quick oven until the surface is well browned and the tomatoes soft.

Savoury Rice

6 cups stock or broth	2 cups rice
tomato sauce	a large piece butter
salt and pepper	25 g. (1 oz.) grated cheese

Put stock or broth into a saucepan. Add a generous portion of tomato sauce and salt and pepper to taste. When it boils, throw in rice well washed and allow to cook until the rice has absorbed the whole of the stock. Melt butter and pour over the rice. Add grated cheese to the mixture; sprinkle some on top and brown in the oven.

Tomato au Gratin

6 tomatoes	seasoning to taste
1 tablespoon flour	15 g. (½ oz.) butter
300 ml. (½ pint) boiling milk	30 g. (1 oz.) grated cheese

Halve the tomatoes and fry them lightly, skin side downwards, in the butter. Add 3 tablespoons of boiling water and cook until tender. Remove the tomatoes to a hot dish and stir in the flour with the butter. When it browns slightly pour in the milk, seasoning and cheese. Cook the sauce for 2 or 3 minutes, stirring all the time, then pour it over the tomatoes.

Tomato Mayonnaise

as many tomatoes as required	watercress
chopped sardines	mayonnaise sauce
olives	lettuce

Scoop out centres of tomatoes and reserve pulp. Fill with chopped sardines, olives and watercress and the tomato pulp. Cover with mayonnaise and serve on lettuce.

Tomato and Sardine Omelette

1 cup rather thin tomato sauce	4 eggs
	½ cup thick tomato sauce
salt and pepper	a little cornflour
1 teaspoon curry powder	a few large sardines
a few cloves, garlic or a little minced onion	

Heat the thin sauce in a saucepan; add salt, pepper, curry powder, skinned and pounded garlic or minced onion and butter. Simmer till the mixture thickens a little; leave to cool. Beat the eggs and stir them in. Heat some fat in a pan, pour in the mixture and fry. Meanwhile heat the thick sauce; mix in the skinned, cleaned and mashed sardines and season to taste. When the omelette is ready, turn it out, spread the sardine mixture on half of it, fold over, and serve hot.

Tomatoes Stuffed with Asparagus

4 large firm tomatoes	salt
a pinch of nutmeg	1 medium chopped gherkin
mayonnaise (thick)	lettuce
150 ml. (¼ pint) green asparagus tips (or a small tin)	

Wipe the tomatoes, removing the centre with the handle of a tea-spoon and rejecting the core. Cook asparagus tips until tender (unless tinned asparagus is used). Drain well. Season and flavour the tomato pulp, add the tips and chopped gherkin and fill the tomato shells with the mixture. Mask with thick mayonnaise and garnish with fancy shapes of gherkin. Serve immediately on a bed of lettuce. When possible chill before serving.

Vegetable and Cheese

6 onions
500 ml. (1 pint) boiling water
1 tablespoon butter
1 tablespoon lard (if no
    lard use 2 tablespoons
    butter)

250 g. (½ lb.) cheese sliced
1.25 l. (1 quart) freshly stewed,
bottled or tinned tomatoes
a little sugar
pepper and salt

Peel and slice onions and put into a pan with the boiling water, butter and lard; cook slowly for at least 1 hour, stirring often. Add tomatoes freshly stewed and cook steadily for about 20 minutes, leaving the pan or saucepan uncovered, so that the liquid in tomatoes may evaporate. Turn the mixture into a well-buttered pie dish; cover the top with slices of cheese and bake in the oven till cheese has melted and become slightly browned. Serve on, or with, hot toast. This recipe is sufficient for 6 persons. If potatoes and cauliflowers or some other vegetables are served at the same time no meat will be required with this dish. A little sugar to counteract the acidity of the tomatoes, also pepper and salt, should be added while the mixture is stewing in the pan.

Welsh Rarebit

125 g. (¼ lb.) cheese
1 egg

2 tablespoons milk
½ teaspoon mustard

Grate the cheese and put into a small pan. Drop in the slightly beaten egg, add milk and mustard. Stir and when thick and creamy pour over 2 slices of buttered toast.

Welsh Rarebit with Beer

1 cup cheese (grated)
1 wineglass beer

slices of toast

This recipe makes 5 rarebits. Take cheese; put in an enamel saucepan; add beer enough to thin the cheese sufficiently. Place on stove and stir until it is melted. Have slices of toast ready for each rarebit (crust trimmed). Put a slice on each plate and pour cheese enough over each piece to cover it. Serve hot.

Golden Buck

A "golden buck" is merely a rarebit with the addition of a poached egg, which is put carefully on top before serving.

Yorkshire Rarebit

Same as "golden buck" only it has 2 thin slices of broiled bacon on top instead of the egg.

Fried Liver and Bacon. *See* Entrées.
Kippers and Haddocks. *See* Fish Dishes.

FIRST AND SECOND TOASTIES

(Hors d'oeuvres and Savouries)

Savoury Butters

Savoury butters are a very essential and important part in the preparation of many savouries; they are also invaluable for king toasties and canapés, as well as for garnishes.

A few suggestions are:—

anchovy (pounded)
curry powder
ham (finely chopped)
lobster
paprika
caviare

garlic (blanched cloves, pounded)
horseradish
mustard (French)
pimento
sardine

The amount of butter used depends on individual taste and according to the type of flavouring used. For example, for the anchovy butter, using the fillets of a dozen anchovies, 125 g. ($\frac{1}{4}$ lb.) butter would be needed. In the case of mustard butter, garlic, horseradish, etc , use as much of the flavouring as the palate dictates. To 125 g. ($\frac{1}{4}$ lb.) butter, 1 teaspoon of paprika would be ample, moistened with a few drops of stock.

Tests for Mushrooms

With mushrooms one cannot be too careful. Commence peeling the outside white skin of the mushroom, from the edge to the crest. If the skin does not come off easily the mushroom is suspect. To make sure, if not certain, put a shilling in the pan of frying mushrooms. It will turn black if they are of a poisonous variety.

Almonds Salted

125 g. ($\frac{1}{4}$ lb.) almonds
pinch of salt

$\frac{1}{2}$ teaspoon butter
a little cayenne pepper

Blanch and prepare the almonds. Melt the butter and add the almonds. Stir well till evenly and lightly brown. Place the almonds on a sheet of clean blotting paper to absorb fat and sprinkle with salt and cayenne mixed together.

Anchovy Croûtes

85 g. (3 oz.) butter
yolks of 2 hard-boiled eggs
1 teaspoon anchovy paste
cayenne pepper
a few drops cochineal
rounds of buttered toast

Beat butter to cream; add paste, eggs, seasoning and colour. Pass the mixture through forcer on to rounds of buttered bread or toast. Decorate with parsley and serve very cold.

Anchovy Eggs (hot)

6 small rounds of buttered
  bread
anchovy or bloater paste
dessertspoon of milk
1 hard-boiled egg
30 g. (1 oz.) grated cheese

Butter the bread, put a dab of paste in centre and cover with a slice of hard-boiled egg. Moisten the cheese with milk and drop $\frac{1}{2}$ teaspoon of this on top of egg. Place on baking tin and put in oven until the cheese is toasted. It ought to spread over the egg. Serve hot.

Anchovy Eggs (cold)

2 hard-boiled eggs
1 dessertspoon anchovy paste
rounds of thin bread and
  butter
30 g. (1 oz.) butter
cayenne pepper
watercress
lemon juice

Remove the shells from the eggs; cut them in half across. Take out the yolks, pound them with the butter and anchovy paste, a few drops of lemon juice and pepper. Pile the mixture in the centre of each white, cut the bottom to stand and put each on a round of bread and butter. Garnish with watercress and serve.

Anchovy Savoury

toast
anchovy paste
1 tablespoon butter
1 tablespoon flour
1 cup milk
2 hard-boiled eggs
pepper

Toast bread, remove crust, butter and spread sparingly with anchovy paste. Cook together the butter and flour, pour the milk on slowly, stirring till the mixture is smooth, then add the hard-boiled eggs, chopped coarsely. When the mixture is thoroughly hot, add pepper to taste, pour over the anchovy toast and serve hot.

Asparagus Toastie

Strain the juice from a small tin of asparagus tips and bring to the boil. Place a dessertspoon of butter in a small bowl, stir in a heaped dessertspoon of dry flour and when blended add asparagus juice and pepper and salt to taste. Place each asparagus tip on a long strip of buttered bread, spread the above mixture on top of the asparagus and dust with grated cheese. Place in a hot oven for 5 to 7 minutes and serve hot garnished with parsley.

Bombay Toasties

slices of bread 5 mm. (¼ inch)
  thick
pounded meat or paste

chutney
cheese

    Stamp out pieces of bread about the size of a 10 cent piece. Spread with a thin coating of any kind of pounded meat or paste, mixed with a little butter and chutney. Put a thin piece of cheese on top, heat in the oven till the cheese is toasted, then serve.

Canapés of Herring Roes

tin of soft roes
3 small onions
1 dessertspoon white wine
150 ml. (1 gill) of Bechamel
  sauce (see "Sauces" page 63)
a pinch of salt and cayenne pepper

anchovy paste
4 slices bread
30 g. (1 oz.) butter
dry breadcrumbs
30 g. (1 oz.) grated cheese

    Toast bread a golden colour and cut into 8 pieces. Peel and slice onions and cook for 5 minutes in boiling water. Strain off water and add butter. Cook another 5 minutes. Add the cheese, wine and Bechamel sauce, seasoning with salt and pepper. Spread each piece of toast with anchovy paste, on the top of which put a layer of onion mixture, on top of that a piece of roe, then the remainder of the mixture, and sprinkle with breadcrumbs. Place for a few minutes in a hot oven and serve very hot.

Canapés de Sardines

5 French sardines
2 eggs
French mustard
5 small gherkins
5 fried croutons.

butter
chives
parsley
Tarragon vinegar

    Fry some pieces of bread about the length and width of a sardine. Skin and fillet the sardines. Lay half of them aside and pound the remainder with the yolks of eggs, a teaspoon of French mustard and about a teaspoon of chopped parsley and Tarragon vinegar. Mix all these and blend them with a little butter. Spread the mixture on the croutons and lay ½ sardine on each. Place in the oven to get quite hot and serve with a pickled gherkin on each.

Cheese Aigrettes

150 ml. (¼ pint) water
15 g. (½ oz.) butter
1 egg

30 g. (1 oz.) flour
45 g. (1½ oz.) cheese
pepper, salt and cayenne pepper

    Put the water and butter into a small saucepan. When boiling remove from heat and stir the flour in quickly. Beat well and cook for 2 or 3 minutes, then cool slightly. Break the egg and beat it in well. Add cheese grated, salt, pepper and cayenne. Cool on a plate, then fry in teaspoonfuls in smoking-hot fat. Drain on paper and serve neatly, sprinkled with grated cheese and cayenne pepper.

Cheese Cake

6 rounds of buttered bread
30 g. (1 oz.) butter
1 teacup flour
pepper, salt

60 g. (2 oz.) grated cheese
1 egg (large)
½ teaspoon baking powder
1 tablespoon milk

Rub butter into flour; add cheese and baking powder. Make into a stiff paste with egg and milk. Heap on buttered bread or pastry and bake in a quick oven. If you line a small patty tin with the bread or pastry, this will ensure a good-shaped cake. Serve hot.

Cheese and Celery Toasts

Cut up some celery into small pieces and boil it with a little milk till quite soft. Add as much grated cheese as liked and season accordingly. Boil up, stirring well, till it is fairly thick, then spread it on pieces of buttered toast. Sprinkle with paprika or cayenne on serving.

Cheese Dip

185 g. (6 oz.) butter
375 g. (12 oz.) cheese
large pinch cayenne pepper

1 teaspoon sugar
6 tablespoons sherry

Cream the butter and beat in grated cheese. Add sugar, cayenne and sherry and beat together to give a soft consistency. Put in a small dish and serve with biscuits, celery sticks, cauliflower sprigs or French bread, cut into a suitable size for dipping into the mixture.

Cheese Eclairs

60 g. (2 oz.) grated cheese
150 ml. (1 gill) cream
150 ml. (1 gill) water
2 eggs

30 g. (1 oz.) butter
90 g. (3 oz.) flour
cayenne pepper and salt
vinegar

Boil the water and butter. Add the flour and stir till it leaves the sides of the saucepan. Let it cool; then add the eggs separately and beat till smooth. Pipe mixture on a greased and papered tin, in 5 cm. (2-inch) lengths. Bake in a moderate oven for ½ hour. When cold cut open the side and fill with cheese mixed with whipped cream and cayenne, salt and vinegar to taste. Arrange on fancy paper d'oyley and garnish with cress.

Cheese Fritters

125 g. (¼ lb.) flour
125 g. (¼ lb.) grated cheese
1 egg
1 teacup warm water

½ teaspoon dry mustard
pepper and salt
1 teaspoon butter

Mix together flour, cheese, mustard, pepper and salt in a basin. Melt butter in a teacup of warm water and add the beaten yolk of egg. Stir the moist mixture into the dry one and beat well. Lastly stir in the stiffly beaten white of egg. Drop the mixture from a dessertspoon into smoking fat and fry to a delicate brown. Drain and serve piping hot.

31

Cheese Pastry

some good pastry
grated cheese
1 egg

pepper and salt
a few grains cayenne pepper

Make some good pastry. Roll it out very thin. Sprinkle with grated cheese. Season with pepper and salt and if liked a few grains of cayenne and roll up tightly. Roll out once more, if possible even thinner than the first time. Sprinkle again all over with cheese. Roll up once more and set aside for ½ hour in a cold place to get crisp. Roll once more into a sheet, cut into straws, rounds or any fancy shapes, prick with a fork and bake quickly in a hot oven. Brush over with beaten egg while hot, sprinkle finely grated cheese over the top and close the oven for a minute just to glaze the biscuits. Take care not to burn them at this stage. Serve hot or cold. This is a good recipe for using up dry pieces of cheese.

Cheese Patties

puff paste
1 egg
cayenne pepper

30 g. (1 oz.) grated cheese
a dessertspoon cream
salt and pepper

Line some patty pans with paste. Beat the yolk of egg with grated cheese. Add cream and seasoning and last of all the white of egg beaten stiff. Fill cases and bake in a quick oven. Serve at once.

Cream Cheese (*See* also page 13.)

(*a*)
sour thick cream

salt, pepper and cayenne pepper

Mix ingredients well together. Put into muslin and hang over bowl till moisture filters through. The cream cheese will be ready for use in ½ hour.

(*b*)
equal parts of milk and cream
½ cup water

⅔ tablespoon essence of Rennet

Stir milk and cream well, then add essence of Rennet in the water. Stir in and let it stand for 12 hours, until nicely set. Skim off the top and lay in layers in a muslin cloth. Hang up until it stops dripping, then change the muslin and hang up again till firm. Knead with spoon. Put into shapes lined with paper, when it will be ready for use.

Cheese Puffs (Savoury)

Fold some finely grated cheese into stiffly whisked egg whites, season and drop in spoonfuls into hot, deep fat. Fry till golden, then drain and serve.

Cheese Roulettes

60 g. (2 oz.) cream cheese
45 g. (1½ oz.) breadcrumbs

1 yolk and 1 egg
salt, pepper, cayenne pepper

Cut up cheese in basin, mix in breadcrumbs and seasoning and add yolk of egg. Turn out on floured board. Knead together and divide into small rolls. Dip in egg and breadcrumbs and fry in deep fat. Serve at once on paper d'oyley.

Cheese Sticks

60 g. (2 oz.) breadcrumbs	60 g. (2 oz.) butter
60 g. (2 oz.) grated cheese	60 g. (2 oz.) flour
pinch of baking powder	salt and pepper
egg to bind	

Rub butter into flour and breadcrumbs, add other dry ingredients and bind with well-beaten egg. Knead carefully and roll out on board. Cut into fingers. Bake in moderate oven.

Cheese Straws

30 g. (1 oz.) flour	cayenne pepper and salt
30 g. (1 oz.) butter	a little yolk of egg and water
45 g. (1½ oz.) dry grated cheese	

Rub the butter into the flour. Add the cheese and seasonings. Bind to a stiff paste with the yolk of egg and water. Roll out thinly and cut into straws and rings. Bake in a quick oven for 5 to 7 minutes. Place the straws through the rings and serve hot.

Cheese Toast

50/60 g. (2 oz.) grated cheese	75 ml. (½ gill) of milk
rounds fried bread	chopped parsley
cayenne pepper, salt	a few crumbs
1 egg	

Melt the butter in a saucepan. Add the beaten egg, milk and crumbs. Stir over a gentle heat till it begins to thicken, then add grated cheese, salt and cayenne. Pile high on small croûtes fried in butter and garnish with chopped parsley. Arrange on hot dish on paper d'oyley. Garnish with sprays of parsley.

Cinnamon Toast with Nuts

3 tablespoons butter	2 tablespoons brown sugar
1 teaspoon cinnamon	3 slices bread
2 tablespoons walnuts	

Cream butter and add cinnamon. Cut stale bread in 5 mm. (¼-inch) slices, remove crusts and cut in 3 pieces, crosswise. Toast on one side. Spread untoasted side with butter mixture and sprinkle with finely chopped walnuts. Put in oven until sugar melts and serve at once on hot plate.

Croûtes à la Garrick

2 hard-boiled eggs	½ teacup of thick white sauce
rolls of bacon	toast

Chop the whites of eggs roughly and mix in sauce. Pile on rounds of toast. Rub the yolks of eggs through a sieve on top of the savoury and place rolls of bacon previously fried on top. Garnish with parsley and serve hot.

Croûtes à l'Indienne

a few round croûtes of
fried bread
30 g. (1 oz.) butter
2 eggs

1 teaspoon curry powder
1 teaspoon chutney
1 teaspoon anchovy essence
1 tablespoon breadcrumbs

Melt the butter; add the beaten egg and breadcrumbs and when it begins to thicken add the chutney, curry powder and anchovy essence. Pile on the croûtes. Arrange on a hot dish and serve, garnished with watercress.

Croûtes of Cod Roes

1 tin cod roes
4 sliced tomatoes
2 tablespoons finely chopped
onion

fried bread
parsley
cayenne pepper

On slices of fried bread place fried, sliced tomatoes and onion. Fry neat pieces of the roe and arrange on the tomatoes and onion. Serve very hot. Drop $\frac{1}{2}$ teaspoon of tomato ketchup or sauce on top of roe and a sprinkle of cayenne pepper. Heat again in oven and serve hot.

Devils on Horseback

rashers of streaky bacon
prunes
rounds of bread
almonds

allow 1
for each
person

butter
chutney
parsley (for garnish)

Stew or steam prunes (previously soaked an hour or two), being careful not to break them. Stone them and stuff with chopped chutney and an almond if liked. Cut the rashers of bacon in half and wrap round each stuffed prune. Place each on a round of buttered bread. Put into a quick oven and when crisp serve with a garnish of parsley.

Sardines, oysters, or fish roe may be used instead of prunes.

Eggs and Caviare

French rolls
butter
caviare

lemon juice
hard-boiled eggs

Cut some French rolls into thin round slices; butter them. Spread them with caviare and sprinkle with lemon juice. Cut some hard-boiled eggs into rounds and lay one on each slice. Serve cold.

Eggs Stuffed

some hard-boiled eggs

a little cream or butter
flavouring if desired

Have ready number of hard-boiled eggs required; cut in half, remove yolks and mash with a little cream or butter. To this mixture can be added grated cheese, anchovy or anchovy and cheese, mashed sardines, grated nuts, curry paste or any potted fish, meat or tomato sauce. Refill the whites with this mixture and place on rounds of buttered bread. Garnish with parsley and a caper or small piece of pickle on top.

Egg and Tomato Toastie

small piece of onion

1 tomato—skinned

pepper, salt and parsley

2 eggs

30 g. (1 oz.) butter

rounds of bread

Chop onion very finely and fry in butter. Add tomato cut up and fry all together. Beat eggs and add to mixture. Cook gently till set. Season and leave till cold. Cut into small portions and place each on rounds of buttered bread. Decorate with parsley and serve cold. Grated cheese may be added to this mixture if liked.

Egg and Ham Tartlets

Line some very small tartlet moulds with pastry. Mince 125 g. ($\frac{1}{4}$ lb.) of lean cooked ham (or bacon) with 3 hard-boiled eggs. Bind with 3 raw egg-yolks and a little cream and season with salt, pepper and a little grated nutmeg. Fill the tartlets with this, place in moderate oven until pastry is cooked.

Eggs Mimosa

Hard-boil the eggs and cut in half. Remove yolks and stuff whites with a purée of foie gras. Cover lightly with a sauce made of one-third Bechamel sauce (see page 63) and two-thirds mayonnaise so that the flavour of the foie gras is not spoiled. Rub the egg yolks through a coarse sieve over the stuffed whites and sauce so that they form little yellow balls from which this very nice savoury derives its name.

Fish Toast

breakfast cup cold boiled

fish

300 ml. ($\frac{1}{2}$ pint) milk

teaspoon flour

30 g. (1 oz.) butter

1 yolk of egg

seasoning and hot buttered

toast

Shred any remains of cold boiled fish, carefully removing all skin and bone. Melt the butter in a saucepan and mix in a tablespoon of flour. Add the milk; stir for a minute or two till smooth and boiling, then put in the fish. Season with salt and pepper. Beat egg and add to fish and stir well, taking care that the egg does not curdle. Spread the mixture at once on some squares of hot buttered toast. Dust with cayenne pepper. Garnish with chopped parsley or slice of hard-boiled egg and serve at once.

Fish Toastie

short crust

toast

chutney

anchovies or sardines

1 hard-boiled egg

butter or a little cream

Make some rounds of short crust or toast. Put round the edge some chopped chutney. Fill in centre with anchovy or sardine mixture, made by mixing the hard-boiled egg, butter or cream with a little of the anchovy or mashed sardine. Serve cold.

French Toast

(a)

rounds of bread	pepper and salt
1 egg	teacup milk

Beat egg with the milk, salt and pepper. Pour over rounds of bread and allow to stand 1 hour. This can be fried and served with bacon or underneath fillet of beef or as a garnish for mince.

(b)

Quick method (*See* page 15 under Baked Eggs and Gravy)

Fried Cheese Sandwiches

slices of bread	cream cheese
butter	salt and pepper

Spread slices of bread with butter and cream cheese, salt and pepper. Cover with slices of buttered bread and cut any shape. Fry in boiling hot butter. Serve very hot.

Gherkin Croûtons

6 croûtons of fried bread	2 teaspoons butter
2 hard-boiled eggs	salt and pepper
3 or 4 small gherkins cut into strips	2 teaspoons grated cheese

Mix butter, cheese and yolk of egg till quite smooth. Season and spread thickly on croûtons. Decorate with gherkins in lattice work round the edge and put a spoonful of white of egg, very finely chopped, in the centre. Serve cold.

Haddock and Cheese Savoury

any quantity of Finnon haddock	teaspoon of chopped parsley
	a little mustard
50/60 g. (2 oz.) grated cheese	pinch of cayenne pepper
1 tablespoon cream	1 egg

Scrape the fish from the bone; mince or pound and mix it with other ingredients. Cook this for a minute or two, then add a beaten egg and boil the mixture for another minute or so. Serve on hot buttered toast. Crab or kippers may be done in this way. Garnish with chopped parsley.

Ham Canapés

1 cup ham	cream
2 tablespoons grated cheese	buttered toast
a little cayenne pepper	brown breadcrumbs

Chop very finely enough ham, with a little fat, to make a cupful. Add grated cheese, cayenne and enough cream to make the mixture of

36

a consistency to spread. Put this evenly on slices of buttered toast; cover top with breadcrumbs. Set in oven to heat through.

Herring Roes en Croûtes

1 tin soft roes
6 small croûtes of fried bread
15 g. (½ oz.) butter
1 egg

1 tablespoon cream
cayenne pepper
lemon juice

Put the butter in a saucepan. Pound the roes until soft and add to the butter with beaten egg and cream. Stir till it thickens. Add lemon juice and cayenne. Serve on hot croûtes. Arrange on fancy paper d'oyley and garnish with parsley.

Herring Roes on Toast

1 tin herring roes
butter
a little French mustard

salt and pepper
hot buttered toast

Heat roes in butter; season with salt, pepper and French mustard and pile on hot buttered toast.

Indian Croûtes

4 or 5 small rounds of bread
8 almonds
50/60 g. (2 oz.) cheese

cayenne pepper
chutney

Fry bread in a little butter, heating butter till it begins to get brown before putting bread in. Blanch and shred almonds; grate cheese and put in a pan with chopped chutney. Add cayenne. Put a little of the mixture on each croûte and decorate with almonds. Put back in the oven and serve hot.

Kidney Savoury

3 sheep's kidneys
30 g. (1 oz.) butter
chopped parsley
1 small onion
15 g. (½ oz.) flour

1 tablespoon Worcester sauce
salt and pepper
thin slices of buttered toast
breadcrumbs mixed with 30 g.
(1 oz.) grated cheese

Prepare the kidneys by splitting in two and removing the sinews and outer skin. Wash them in salted water, afterwards mincing finely. Put a little butter into a stewpan and add some chopped parsley and chopped small onion. Let these fry together for a few minutes, then add Worcester sauce. Sprinkle in flour and boil up again for 2 minutes. Whilst boiling, stir in the minced kidneys, with salt and pepper to taste. Butter some thin slices of toast and cover with the mince; sprinkle over a thick layer of breadcrumbs and grated cheese. Place in a quick oven for about 10 minutes and serve very hot.

Smoked Salmon en Croûtes

1 small tin of smoked salmon	30 g. (1 oz.) butter
round croûtes fried bread	1 small onion
cayenne pepper	1 teaspoon Worcester sauce
parsley	

Fry the croûtes. Keep them hot. Take out the salmon and allow 2 or 3 pieces for each croûte. Put the butter in a stewpan; add the salmon, chopped small onion and chopped parsley. Stir till it heats thoroughly; add the cayenne and Worcester sauce. Place on the croûtes and serve hot.

Devilled Poultry Liver

3 chicken livers or	streaky bacon
1 turkey liver	1 teaspoon anchovy essence
30 g. (1 oz.) butter	seasoning of mustard, salt,
1 small onion	cayenne pepper, pinch of
	nutmeg or mixed herbs

Mince liver and onion and fry in a small saucepan till brown. Add other ingredients and thicken with one teaspoon of dry flour. Form into small sausages and wrap around with thin slices of bacon, tying them with a small piece of white thread. Fry in pan till bacon is cooked and serve on hot toast. Garnish with parsley and chopped almonds.

Liver Paté

250 g. (8 oz.) calves' liver	90 g. (3 oz.) butter
or chicken livers	1 small onion, finely chopped
1 rasher fat bacon	parsley and herbs
2 tablespoons water or stock	1 dessertspoon brandy or
	sherry, if liked

Fry the onion gently in a saucepan with 30 g. (1 oz.) butter without browning. Add liver and bacon chopped, also herbs, salt and pepper. Add water and simmer very slowly until tender, either in a saucepan or a casserole in the oven. When cold, mince finely twice. Blend in rest of butter and brandy or sherry. Place in small dish and chill. Serve with crisp toast and butter.

Marmite and Cheese Toasties

30 g. (1 oz.) grated cheese	seasoning
½ teaspoon Marmite	buttered toast
1 teaspoon butter	

Put the cheese into a small saucepan with the Marmite, seasoning and butter. Stir over a low heat. When melted, spread on rounds of buttered toast and serve hot.

Marrow Bone Savoury

(a)

marrow bones, 1 for each	parsley
person	toast
salt	

Ask the butcher to cut marrow bones 7.5 cm. (3 in.) thick and scrape the sides perfectly clean. Place in a hot oven for 10 minutes. Salt and send to the table at once, arranged in a folded serviette. Garnish with parsley and serve with small strips of toast.

(b)

marrow bones, 1 for each person
a little dry flour

dry toast
pepper and salt

Dust ends of marrow bones with dry flour. Place in boiling water or in soup pot and boil for about 1 hour. Shake marrow out of bone; spread on dry toast; sprinkle with pepper and salt. Place in oven for a few minutes and serve very hot.

(c) Or sprinkle with lemon juice, cayenne, pinch of curry powder and chopped parsley. Return to oven and serve very hot.

Messina Toasties

6 rounds buttered bread
chutney, grated cheese
mustard, capers

12 sardines, 2 eggs
teaspoon of lemon juice
chopped parsley

Bone and skin the sardines. Pound them with chutney and yolks of hard-boiled eggs. Add mustard, lemon juice and seasoning to taste. Arrange on bread; sprinkle with grated cheese. Put in quick oven and serve hot, garnished with capers and parsley.

Mushroom Savoury

(a)

mushrooms
butter

salt and pepper
rounds of hot buttered toast

Peel mushrooms and cut off crest. When all are peeled and washed, place in frying pan with hot butter, white side of mushroom down. Sprinkle with salt and pepper. When crisp, turn and fry on other side and serve on rounds of hot buttered toast.

(b)

24 mushrooms
1 small onion

chopped parsley
salt and pepper

Peel the mushrooms; chop them. Melt the butter. Fry the chopped onion. Add mushrooms, parsley, salt and pepper and fry for 10 minutes. Pour into warm china soufflé cases; serve hot, garnished with parsley or on buttered toast.

Mushroom and Tomato Savoury

oblong pieces of bread
mushrooms
seasoning

tomato sauce
hard-boiled egg
chopped parsley

Fry bread and cover with tomato sauce. Put a fried mushroom on each croûte. Sprinkle with pepper and salt. Chop the white and yolk of egg separately; scatter over top of mushrooms. Reheat and serve garnished with parsley.

Olives Stuffed

small fried croûtons of bread

a few olives

1 hard-boiled egg

anchovy paste

1 tablespoon cream

lemon juice, cayenne pepper

Fry some small rounds of bread; spread over a little anchovy paste. Whip the cream; mix in a dessertspoon of anchovy paste; season with cayenne and lemon juice. Stone the olives; fill with the mixture, place an olive on each fried croûton and border the edge with chopped yolk of egg.

Rajah's Toast

Spread toast with ham paste flavoured with curry powder and sprinkle with chopped chutney.

Oysters on Toast

1 tin oysters

tablespoon lemon juice

30 g. (1 oz.) butter

½ teaspoon chopped parsley

salt and pepper

Put the butter in a saucepan. When dissolved, add the lemon juice, parsley and the liquor from the oysters. Let it boil up, add the oysters and cook them carefully. Season with pepper and salt and serve on toast.

Pineapple and Cream Cheese

Make some cream balls by working enough cream cheese into some salad cream for the mixture to bind and then rolling it on a wet board with a wet knife. Put some lettuce leaves on a dish, place pineapple rings on top and put a cream cheese ball in the centre of each. Arrange some watercress between the rings and serve.

Sardine or Anchovy Straws

short pastry

boned anchovies or sardines

cayenne pepper

Make some short pastry (see page 160). Roll out thinly and cut into strips. Twist each round a boned anchovy or sardine and season with cayenne. Bake until crisp. Sardines may be dipped in grated cheese or tomato sauce and the pastry rolled round.

Sardine Butter

125 g. (4 oz.) butter

1 tin of sardines

cayenne pepper

anchovy

salt

Take a small tin of sardines and wash the fish quickly in cold water. Scrape off the skins; remove the flesh from the bones and pound in a mortar with fresh butter. Add 125 g. (4 oz.) of butter gradually. Season with salt, cayenne and a few drops of anchovy. Work all into a smooth paste. Form the paste into small balls or cakes and serve on cracked ice with buttered water biscuits.

Sardine Toast

4 sardines	black pepper
4 eggs	salt
90 g. (3 oz.) butter	bread

Skin and pound the sardines. Warm them with a little butter and pepper. Spread on squares of buttered toast. Heat the yolks of 4 and the whites of 3 eggs in a small saucepan with the butter; season with pepper and salt. Put a thick layer of this over the sardine and pile the stiffly whisked white of egg on the top of each square to cover it. Brown in a very quick oven and serve hot.

Savoury Aspic

1 egg	aspic	1 cooked carrot
chopped parsley	lettuce	a few cooked peas

Place slices of hard-boiled egg at the bottom of small moulds and add peas, chopped parsley, slice of carrot, a couple of prawns, sardines, or any fish available. Fill up the cup with aspic jelly (see page 101) and when set turn out and serve on bed of lettuce with mayonnaise sauce.

Savoury Cheese Biscuits

a few water biscuits or cheese biscuits	80 ml. (½ gill) cream
	30 g. (1 oz.) Parmesan or grated cheese
slices of beetroot pickled	cayenne pepper and salt

Butter the biscuits. Place thin slices of pickled beetroot or gherkin on each biscuit. Whip the cream. Add the grated cheese, cayenne and salt. Put mixture into a piping machine and decorate biscuits with it. Colour a little with a few drops of carmine. Pipe a rose in the centre of each. Serve on paper d'oyley.

Scotch Toast

haddock	curry powder
butter	lemon juice
cayenne pepper	

Pick all the flesh from a cold, boiled, dried haddock. Mince the fish. Add a little butter, cayenne pepper, a pinch of curry powder and a dash of lemon juice. When all are blended, put the basin in a warm oven, with a plate over it, for ½ hour. If you wish to keep the mixture, place in a jar, press down and cover with melted butter. Have ready rounds of fancy shaped pieces of buttered toast, spread thickly with the fish mixture, garnish with chopped yolk of egg and serve very hot.

Scotch Woodcock
(a)

fried croûtes bread	1 yolk of egg
2 tablespoons cream	anchovy paste
15 g. (½ oz.) butter	cayenne pepper

Spread the croûtes with anchovy paste; put butter in a stewpan; add the yolk of egg and cream. Stir gently till it begins to thicken. Season with cayenne. Pour hot on to croûtes. If allowed to boil it will curdle. Arrange on fancy paper d'oyley and serve hot.

(b)

anchovy paste	hot buttered toast
150 ml. (1 gill) milk	1½ teaspoons flour
30 g. (1 oz.) butter	2 yolks of eggs
1 flat teaspoon chopped parsley	salt and cayenne pepper

Make hot buttered toast and cut into small rounds or squares. Spread each with anchovy paste and keep warm. Heat the butter in a saucepan. When hot, stir in the flour and add hot milk. Simmer a few minutes, keeping it well stirred, then cool slightly. Add the yolks separately. Beat the first one in thoroughly before adding the second. Stir over a warm heat to cook the eggs. Do not boil. Season and add parsley. Spread neatly on the prepared pieces of hot toast and serve very hot.

Toasted Cheese

small pieces of bread	slices of cheese
butter	tomato sauce

Butter pieces of bread and lay a slice of cheese on each; or moisten a teacup of grated cheese with a tablespoon of milk and spread on bread. Pour ½ teaspoon of tomato sauce on top of cheese. Put on dish; heat in oven till cheese is melted and serve.

Tomato Anchovy and Cream Savoury

a few rounds of brown bread and butter	lemon juice
2 tomatoes	boned anchovies
75 ml. (½ gill) cream	cayenne pepper, parsley
	butter

Cut some rounds of thin bread and butter. Dip the edges in liquid butter and chopped parsley. Spread a little whipped cream on top. Skin the tomatoes. Cut in slices and drain. Put a slice of tomato on each, with a boned anchovy rolled in centre. Pipe a pattern with remainder of cream, seasoned with cayenne and lemon juice. Arrange on fancy paper d'oyley.

Tomato Toast
(a)

rounds of toast	25/30 g. (1 oz.) grated cheese
30 g. (1 oz.) butter	2 or 3 tomatoes
Tarragon vinegar	chopped parsley
pinch of cayenne pepper	

Pour boiling water on tomatoes and remove skins. Put into stew-pan with butter and seasoning. Add cheese and Tarragon vinegar to taste and thicken with a little dry flour if tomatoes are very watery. Pour on to buttered toast, sprinkle with parsley and serve.

(b)

2 tomatoes	½ cup breadcrumbs
30 g. (1 oz.) butter	1 oz. grated cheese
1 egg	salt, cayenne pepper
croûtes of fried bread	

Put the butter in a stewpan. Let it melt and add the skinned and sliced tomatoes. Fry to a pulp; add breadcrumbs, beaten egg, salt, cayenne and cheese. Stir till hot but do not let it boil. Pile on hot fried croûtes.

Other suggestions for toasties

Small sausage rolls.

Pastry cases filled with minced meat or fish, well seasoned.

Minced ham, chicken brains or chopped cooked celery put into a well-seasoned white sauce served on pieces of toast or French toast.

Chopped liver and bacon, with a little minced onion, on toast.

Devilled ham, i.e. grilled ham sprinkled with grated cheese and cayenne.

Prawns, curried or plain, on toast.

Grilled tomatoes sprinkled with grated cheese or chopped pickled walnut.

Scrambled egg cooked with seasoning and chopped parsley or thyme, to which grated cheese or cream cheese is added. Allow this to cool and use for toasties or sandwiches.

Cream cheese, plain or coloured, piped on to a biscuit.

Cream cheese and pickle on a biscuit.

Cream cheese, mixed with a little vinegar, to which add asparagus tips, chopped celery, celery salt, chopped cucumber, pickled onion, pickled cabbage, tomato, mushrooms, pineapple, nuts, chicken or ham. Serve hot or cold.

NOTE:—*See* also Savoury Sandwich Fillings, many of which are suitable for toasties.

COCKTAILS

Grapefruit, a piece of melon or a fruit cocktail makes a delicious first course for lunch or dinner and in hot weather is often more acceptable than the usual hors d'oeuvres.

Juice from tinned fruits provides delicious cocktails, too. Mix them as you wish, then add some dry ginger ale and, if you have it, a little raspberry vinegar. Tiny pieces of fresh fruit make the best garnish after the drink is iced and poured into glasses. If a thicker cocktail is liked use equal parts of the pulp of grapefruit and oranges, breaking it into small pieces and removing skin and pips. Add a few halved and skinned grapes and a little sugar and lemon juice and cool with ice.

Fruit Cocktail

(a)

2 grapefruit	2 tangerines
2 oranges	½ cup lemon juice, sweetened
a little gin (if liked)	to taste

Divide fruit into sections and remove skins and pips. Place in glasses with their juice and the lemon juice. Decorate with a Maraschino cherry.

(b)

1 cup diced bananas	2 tablespoons diced pineapple
¼ cup orange juice	1 cup diced peach or pawpaw
¼ cup grenadilla juice	2 tablespoons icing sugar
a little preserved ginger	

Mix together peach, banana and pineapple and sprinkle with sugar. Strain over these the orange and grenadilla juice. Serve in sundae glasses. Sprinkle with a little preserved ginger, chopped finely.

Grapefruit

Cut the grapefruit in half. Remove core and pips. Loosen all the sections and carefully remove their skins. Put the pieces into glasses or little bowls or replace in the shell of the fruit with all the juice. Sprinkle about 3 teaspoons of fine sugar over each and leave in a cool place for some hours. A dash of Maraschino may be added if liked. Place a cherry on top for decoration or sprinkle with minced preserved ginger or a little chopped and sugared mint. Blanched almonds or muscatel raisins added to grapefruit also make a variation.

Pineapple Cocktail

Cut pineapple in very small cubes; fill glasses ¾ full; mix with a little salt and cherry brandy. Keep in a cool place and serve with a cherry on top of each glass.

Tomato Juice Cocktail

(a)

2 cups tomatoes (raw or tinned)	½ teaspoon salt
½ cup water	⅛ teaspoon pepper
1½ teaspoons sugar	celery tops
⅛ teaspoon Worcester sauce	3 cloves
5 drops Tabasco sauce (or Chilli vinegar)	1 teaspoon lemon juice

Combine all the ingredients except the lemon juice and boil slowly for 20 minutes. Press through a sieve, forcing through as much pulp as possible. Add lemon juice and chili thoroughly. Serve very cold in glasses. Garnish each glass with an olive.

(b)

2 cups tomato juice	1 teaspoon lemon juice
salt to taste	

See that the tomato juice is ice cold. Stir in lemon juice and salt. Pour into cocktail glasses and serve.

Tomato and Orange Cocktail

2 ripe tomatoes   Tarragon vinegar
2 oranges   olive oil
parsley

Put the tomatoes into hot water for a minute or two then remove skins. Peel the oranges. Slice the tomatoes and oranges thinly and put into glasses in alternate layers. Cover with a sauce made of orange juice, a little Tarragon vinegar and olive oil. Sprinkle with chopped parsley. Serve very cold.

Athol Brose

Make a brew of 500 g. (1 lb.) oatmeal and water, i.e. enough water to make the oatmeal "soft". Allow to stand for at least 2 days. On the day of the party strain the solution into a large jug, preferably through muslin. Add 1 to 2 tablespoons of liquid honey. Stir well until honey is dissolved, then add 500 ml. (1 pint) of cream. Lastly add just over $\frac{1}{4}$ bottle whisky.

Now begin tasting! If found too sweet, add more cream and whisky. The brose should have the full creamy flavour of the whisky.

This should be enough for 8 people.

In hot weather the brose should be kept in a refrigerator.

SOUPS

Stock is the liquid into which the juice and flavour of meat, vegetables, etc., has been drawn out by long and gentle cooking. It serves as a foundation for all kinds of soups, stews and gravies.

Thickenings for Soup

The usual method of thickening soup is with flour with the addition of browning for brown soups. Add milk and flour for white soup, but the better plan is to have a stock of brown and white thickening ready for use. It is usually called by its French name, "Roux". It is far superior to any other form of thickening, as it flavours the soup and sauces at the same time and it is a great help if soup is needed in a hurry (*see* page 51 for recipe).

Purées are thickened by vegetables rubbed through a sieve and added to soup.

Colourings

The importance of appearances in food is obvious and this applies equally to soups.

If your soup is brown see it is a rich golden-brown. If green, a pale delicate shade. If white or cream, see it is truly so and not tinged with grey or brown. Browning is useful and easy to make.

Green Colouring

This greatly improves the appearance of bean and green pea soups. It will not keep but must be made and used at once. Take some spinach and wash well. Large, full-grown leaves are best. Put them quite wet into a mortar and pound thoroughly. Strain off juice that flows from them and add to the soup a minute or two before serving, just enough to make a delicate, not full, shade of green. If you have no mortar, use a basin and round end of a rolling pin.

To Clarify Soups

Put stock in a saucepan and add the shell and white of 1 egg beaten. Mix well and go on stirring until it boils. Simmer for 15 minutes. Then strain through double thickness of butter muslin.

Over-salted Soup

Add a large potato cut in halves to soup which has been over-salted, and cook for a further 15 minutes. The potato, having absorbed most of the surplus salt, can then be taken out.

To Fry Croûtons

Cut stale bread into small squares and drop into boiling butter. Fry till brown. Serve very hot on a separate dish.

Bone Stock

1 kg. (2 lb.) raw bones	salt
2.5 l. (2 quarts) cold water	1 onion
1 carrot	

Wipe bones, remove fat, break bones into pieces. Put them into a saucepan with salt and water. Bring slowly to boiling point and skin well. Add vegetables cut into good-sized pieces. Boil slowly from 4 to 5 hours. Strain through sieve into large basin. When cold remove all fat from top. It ought to form a good jelly which is very nourishing.

Brown Stock

1 kg. (2 lb.) shin of beef	$\frac{1}{2}$ teaspoon salt
2.5 l. (2 quarts) cold water	stick of celery or $\frac{1}{2}$ teaspoon
1 carrot	celery seeds
small onion	parsley and thyme
10 white peppercorns	

Measure the water into a stock-pot or large pan and add salt. Wipe the meat and remove fat and outer skin. Cut meat into small pieces and add to water. Bring slowly to boiling point, then remove all grey scum. Add onion whole and carrot in large pieces. Simmer stock from 5 to 6 hours. Strain and allow to become cold. Remove all fat. The addition of Bovril adds to flavour.

White Stock

Prepare as for brown stock, using knuckle of veal instead of beef. Omit carrot. Trimmings and carcasses of chicken may be added.

Browning

500 ml. (1 pint) water   50 g. (2 oz.) loaf sugar or ordinary
                                                      sugar

Crush the sugar to a powder if loaf is used or roll ordinary sugar
finely and put into a strong saucepan with 1 tablespoon of water.
Stir it over gentle heat until it begins to colour, then put at the side of
stove and stir until it is black **but it must not burn.** Add 500 ml.
(1 pint) of cold water, bring to boil and boil for 5 minutes. Leave until
cold, strain and bottle and cork securely.

Consommé à la Princesse

Beat up 1 egg with 3 tablespoons of milk (or stock with a little green
colouring in it) and a pinch of salt. Butter a shallow dish, pour custard
in and set in a slow oven. Cut into squares or fancy shapes and add to
clear consommé soup.

As long as you have good stock you can vary soup by adding
different vegetables cut up or macaroni, barley, rice, etc.

Chicken Soup

1 chicken   2 leeks   cup of milk
2 tablespoons rice   6 breakfastcups water   parsley
                                  salt and pepper

Put chicken (cleaned and trussed) into cold water, with leeks and
seasoning. Simmer 4 or 5 hours. Strain the soup. Return to pot and
add rice, well washed, or, if preferred, vermicelli. Just before serving,
add milk and parsley chopped very finely.

Cock-a-Leekie

1 fowl   pepper and salt
3 leeks   2.5 l. (2 quarts) water

Wash the leeks well, take off part of the heads and roots. Scald
in boiling water for 5 or 6 minutes, then cut them into small pieces.
Put fowl trussed as for boiling into a stewpan with the pieces of leek,
pepper and salt and 2.5 l. (2 quarts) water. Let the whole simmer very
slowly for 3 or 4 hours, keeping it well skimmed. When ready to
serve take out the fowl which can be served separately with parsley
or egg sauce.

Cream of Barley Soup

1.25 l. (1 quart) white stock   300 ml. ($\frac{1}{2}$ pint) milk
1 teacup barley   yolk of 1 egg
2 onions   pepper and salt
1 turnip

Wash the barley well and put it into the stock when it comes to
the boil. Add the chopped up onions and turnip, pepper and salt.
Simmer for 4 hours, then strain through a hair sieve. Add the milk
thickened with a little flour. The egg yolk beaten into a little cooled
soup should be poured into the tureen before pouring in the rest of
the soup.

French Spinach Soup

500 g. (1 lb.) spinach
15 g. (½ oz.) butter
yolk of egg
milk

tapioca
1.25 l. (1 quart) good stock
seasoning

Wash spinach and melt butter. Shake spinach free from water and put in saucepan with butter and stock, add seasoning and cook till tender. Sieve, add some milk and a little fine tapioca (or blended flour). Simmer till tapioca is cooked. Beat yolk of egg. Pour soup over it and stir well. Serve without cooking again.

Game Soup

½/1 kg. (1 or 2 lb.) oribi,
  bushbuck, or any available
  game
2 onions
butter or dripping

1 dessertspoon flour
4 cloves
½ bay leaf
pepper and salt
1.25 l. (1 quart) water

Cut up the game and wash it in water with a little vinegar in it. Dry the meat and dust it with flour. Brown it and the onion in the butter or dripping. Strain off the fat and add water, seasonings and any vegetables at hand. Simmer for 5 or 6 hours. Strain and thicken the soup with a dessertspoon of flour mixed with a little cold water. A wineglass of port wine or 2 teaspoons Bovril added at the last improves the flavour.

Golden Soup

bacon rinds (or
  30 g. (1 oz.) butter)
250 g. (½ lb.) tomatoes
125 g. (¼ lb.) onions
300 ml. (½ pint) milk
15 g. (½ oz.) flour
pepper and salt

1 kg. (2 lb.) vegetable marrow or
  pumpkin
1 stick celery
1.25 l. (2 pints) water
1 egg yolk
chopped parsley or grated
  cheese if liked

Fry bacon rinds in saucepan. Add all vegetables sliced very thinly and fry with the lid on till all fat is absorbed but do not brown. Shake saucepan often. Add water, salt and pepper and simmer gently for 1½ hours. Remove bacon rinds and rub soup through a sieve. Add flour blended with half the milk. Boil 5 minutes. Add beaten yolk with rest of milk and reheat. Do not boil as egg will curdle. Sprinkle on parsley or cheese. Serve with cubes of fried bread.

Gravy Soup

500 g. (1 lb.) lean shin
1.25 l. (2 pints) stock or water
250 g. (½ lb.) carrots and
  turnips
1 or 2 teaspoons Bovril

a piece of celery
1 teaspoon salt
mixed herbs (tied in a piece of
  muslin)

48

Garnish:—30 g. (1 oz.) vermicelli or cooked macaroni cut in tiny rings.

Shred meat, add water and salt. Stand ½ hour. Bring slowly to boil. Add prepared vegetables. Simmer 1½ hours. Strain through a hair sieve. Season. Add garnish. If a thick gravy soup is required, fry 30 g. (1 oz.) flour in 30 g. (1 oz.) fat till brown and add soup to this after straining. Add Bovril if desired.

Hollandaise Soup

1.25 l. (2 pints) good white stock	30 g. (1 oz.) butter
	30 g. (1 oz.) flour
2 or 3 yolks of eggs	1 teaspoon salt
150 ml. (1 gill) milk or cream	

Garnish:—Small fancy shapes of cooked carrot, turnip, peas, etc.

Prepare garnish and cook in salt water. Melt butter, add flour; then add stock and boil 10 minutes. Cool and add yolks beaten up with the milk or cream. Add seasoning. Stir over moderate heat till soup thickens (do not let it boil). Add garnish and serve very hot.

Julienne Soup

To brown clarified stock add small quantity cooked and shredded turnips, carrots and celery or add Bovril sufficient to give required colour.

Kidney Soup

3 sheep's kidneys	1.25 l. (1 quart) water or stock
onion	salt and pepper
flour	

Wash kidney in salted water and cut it up into small pieces. Fry in fat with onion cut small. Add 1.25 l. (1 quart) of water and boil for 2 or 3 hours gently. Before serving thicken with tablespoon flour and seasoning mixed with cold water. Serve very hot.

Lentil or Split Pea Soup

2 cups lentils or peas	1 fried sliced onion
1 ham bone or meat bone	carrots, turnips
2.5 l. (2 quarts) water	a little parsley
	salt and pepper

Wash lentils or peas and put to soak overnight in 2.5 l. (2 quarts) of water. Put into a large soup pot, ham or meat bone, carrot, turnip, onion and lentils with liquid in which they have been soaked. Cook slowly for 3 or 4 hours, then strain and add a little milk thickened with flour and seasoning. Chopped parsley should be added just before serving. Serve with fried croûtons on a separate dish.

Minestrone Soup

125 g. (¼ lb.) haricot beans (soaked overnight)	2 tablespoons olive oil
	1 garlic clove
white part of 1 leek	1 onion
2 potatoes	2 carrots
handful of peas or finely chopped spinach	1 turnip
	handful of rice
salt	pinch of sugar
1 concentrated beef cube	small tin of tomato purée
Parmesan or grated Tavern cheese	2.5 l. (4 pints) hot water or stock

Boil the haricot beans and while they are cooking prepare the other vegetables. Heat the oil in a heavy frying pan; cut up and slice the onion, leek, garlic clove and sauté them on a low flame without browning; add the sliced carrots, potatoes cut up into little cubes and the turnip. After a few minutes empty the contents of a small tin of tomato purée into the pan; dilute with a cup of hot water; season with a pinch of sugar and a little salt; transfer the vegetables to the saucepan in which the haricot beans are cooking; add the rice and beef cube and simmer the soup for 1 hour. Add Parmesan or grated Tavern cheese just before serving.

Mulligatawny Soup

500 g. (1 lb.) scrag-end neck of mutton	45 g. (1½ oz.) flour
	½ tablespoon curry powder
1 small apple or banana	1 teaspoon lemon juice
onion, carrot, turnip	salt
60 g. (2 oz.) rice	30 g. (1 oz.) dripping
1.25 l. (1 quart) water	

Slice vegetables and fry in dripping. Add flour and curry powder and fry slightly. Add apple or banana chopped, meat cut in small pieces, bones, water and salt. Simmer for 2 hours. Skim well. Strain through hair sieve and reheat. Add lemon juice. Serve with plain boiled rice.

Scotch Broth

½ to 1 kg. (1 or 2 lb.) neck of mutton	1 teacup peas
	2 good-sized leeks
½ teacup barley	2 good-sized carrots
2 small turnips, parsley	2.5 l. (2 quarts) water
salt and pepper	

Soak dried peas overnight, when fresh peas are not in season. Put mutton in soup pot with water. Bring to boil and skim well. Cut vegetables into small dice and grate ½ carrot. Add barley, peas and vegetables. Boil 3 hours or longer. Chop parsley well and put in before serving. Add pepper and salt last.

Tapioca Cream Soup

Same as Hollandaise soup but instead of using butter and flour cook 30 g. (1 oz.) fine sago or tapioca in the stock for 15 minutes before adding the yolks and milk.

Thick Oxtail Soup

1 oxtail	carrots, turnips, etc.
onions	salt and pepper
flour	

Cut the oxtail into sections and soak it in cold salted water for some hours. Take out, dry well, dust with flour and brown it with the onions. Drain off the fat, add water and simmer for 5 or 6 hours. Then put in the cut-up vegetables and boil 1 hour longer. Flavour to taste. Serve as it is or thickened with a little flour. Bovril is sometimes added.

Thickening, Brown or Roux

125 g. (4 oz.) butter   125 g. (4 oz.) flour
   and a slice of a large onion

Put the butter into a small saucepan over very gentle heat and let it melt slowly until it is quite liquid but **on no account** must it boil. Skim the white froth off the top, being careful not to take butter as well. Pour off liquid into another pan leaving white sediment behind. See the flour has no lumps, then stir it little by little into the liquid butter until it is a creamy mass. Continue stirring over **gentle** heat until it is a rich golden-brown. Then stand the pan on a table and put in slice of onion. Continue stirring until it has ceased to bubble. Pour off liquid into small earthenware or glass jars. Cover when cold. Time: 20–30 minutes.

Thickening, White or Roux

This is made in the same way as brown thickening but it is taken off the fire before it acquires any colour.

Vegetable and Tomato Soup

$\frac{3}{4}$ to 1 kg. ($1\frac{1}{2}$ to 2 lb.) of

soup meat	2.5 l. (2 quarts) water
2 carrots	2 turnips
2 leeks or onions	$\frac{1}{2}$ cup peas
1 large tin tomatoes	salt and pepper

If dry peas are used, soak overnight; put beef in pot with water; bring to boil and skim well; cut up vegetables, add to the liquid; boil gently, 2 hours or longer if necessary. 20 minutes before serving add tomatoes, pepper and salt. ————————————

MEATLESS SOUPS

Cream Soup

1 carrot	1 level tablespoon flour
2 onions	1 breakfast cup milk
4 potatoes	1 tablespoon butter
pepper and salt	1.25 l. (1 quart) water

Grate the carrot, chop the onions, peel and slice the potatoes. Sauté all these in the butter and then add water. Cook until soft enough to mash with a wooden spoon. When well mashed, add the flour mixed with a little milk. Stir in the remainder carefully, season with salt and pepper and serve hot. A little cream put in the tureen and soup poured over when serving improves the flavour of the soup.

Cream of Tomato Soup

1 kg. (2 lb.) ripe tomatoes
2 onions, about 250 g. (½ lb.)
1 tablespoon flour
rind of bacon or 2 or 3 rashers
  of bacon

1 breakfast cup milk
3 breakfast cups stock or water
salt, sugar and a pinch of soda
  bicarb.

Put bacon rind or bacon into a soup pot and when hot add the onion, cut into slices. When the onion begins to turn a light brown, add tomatoes, also sliced finely. Keep stirring until the fat of the bacon is well absorbed and then close the pot and allow the ingredients to stew gently in their own juice for about 1 hour. The water or stock should then be added and a pinch of soda to counteract acidity. Simmer for another ½ hour, strain, return to pot and add carefully the milk previously thickened with the flour. Before serving season to taste, adding sugar as required.

Emergency Soup

2 l. (3 pints) water
2 onions
2 large tomatoes
2 carrots
2 turnips

60 g. (2 oz.) dripping
½ teaspoon sweet herbs
2 teaspoons Bovril (gravy
  or stock may be substituted)
pepper and salt

Shred onions. Skin and cut finely tomatoes and fry both in dripping until onions are a nice brown. Scrape or mince carrots and turnips. Put into boiling water, add sweet herbs and gravy, stock or Bovril. Season to taste.

Fish Soup or Bouillabaisse

1 kg. (2 lb.) any white sea-fish
½ clove of garlic
1 teaspoon olive oil
½ teaspoon saffron

1 large onion
a few tomatoes
pepper and salt
water

Put in a saucepan fish, garlic, onion, tomatoes skinned and sliced, pepper and salt, teaspoon olive oil and enough water to cover. Bring to boil quickly, continue stirring almost constantly for about 15 minutes. Stir in ½ teaspoon of saffron. Serve fish on a dish and soup in tureen.

Ground Nut Soup

50 g. (⅛ lb.) nuts
  (skinned and ground)
1 onion
1 stick celery
3 cups white stock

600 ml. (1 pint) milk
30 g. (1 oz.) butter
30 g. (1 oz.) flour
60 g. (2 oz.) cream
seasoning

Put nuts in a pan with chopped onion, celery and milk. Simmer 1 hour and rub through sieve. Melt butter and flour and cook slightly. Add stock and boil, stirring all the time. Add rest of milk and nuts. Boil again and before serving add cream and seasoning.

Normandy Soup

125 g. (¼ lb.) haricot beans	1 turnip
1.25 l. (1 quart) water	celery
2 onions	parsley
1 carrot	30 g. (1 oz.) butter
pepper and salt	

Soak haricot beans all night. Put in a saucepan with 1.25 litres (a quart) of water and add onions, carrot, turnip, celery and parsley, all cut up very small. Boil until the beans are tender, then rub through a fine sieve. Add pepper and salt and 30 g. (1 oz.) butter. Heat up and serve.

Potato Soup

8 potatoes	50 g. (2 oz.) butter
3 leeks	parsley
½ cup milk	1.25 l. (1 quart) cold water

Put whole potatoes into the water with the chopped-up leeks. When cooked, add the butter, mash the potatoes and pass all through a sieve. Then add the chopped-up parsley; and lastly, just before serving, pour in carefully the milk.

NOTE: Can be served with oatcakes and grated cheese.

Vegetarian Soup

2 l. (3 pints) water	1 potato	parsley
1 carrot	15 g. (½ oz.) butter	grated cheese
1 turnip	15 g. (½ oz.) flour	pepper
1 parsnip	300 ml. (½ pint) boiling milk	salt

Mince all vegetables and cook in water until tender. Then prepare white sauce with butter, stir in flour and add boiling milk. Add the vegetable stock with a little chopped parsley and serve with grated cheese. Pepper and salt to taste.

FISH

There are 3 classes of fish:—

(a)

Oily Fish

E.g., herring, salmon, sardines, pilchards, kippers and trout.

These fish have fat distributed throughout their flesh and are very nutritious and with the exception of salmon and trout are usually inexpensive.

Flesh of oily fish is composed of protein, fat and water. It is rich in vitamins A and D.

(b)
White Fish
E.g., fish fillets, tilapia, cod.

The flesh of these fish is composed of protein and water. The fat is found, almost entirely, in the liver which is removed when the fish is cleaned. (Cod-liver oil is produced from cod's liver.)

(c)
Shell Fish
E.g., crabs, lobsters, oysters, prawns.

The flesh is composed of protein, some fat and water. Most of the fat is in the liver. Shell fish is rather difficult to digest owing to the closely knit long fibres.

All sea-fish supply iodine in the diet.

Choice of Fish
The following points should be noticed:—
i.   There should be no unpleasant smell.
ii. The gills should be red.
iii. The eyes bright and prominent.
iv. The flesh firm and the tail stiff.

To Thaw Frozen Fillets
Place in warm water. When thawed use immediately.

Brown Crumbs
Take odd crusts of bread, break up into fairly small pieces and toast in oven till dry and crisp and golden-brown in colour. Crush, sieve and put into dry jar till wanted.

To prepare Prawns, Lobsters, Crabs, etc.
Wash the fish well and place them in very salt water, which *must* be boiling. Lobsters and crabs should be cooked for 15 to 20 minutes; prawns only for 5 to 10 minutes, as they become tough if cooked too long. Remove shell and head of prawn with a sharp knife, then remove the black thread down the back. Replace in salt water and wash well.

Fish and Avocado Pear
Allow for each person:—

½ avocado pear ⅓ cup prawns, shrimps or other
lemon juice or vinegar (white) suitable fish flaked or chopped
lettuce pepper and salt

Mix fish and a little sauce together (*see* Fish Cocktails with Sauce below).

Cut avocado pears in half and remove stone. Sprinkle pear with lemon juice or white vinegar, salt and pepper. Fill with fish and

54

sauce. Decorate with parsley or olive and serve very cold on lettuce leaves.

Fish Baked

1 fish	savoury herbs	yolk of 1 egg
1 onion	1 cup breadcrumbs	dripping
parsley	a little butter	black pepper and salt

Clean a fresh fish and soak in milk and water for ½ hour. Then stuff with the following: onion chopped. parsley and savoury herbs, cup of breadcrumbs, pepper and salt. Work all together with a little dripping or butter and the yolk of egg. Place fish in a baking tin with dripping; scatter breadcrumbs over fish and bake for ½ hour. Baste often and serve with boiled potatoes.

Fish Boiled Whole

Wash and trim fish. Tie in muslin cloth if fish kettle is not procurable. Put in boiling salted water to which add dessertspoon vinegar. Boil quickly for 5 minutes; reduce heat by adding cup of cold water. Remove to side of stove to cook slowly for ½ hour. Drain well and remove cloth. Serve with appropriate sauce. (*See* Sauces.) Garnish with parsley.

Fish Cocktails with Sauce

For each person allow about:—
⅓ cup dried lobster **or**
⅓ cup shredded crab **or**
⅓ cup whole shrimps or oysters.

Mayonnaise sauce coloured pink with tomato sauce or puree and sharpened with Worcester sauce.

Parsley, celery tops or cucumber slices to decorate.

Add prepared fish to the above sauce till fairly stiff. Line glass bowls with lettuce leaves (whole or shredded). Fill with fish mixture and garnish with parsley or celery tops.

Prawn cocktails may be decorated with whole prawns or sliced cucumber put round the edge of the glass.

Chill thoroughly before serving.

Fish Fried

fish	dripping, lard or oil
1 egg	pepper and salt
flour, breadcrumbs, maize meal or oatmeal	

Fillet fish; wash and dry in cloth. Sprinkle with salt and pepper. Dip into beaten egg, then roll in flour, breadcrumbs, maize meal or oatmeal and fry in smoking-hot dripping, lard or oil. Turn when one side is golden-brown. Drain on paper and serve on d'oyley. Garnish with lemon.

Fish Grilled

slices of fish
6 tablespoons melted butter
    to every kilogram (2 lb.)
    of fish

flour
salt and pepper

Cut the slices of fish about 2.5 cm. (1 inch) thick, season with pepper and salt and lay them in the melted butter for ½ hour; then roll them in flour and grill 15 minutes. Serve very hot.

Fish Pickled (Curried)

4 medium-sized lake fish
olive oil or butter
4 onions
salt

60 g. (2 oz.) curry powder
½ tablespoon flour
300 ml. (½ pint) vinegar

Fillet fish and cut to size desired, dip in egg and flour and fry till a nice brown in olive oil or butter (do not use fat). Slice finely 2 of the onions and fry them also. Add 30 g. (1 oz.) curry powder. Mix flour, remainder of curry powder and a little salt with the vinegar. Put this in a saucepan with the other 2 onions sliced and boil till onions are tender. Mix with the other onion and curry and pour all over the fish. This fish can be preserved for some time in airtight jars. Serve cold.

Fish Steamed

fish
milk

a little butter
pepper and salt

Fillet the fish; sprinkle with pepper and salt and then roll, securing the rolls in place with a skewer or sharpened match. Place in a soup plate and cover with milk, putting small dabs of butter on top. Place the soup plate on top of a pan of boiling water and cover with lid. Allow to steam ½ hour and serve either with the milk in which the fish has been cooked or with white sauce made with the milk.

Fish and Tomato

1 fish
a few tomatoes
a little lemon juice
breadcrumbs

1 teacup water
15 g. (½ oz.) butter
salt

Fillet the fish and place in a pyrex dish. Add salt, lemon juice, butter and water. Take tomatoes, scald and remove their skins, cut in slices and lay on top of the fish. Sprinkle with breadcrumbs, and bake for ½ hour.

Haddock Smoked

(a)
haddock
1 egg
breadcrumbs
fat

grated orange peel
thin potato chips
parsley

Cut haddock into suitable pieces and soak in cold water ½ hour. Remove and dry. Skin each piece and dip first in the beaten egg and then in a mixture of breadcrumbs and grated orange peel. Fry in smoking-hot fat and serve with potato chips and parsley.

(b)

haddock	1 cup milk
1 tablespoon butter	level tablespoon flour
pepper	

Cut haddock into suitable pieces, put in a deep dish and pour boiling water over the pieces. Leave soaking 3 or 4 minutes. Remove and dry. Dip each piece in flour to which pepper has been added. Put butter in frying pan and when quite hot fry the fish on both sides. Add the milk, cover the frying pan and allow to simmer for 10 minutes. Serve neatly on a flat meat dish with the sauce poured on top. If a more substantial dish is required poached eggs may also be served, placed on the slices of fish.

(c)

haddock	milk
butter	flour
pepper	

Cut haddock into suitable pieces and soak in cold water to extract salt. Remove and dry. Dip in the flour and pepper. Place in a pyrex dish, cover the fish with hot milk and put dabs of butter on top. Close the pyrex dish and cook in a hot oven for about 20 minutes or until fish is cooked.

Kippers
(a)

Soak the kippers 10 minutes in cold water, dry well, put in frying pan with hot butter or oil, being careful to place the fish skin side down first. Fry well, turn and serve on a hot dish with a little of the melted butter poured over.

(b)

Place the kippers face to face (skins outwards) and fry in a small piece of butter. When lower fish is cooked completely, reverse and fry on the other side.

Lobster Newburg

1 cooked lobster	150 ml. (¼ pint) cream
30 g. (1 oz.) butter	salt and pepper
yolks of 2 eggs	pinch of nutmeg
1 glass sherry	triangles of toast or pastry

Remove meat from cooked lobster and flake or break into pieces. Heat lobster in butter for 2 minutes. Add sherry, nutmeg, salt and pepper. Beat egg yolks, add cream and gradually mix into lobster. Cook slowly, stirring constantly till thick, but do not boil. Remove from heat. Serve with triangles of toast or pastry.

NOTE: Crayfish, scallops or oysters are all excellent cooked as Lobster Newburg but oysters need to be cooked in the sauce, not just heated.

Lobster Thermidor and Sauce

1 fresh lobster (cooked)
  or 1 tinned lobster
30 g. (1 oz.) butter
30 g. (1 oz.) flour
60 g. (2 oz.) grated cheese
salt and pepper to taste

150 ml. ($\frac{1}{4}$ pint) milk
150 ml. ($\frac{1}{4}$ pint) lobster stock
$\frac{1}{4}$ teaspoon mustard
If liked, add yolk of egg.

    Make white sauce with butter, flour, milk and lobster liquid and season well. Add cheese and chopped-up or flaked lobster. Arrange in a fireproof dish or in $\frac{1}{2}$ lobster shells. Sprinkle with breadcrumbs and a little grated cheese and brown in hot oven or under grill.

Prawns à l'Anchovie

prawns
white sauce

anchovy sauce
mashed potatoes

    Cook prawns as described on page 54. Flavour the white sauce (*see* Sauces) with anchovy sauce to taste. Add the prawns and simmer for a few minutes. Serve in a well of mashed potatoes.

Prawns in Aspic

500 g. (1 lb.) prawns
600 ml. (1 pint) aspic jelly
  (*see* page 101)
sliced hard-boiled eggs

truffles
carrots
a few boiled peas

    Prepare prawns by boiling them as above. Place the cooked prawns in the aspic jelly. Line a mould with sliced hard-boiled eggs, truffles, peas and the carrots cut into fancy shapes. Pour the jelly mixture into the mould and leave till set.

Trout (Kinangop)

(*a*)
trout
butter

pepper and salt

    Clean the trout well, being careful not to injure the skin. Sprinkle with salt and pepper and bake in oven with butter. Trout can also be fried after being dipped in oatmeal.

(*b*)
    If trout are very small, after being well cleaned and sprinkled with salt and pepper they can be packed closely in a pie dish and covered with vinegar. Cover dish with greased paper and put into a slow oven. Cook for 1 hour. Can be served hot or cold.

Zanzibar Fish

1 kg. (2 lb.) fish
milk of 1 coconut
1 cup water
1 coconut grated
2 bay leaves

3 peppercorns
3 cloves
30 g. (1 oz.) butter
salt and pepper

Wash fish; fillet it and put aside in cold salted water. Take the bones and skin and put them into a saucepan. Add milk of coconut, water, grated coconut, bay leaves, cloves, salt and pepper. Boil for 2 hours, strain and place fish in the liquid. Simmer for 15 minutes, add butter and serve hot.

COOKED FISH DISHES

(Ways of Doing Up Cooked or Tinned Fish)

Fish au Gratin

about 250 g. (½ lb.) boiled fish	300 ml. (½ pint) milk
1 cup grated cheese	1 teaspoon mustard
60 g. (2 oz.) butter	pepper and salt
60 g. (2 oz.) flour	breadcrumbs

Fillet the fish and place it in a buttered pie dish. Make a white sauce of the butter, flour and milk, flavouring it with the grated cheese, mustard, pepper and salt. Pour this over the fish. Sprinkle the top with breadcrumbs and a little more cheese. Bake in a hot oven until brown on top.

Fish Cakes

250 g. (½ lb.) cooked or tinned fish	pepper and salt
	lemon juice
125 g. (¼ lb.) mashed potatoes	a little white sauce or 1 egg
15 g. (½ oz.) butter	
1 teaspoon chopped parsley	

Remove skin and bone from the fish and flake it finely. Place in a basin. Add the potato, parsley, seasoning, butter and lemon juice. Mix well, then stir in the sauce or egg to bind it together. Divide into equal-sized pieces and form these into neat, flat, round cakes. Coat the cakes with beaten egg and dry white crumbs. Fry in deep fat and drain well. Serve on a d'oyley, garnished with parsley and lemon.

Fish Creamed

1 kg. (2 lb.) steamed fish	chopped parsley
600 ml. (1 pint) white sauce	lemon juice or a few drops vinegar
salt and pepper	

Break the fish into flakes, removing skin and bones. Grease a pie dish and fill it with alternate layers of fish and sauce, seasoning with salt, pepper, chopped parsley and lemon juice.

Fish Custard

(*a*) Baked

350 g. (¾ lb.) cooked fish	500 ml. (1 pint) milk
3 eggs	salt and pepper
a little butter	

Have ready some cooked fish, preferably boiled or steamed. Flake the fish and if large divide the flakes into 2 or 3 portions. Beat 3 eggs till creamy and add milk and seasoning. Put fish into a greased pie or pyrex dish and pour over egg mixture. Add a few dabs of butter on top. Cover with greased paper and bake in a very slow oven till firm. 15 minutes before serving, remove paper, in order to brown top slightly.

(*b*) Steamed

Proceed with fish as in above recipe, using same ingredients only divide whites from yolks of eggs and beat separately. The whites should be added last of all. Pour mixture in a greased pudding bowl, cover with greased paper and steam for 1 hour, or till custard is set. A little finely chopped parsley may be added to give flavour.

Fish Mousse (Cold)

1½ cups well-beaten fish, mix with ¾ cup aspic jelly and ½ cup whipped cream. Season sharply with salt, paprika, vinegar and Worcester sauce.

Fish Pie

250 g. (8 oz.) cooked fish	cooked potatoes
or small tin of salmon	salt and a little cayenne pepper
60 g. (2 oz.) flour	2 teaspoons lemon juice
60 g. (2 oz.) butter	1 cooked onion sliced
600 ml. (1 pint) milk	chopped parsley

Break up the fish with a fork. Make a sauce with the flour, butter and milk, seasoning it well. Add the fish, lemon juice, chopped onion and parsley. Place this mixture in a pie dish. Mash the potatoes with a little milk, butter and salt. Put this in a thick layer on top of the fish mixture or force through a vegetable rose pipe on to it. Brown in a hot oven.

Fish Pudding

250 g. (8 oz.) cold boiled or	60 g. (2 oz.) butter
tinned fish	a piece of onion
60 g. (2 oz.) breadcrumbs	chopped parsley
a little milk	pepper and salt
2 eggs	

Soak breadcrumbs in the milk and add to it the fish broken into small pieces. Mix with it the eggs well beaten, the butter warmed, the onion chopped finely, the parsley, pepper and salt. Put the mixture into a well-buttered mould and steam for 1 hour. Turn out and serve with anchovy or oyster sauce.

Fish Soufflé

2½ cups cold boiled or tinned fish
2 tablespoons butter
2 tablespoons flour
300 ml. (½ pint) milk
juice of ½ lemon
2 eggs
seasoning

Melt butter, add dry flour and mix to a smooth paste being careful not to brown it. Add the milk gradually until it boils. Now add the fish mashed up and the lemon juice. Take from the stove and, when cooled a little, stir in the egg yolks. Lastly, fold in the stiffly beaten whites and pour all into a buttered mould. This can be steamed or baked for ¾ hour. Serve at once.

Fish Soused

any quantity boiled fish
2 onions
250 to 300 ml. (½ pint) vinegar
2 bay leaves
1 blade mace
1 teaspoon sugar
½ teaspoon salt
½ teaspoon whole pepper
1 whole pimento

Slice and boil the onions. Arrange the fish as flat as possible in a dish; place the prepared onion on top of it. Put the vinegar, sugar, salt, pepper and other seasonings in a pan and simmer for ¼ hour. Pour this over the fish and onion and leave to become cold.

Fish Kedgeree

125 g. (¼ lb.) rice
250 g. (½ lb.) cooked or tinned fish
1 egg
60 g. (2 oz.) butter
1 tablespoon chopped parsley
pepper and salt

Remove skin and bone from the fish, boil the rice and drain. Boil the egg hard. Melt the butter in a saucepan and add to it the fish, rice and white of egg chopped up. Season to taste and when thoroughly hot pile on a warm dish, sprinkling over it the parsley and egg yolk sieved on top.

Mayonnaise of Lobster or Salmon

1 cooked lobster or a tin of salmon
150 ml. (1 gill) mayonnaise
2 hard-boiled eggs
beetroot or tomato
cucumber and radish
lettuce

WITH LOBSTER. Split the tail and remove the flesh. Take the flesh from the claws and cut all into neat pieces. Put aside some of the salad, etc., and the claws for decorating. Mix remainder of salad and pieces of lobster with mayonnaise. Pile in a salad bowl and garnish with reserved pieces of salad, the eggs and the claws.

WITH SALMON. Coat the fish evenly with mayonnaise and arrange on fresh green salad, decorating with radish, tomato, cucumber and beetroot according to taste.

Oyster Patties

1 tin oysters	salt and pepper
puff pastry	egg
chopped parsley	coating sauce

Season the coating sauce (*see* page 64) with chopped parsley to taste. Drain the oysters and add to the sauce. Make patties (*see* page 167), and just before serving fill them with the oyster and sauce mixture.

Reheating Cold Fish

(*a*) Over 250 g. (½ lb.) of fine breadcrumbs pour 1 teacup of hot milk and after 20 minutes of soaking beat well with a wooden spoon. Add 250 g. (½ lb.) of cooked fish previously flaked, 2 tablespoons of liquid butter and seasoning to taste. Stir in 2 beaten eggs, turn all into a buttered pie dish and bake in a moderate oven until lightly set—about ½ hour.

(*b*) Separate the white of the eggs as in the above recipe, whip them stiffly and then add them at the last moment to the fish and bread mixture. Turn into a buttered mould or pie dish and either steam or bake in a moderate oven for about ½ hour. Serve with a white sauce containing coarsely chopped gherkin, halved capers, or nasturtium seeds.

(*c*) Make a white sauce and flavour it with grated cheese. Flake the cooked fish and arrange it in a buttered pie dish. Pour over it the cheese sauce and grate more cheese on it. Bake till nicely browned.

(*d*) Make a French batter as follows: beat together 25 g. (1 oz.) butter, 1 tablespoon boiling water and 1 tablespoon flour, adding a very little cold water if necessary, as it should be of the consistency of thick cream. Lastly fold in the stiffly beaten white of an egg. Prepare a pan of smoking-hot fat. Cut the fish to the desired size and dip it into the batter. Fry in the hot fat until a light brown.

(*e*) The fish may be warmed in a little butter and served on rounds of toast. This method is good when the remains of a tin of salmon or kippered herrings have to be used up.

Salmon Baked

1 tin of salmon	salt and pepper
1 teaspoon chopped parsley	grated nutmeg
1 small glass red wine	tomato sauce
2 small onions peeled and chopped.	a little butter

Cut the fish into even-sized pieces and place them in a buttered pyrex or pie dish. Season with salt, pepper and a little nutmeg. Sprinkle the onions and parsley over and place small dabs of butter on top. Moisten with the wine and bake for about 15 minutes, basting frequently. When done, pour some tomato sauce over the fish and serve hot.

SAUCES

Sauces can be kept hot either in a double saucepan or, where several pans have to be kept hot, they should be covered and placed in a meat tin containing hot water.

In this way the sauces keep hot without forming a skin on the surface, going lumpy or becoming cold and only the requisite flavouring and colouring need be added at the last minute.

The pans for making white sauces should be either white-lined iron or aluminium and they, like the rest of the utensils used, should be scrupulously clean. A stained spoon or one used, say, for measuring chopped onion, would naturally affect the sauce.

Apple Sauce

2 apples or 50 to 60 g. (2 oz.)   sugar
    dried apples   butter

Prepare apples as for a pie. Put into a saucepan with a tablespoon of water. Simmer until soft and beat to a pulp. Stir in a little butter and moist sugar.

Bechamel Sauce

1 litre (1½ pints) milk   1 onion   10 peppercorns
60 g. (2 oz.) butter   a little parsley   1 blade mace
45 g. (1½ oz.) flour   thyme and bay leaf   salt, cayenne pepper

Boil milk with onion and all the seasonings. Melt the butter, stir in flour and strain on the hot milk. Whisk well until it boils; simmer 20 minutes and strain. Season with salt and cayenne pepper.

Bread Sauce with Cream

125 g. (4 oz.) breadcrumbs   30 g. (1 oz.) butter
1 small onion   3 tablespoons cream
blade of mace   300 ml. (½ pint) water
3 cloves

Stick cloves into onion. Cook onion, mace and pepper in the water. Strain this seasoned water over the breadcrumbs; cover and just before serving add butter and cream.

Bread Sauce without Cream

60 g. (2 oz.) breadcrumbs   2 or 3 cloves
15 g. (½ oz.) butter   blade of mace
300 ml. (½ pint) milk   salt and pepper
1 small onion   a stick of cinnamon (if liked)

Stick cloves into onion. Put the milk, onion, cinnamon and mace in a saucepan. Let it stand 1 hour or so, boil up and simmer 15 minutes. Strain and pour milk over the breadcrumbs. Add the butter, salt and pepper. Reheat until the crumbs swell.

Cheese and Onion Sauce

30 g. (1 oz.) butter
150 ml. (1 gill) milk
60 g. (2 oz.) cheese
seasoning

1½ dessertspoons flour
150 ml. (1 gill) onion liquor
some finely chopped onion

Melt the butter in a saucepan, add the flour and when well blended stir in the milk and onion liquor and bring to the boil. Chop up some of the inside part of the onions, choosing the best-cooked pieces, and add to the sauce. Boil gently for a few minutes, take mixture off, stir in the cheese and seasoning, reheat and serve in sauceboat.

Curry Sauce for Meat, Poultry or Fish

500 ml. (¾ pint) good stock
45 g. (1½ oz.) butter
1 tablespoon curry powder
1 dessertspoon flour

1 tomato sliced
1 dessertspoon jam
1 small onion sliced
salt

Melt the butter in a saucepan, fry the onion until lightly browned. Add the flour and the curry powder. Stir and cook gently for a few minutes, then add the stock and bring to the boil. Put in the tomato and season to taste. Cook gently for 20 minutes, then strain and serve.

Fish Sauce

1 tablespoon butter
1 teaspoon dry mustard
½ tablespoon flour

½ teacup water or milk
1 dessertspoon vinegar
salt

Melt half the butter in a saucepan; stir in flour and mustard, mixing till smooth. Pour on the water and stir till boiling. Season with salt and vinegar and add the rest of the butter just before serving.

Foundation Sauces:—

Panada or Binding Sauce

50 g. (2 oz.) butter
50 g. (2 oz.) flour

250 ml. (½ pint) milk or other
    liquid
pinch of salt

Coating Sauce

25 g. (1 oz.) butter
25 g. (1 oz.) flour

250 ml. (½ pint) milk or other
    liquid
pinch of salt

Game Sauce

2 eggs
salt and pepper
1 tablespoon vinegar
6 drops olive oil

½ tablespoon chopped parsley
2 tablespoons water
1 teaspoon sugar

Beat eggs well. Add salt, pepper, vinegar, parsley, sugar and cold water. Beat all in a basin over boiling water. When creamy, remove and stir in oil drop by drop. If desired add ½ wineglass of sherry.

Ginger Sauce or Filling

1 cup boiling water
1 heaped teaspoon ground ginger
2 tablespoons cold water
1 cup golden syrup
1 tablespoon custard powder

Mix custard powder and cold water in a bowl; add syrup and ginger to the boiling water and, when boiling, add custard powder mixture and boil for 3 minutes.

Gubbins Sauce

1 teaspoon mustard
salt, cayenne pepper
1 tablespoon Tarragon vinegar
1 tablespoon butter
2 tablespoons cream
1 tablespoon malt vinegar

Melt the butter, add other ingredients and lastly the cream. Serve this sauce with grills.

Hollandaise Sauce

4 tablespoons vinegar
8 peppercorns
60 g. (2 oz.) butter
a little salt
2 bay leaves
2 yolks of eggs
about 1 tablespoon Tarragon
vinegar (if liked)

Put vinegar, bay leaves and peppercorns in a saucepan and boil till reduced to half the quantity. Put yolks of eggs in a double pan or jam jar; strain vinegar very carefully on to the eggs, stirring all the time until it thickens. Be very careful not to overheat. Just melt butter and add gradually to the mixture. Add salt and a little Tarragon vinegar. Serve with any boiled fish, asparagus, etc.

Horseradish Sauce

grated horseradish
cream
a little salt
½ tablespoon vinegar
1 small teaspoon sugar

Mix the grated horseradish, vinegar, sugar and salt together. Add them to the cream, slightly whisked. Serve cold. Dried horseradish may be used: for this follow directions on bottle.

Mayonnaise

yolks of 2 eggs
salt, pepper, mustard
1 tablespoon white vinegar
1 teaspoon castor sugar
250 ml. (½ pint) salad oil
2 teaspoons Tarragon vinegar

Beat eggs well with a little made mustard, salt and pepper. Add oil drop by drop, whisking all the time. When well mixed, add the sugar and vinegar. Should the mayonnaise curdle, add another egg yolk and beat well.

Mayonnaise without Oil

1 saltspoon mustard	½ cup vinegar
½ teaspoon salt	2 tablespoons butter
¼ teaspoon pepper	2 large or 3 small eggs

Put in a saucepan the mustard, salt, pepper, vinegar and 1 tablespoon butter; heat gently—do not boil. Into a double boiler drop the eggs; beat them just enough to mix them and add the other tablespoon butter. Stir until the egg is warmed and the butter begins to melt. Then gradually add the vinegar mixture, stirring all the time. Continue stirring until it thickens, cooking very gradually, as it will curdle if cooked too rapidly.

Mayonnaise (Easy Method)

Make a coating sauce (*see* page 64) and when cold add salt, pepper, made mustard, sugar, vinegar, oil and well-beaten yolk of egg. Mix all well together.

Mint Sauce

½ cup vinegar	2 tablespoons sugar
3 tablespoons chopped mint	1 tablespoon boiling water

Chop mint and put into the sauceboat with the sugar. Add boiling water and stir till the sugar is dissolved. Lastly add vinegar. Serve cold.

Salad Dressing (with hard-boiled eggs)

yolks of 4 hard-boiled eggs	sugar
salt and mustard	vinegar
salad oil	

Mash the egg yolks with the back of a wooden spoon. Add salt, mustard and sugar to taste; then gradually stir in salad oil till the mixture is the consistency of thick cream. Add sufficient vinegar to give the required flavour.

Salad Dressing for Bottling

1 dessertspoon flour	¾ cup milk
1 teaspoon mustard	1 tablespoon olive oil or butter
1 teaspoon sugar	¼ cup vinegar or lemon juice
1 egg	salt and cayenne pepper

Put all the dry ingredients together and stir in the milk gradually. Add the egg and mix thoroughly; then stir in the vinegar or lemon juice and the oil or butter. Put the bowl in which they are mixed into a pan of boiling water or into a double boiler. Stir till the mixture thickens. Cool and bottle.

Salad Dressing (Easy Method)

2 eggs	25 g. (1 oz.) butter
2 tablespoons vinegar	2 tablespoons cream or milk
1 tablespoon sugar	1 teaspoon mustard
pepper and salt	

Beat eggs. Mix all ingredients together and put in a basin over hot water. Beat well (or whisk) until egg thickens.

Scotch Salad Dressing (without Oil)

yolks of 2 hard-boiled eggs
1 teaspoon castor sugar
1 teaspoon dry mustard
pepper

¼ teaspoon salt
125 to 150 ml. (¼ pint) cream
   (fresh or sour)
1 tablespoon vinegar

Pound the egg yolks into a powder. Put in a basin with the sugar, mustard, salt and pepper. Mix well, then add slowly the cream, stirring all the time. Lastly stir in the vinegar.

Sweet Sauces for Steamed Puddings

(a) WITH JAM

1 teacup water
1 tablespoon sugar

1 heaped tablespoon red jam
1 teaspoon cornflour

Put water, sugar and jam into a saucepan. Mix cornflour in a little cold water and add to the water when it boils. Boil all for 2 or 3 minutes till quite clear. A squeeze of lemon juice improves the flavour.

(b) WITHOUT JAM

1 teacup milk
1 tablespoon butter
½ tablespoon flour or cornflour

1 egg yolk
1 tablespoon sugar

Melt butter, stir in the dry flour and, when mixed, the milk and sugar. When it has boiled, cool and beat in the egg yolk.

This foundation sauce can be varied by adding chocolate, cocoa, vanilla or lemon essence, strained coffee instead of milk and syrup instead of sugar.

Tomato Sauce

3 or 4 tomatoes
2 small onions
small piece of bacon or
   bacon rinds

½ tablespoon flour
salt and pepper
½ teaspoon sugar
a little water or stock

Fry bacon or rinds, then add onion and tomato sliced. Boil, then simmer gently till pulpy. Put through a sieve. Return to saucepan and thicken with flour blended with water or stock. Add sugar and seasoning. Serve hot.

Velour Sauce

2 tablespoons butter
1½ tablespoons milk

small ½ cup castor sugar
½ teaspoon vanilla essence

Beat butter to a cream. Slowly stir in sugar. Stir in milk and then vanilla, even more slowly. Cream may be used if richer sauce is desired.

Sauces for Christmas Pudding

(1) 125 g. (¼ lb.) sugar icing   1 wineglass brandy or rum
     125 g. (¼ lb.) butter   or other flavouring
  Mix butter and sugar together till they cream. Add brandy gradually.

(2) 1 tablespoon sugar   sherry or brandy to flavour
     a little water
  Thicken with cornflour, boiling 3 or 4 minutes to cook it.

(3) 2 yolks eggs   2 tablespoons cream
     1 tablespoon brandy   15 g. (½ oz.) castor sugar
     1 tablespoon water

Put all the ingredients into a small stewpan and whisk them over a gentle heat till they are thick and frothy. Do not boil or it will curdle.

(4) 250 ml. (½ pint) double cream   45 g. (1½ oz.) castor sugar
     1 good dessertspoon brandy   1 good dessertspoon sherry
     the juice and finely grated rind of 1 lemon

Put the sherry, brandy, sugar, lemon juice and rind into a basin and stir until the sugar is dissolved. Add the cream and whip slowly at first and afterwards more quickly, until firm. Raisin or other sweet wine may replace the sherry and brandy. Sufficient for 7 or 8 persons.

Flowing or Pouring Sauce and Foundation of the following Sauces

15 g. (½ oz.) butter   300 ml. (½ pint) milk or other
15 g. (½ oz.) flour   liquid
                                pinch of salt

Melt butter, stir in dry flour, add milk gradually, stirring well, and bring to boil. Boil 3 minutes. Add salt.

(a) Anchovy Sauce

Add 1 teaspoon anchovy sauce, a small pinch cayenne and a little lemon juice.

(b) Caper Sauce

Add 1 tablespoon capers.

(c) Celery Sauce

Wash and scrape celery, cut into thin slices and cook 3 cups of it in boiling salted water until soft. Drain, rub through a sieve and add to 2 cups of rather thin white sauce.

(d) Cheese Sauce

Add 1 teacup grated cheese and a little mustard.

(e) Egg Sauce

Add hard-boiled chopped egg.

(*f*) **Mock Hollandaise or Dutch Sauce for Fish**

Just before serving add 1 raw yolk of egg and the juice of 1 small lemon. Add a little vinegar if liked.

(*g*) **Mustard Sauce**

Add teaspoon of vinegar, salt and pepper to taste and 1 tablespoon made mustard.

(*h*) **Onion Sauce**

Add 2 onions cooked and chopped.

(*i*) **Parsley Sauce**

Add chopped parsley.

(*j*) **Piquante Sauce**

Brown flour. Add stock instead of milk. 2 teaspoons minced onion, a little mustard, some chopped gherkins or mushrooms.

CHOOSING AND COOKING MEAT

Success in cooking meat, it is said, begins at the butcher's shop, for the right cut must be selected for its own particular method of preparation, be it roasting, grilling, stewing or any other of the innumerable forms in which it may be served. To succeed, however, the housewife herself must visit the butcher's shop and be guided by the butcher as he is the expert.

Quality in meat is determined by a number of important factors but for consumers it may be measured in terms of tenderness and flavour—a matter of individual taste. Some prefer a full flavour, which is a characteristic of increasing age, others prefer a less marked flavour, but practically all are agreed that the tenderest meat is the best.

Tenderness, which is largely influenced by age, depends upon the structure of an animal's muscles, the latter being composed of bundles of cells held in position by connective tissues, the tough fibrous material from which the tendons and ligaments are formed. It is the amount and condition of the connective tissues, governed by the activity of the animal during its life, which account for the toughness or otherwise of meat and, of course, underline the importance of early maturity. The tenderness of beef is improved by hanging for several days. At the time of purchase the housewife should ascertain from the butcher whether or not he recommends additional hanging.

To judge the quality of meat in the carcass, therefore, is a matter of long experience which the retail butcher gains in the normal course of his business and stores for the future benefit of his customers.

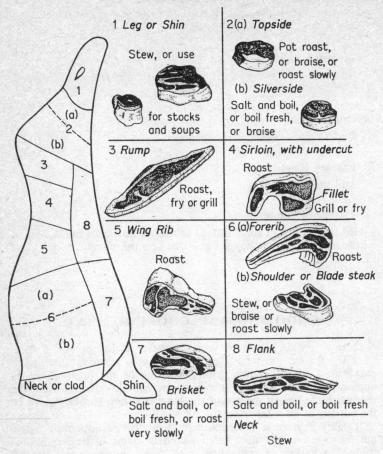

1 *Leg or Shin*

Stew, or use

for stocks and soups

2(a) *Topside*

Pot roast, or braise, or roast slowly

(b) *Silverside*

Salt and boil, or boil fresh, or braise

3 *Rump*

Roast, fry or grill

4 *Sirloin, with undercut*

Roast

Fillet
Grill or fry

5 *Wing Rib*

Roast

6 (a) *Forerib*

Roast

(b) *Shoulder or Blade steak*

Stew, or braise or roast slowly

7

Shin

Brisket

Salt and boil, or boil fresh, or roast very slowly

8 *Flank*

Salt and boil, or boil fresh

Neck

Stew

Neck or clod

Nevertheless, there are some characteristics of which the housewife can acquire a knowledge and so ensure that the meat she purchases has all the qualities she requires. In selecting cuts the housewife should ensure that the meat has a reasonably even distribution of fat which, however, should not be excessive. She can learn to recognise the numerous retail cuts by their appearance as well as by name and a knowledge of the structure of meat is a great help to an understanding of how it should be cooked. Then, with a knowledge of the basic principles of cooking, she will find that the less tender and therefore less expensive cuts can be made tender and palatable by proper cooking. In short, she will find that while being able to buy more economically she can prepare and serve an infinite variety of attractive and nutritious meat meals.

There is no known short cut to becoming a good cook, but with a

CUTS OF PORK

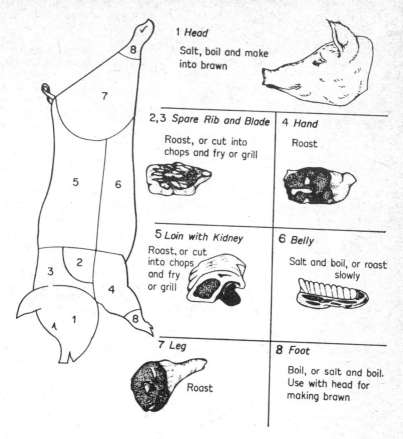

1 Head

Salt, boil and make into brawn

2,3 Spare Rib and Blade

Roast, or cut into chops and fry or grill

4 Hand

Roast

5 Loin with Kidney

Roast, or cut into chops and fry or grill

6 Belly

Salt and boil, or roast slowly

7 Leg

Roast

8 Foot

Boil, or salt and boil. Use with head for making brawn

knowledge of the basic principles of cooking, the proper selection both of meat and the method of its cooking, the modern housewife should be able to master culinary art.

All cooking, the effect of which on meat is to coagulate the proteins, to increase the intensity of its flavour and to bring about a loss of weight, mainly in the water content, is based on two fundamental principles—DRY HEAT and MOIST HEAT. In cooking by dry heat, i.e. roasting, grilling, etc., the meat is surrounded by hot air in an oven or under a broiler; a system employed for cooking the more tender cuts. In cooking by moist heat, steaming, stewing or pressure cooking, the meat is in contact with or immersed in hot water, hot fat or steam, a method more suitable for the less tender cuts.

The loss of water has an important bearing on the subsequent keeping qualities of the meat and it is, of course, well known that a cooked joint will keep longer than an uncooked one.

71

CUTS OF MUTTON AND LAMB

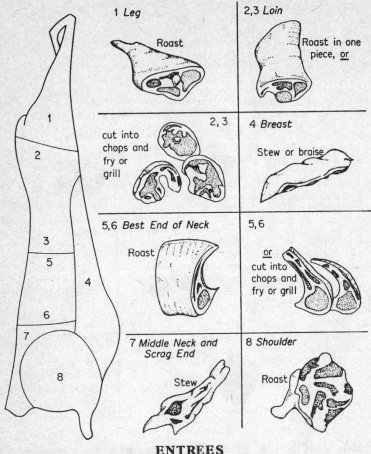

1 Leg — Roast

2,3 Loin — Roast in one piece, or

2, 3 — cut into chops and fry or grill

4 Breast — Stew or braise

5,6 Best End of Neck — Roast

5,6 — or cut into chops and fry or grill

7 Middle Neck and Scrag End — Stew

8 Shoulder — Roast

ENTREES

Methods of Frying Meats

Meat is fried either by "dry" or "deep" fat method. (1) The first is used for sausages, kidneys, chops, steaks, etc.; (2) the second for cutlets, rissoles and any meat that is enclosed in batter or egg and breadcrumbs.

(1) For "dry" frying, place a small quantity of fat (1 or 2 table-spoons) in frying pan and, when really hot, meat is fried on one side and then turned. This method of cooking chops and steaks is not as good as "grilling" which is far more digestible.

(2) Deep frying. Wipe and dry meat with a cloth, flour lightly and shake off superfluous flour. Well beat egg on a plate, dip meat into egg and brush it well over to cover all. Have ready a sheet of kitchen paper full of fine breadcrumbs and ¼ saltspoon salt to a break-fast cup of crumbs. Well cover meat with crumbs and pat to make them adhere. Use a deep pan and enough fat to cover meat. Salad oil, clarified

72

dripping or lard may be used. If carefully strained this fat can be used many times, so it is not extravagant. See fat is boiling. It is not boiling when it bubbles. When boiling it is quite still with a faint blue smoke rising. Fry a golden-brown, drain on sieve or kitchen paper. Dish on paper d'oyley.

Methods of Grilling Meat (To make tough meat tender wrap it in pawpaw leaves for 1 or 2 hours before cooking.)

The gridiron or frying pan must be perfectly clean; grease it well, then heat it and rub off grease with paper. See the gridiron or frying pan is red hot and have a clear, fierce, smokeless fire ready. Well grease gridiron, put steak on, let it be close to heat for first 4 minutes to harden albumen and keep in juices, then slacken heat. When cooked one side turn with a fish slice. Never stick a fork in meat being grilled or goodness will run out. Serve immediately the meat is cooked. Time to grill chop or steak 4 cm. (1½ inch) thick—5 minutes on each side or 10 minutes turning frequently. For a kidney, 3 minutes each side.

Beef Olives

500 g. (1 lb.) top cut of sirloin or good steak	¼ teaspoon grated lemon rind
	salt and pepper
60 g. (2 oz.) finely chopped beef suet	nutmeg
	1 egg
100 g. (3 oz.) breadcrumbs	500 ml. (¾ pint) stock
1 teaspoon chopped parsley	Worcester sauce
30 g. (1 oz.) butter	
flour	

Mix suet with the breadcrumbs, parsley, lemon rind, salt, pepper and nutmeg and bind together with egg. Bone top of sirloin and cut into long thin strips, with the grain running down, not across. Place a little of the stuffing on one end of it and roll up, tying with thread. Put 30 g. (1 oz.) of butter in a saucepan and when hot put in the olives and turn about for 2 or 3 minutes until nicely browned. Add 500 ml. (¾ pint) of good stock, simmer gently for 1½ hours and 5 minutes before serving add ½ tablespoon of flour mixed with a little Worcester sauce and water.

The fillet of the sirloin can be used for grilling and the bone goes in the soup.

Brains

1 set of calf's brains or 2 sets sheep's brains	egg and crumb
	straw potatoes
deep fat	pepper and salt

Wash the brains in salt and water. Blanch them and leave in salt water till wanted. Dry thoroughly; halve the egg and crumb and fry 3 minutes in deep fat. Meanwhile cut the potatoes in thin slices and straws; dry thoroughly. Fry them till tender in hot fat; take them out of the fat and make it smoking hot again; fry them again till brown and crisp. Sprinkle them with pepper and salt; dish the brains in the centre of a hot dish, the straws round them or in clumps. Tomato or other sauce may be served.

Buck (or Mutton) Macedoine

1 kg. (2 lb.) buck or mutton	salt and pepper
1 onion	celery
a few skinned tomatoes	a little vinegar
stock or water	carrots and turnips
sprig of parsley	Worcester sauce

Cut up meat into neat pieces. Dust with flour and fry in dripping till a nice brown, then add onion and tomatoes. When browned, drain off fat and put meat in saucepan; add some stock or boiling water to the browned flour in the frying pan, also parsley, salt and pepper and celery, a little vinegar and Worcester sauce. Bring to boil and strain over the meat. Add carrots and turnips cut up and simmer gently for an hour or so. A few fresh peas or tinned peas add to the flavour. Thicken the sauce with flour and serve with mashed potato.

Grilled Chops or Fillet

chops or fillet	chopped parsley
butter	

Cut chops or fillet about 2 cm. (¾ inch) thick. Dip quickly into melted butter. Lay on well-heated gridiron over clear fire. Turn frequently and cook about 8 minutes. Serve with maitre d'hotel butter, i.e., a pat of butter mixed with some finely chopped parsley.

With this dish, green peas or mashed potatoes and tomato sauce may be served.

Stewed Chops

chops	pepper and salt

¼ cup of hot water or gravy or 1 teaspoon Bovril

Brown the chops by frying slightly in a pan, put them into a saucepan with hot water or gravy and simmer gently till tender. Thicken the gravy with a little flour mixed smooth in cold water.

To this dish, green peas, mushrooms, a few slices of fried onion, tomatoes from which the outer peel has been removed or a few sliced potatoes may be added.

Cornish Pasties

250 g. (½ lb.) flour	cold water	1 teaspoon salt
90 g. (3 oz.) lard or	125 g. (¼ lb.) mutton	¼ teaspoon pepper
dripping	125 g. (¼ lb.) potatoes	½ teaspoon baking powder

Cut meat and potatoes into dice. Mix with salt and pepper and divide into 8 portions on a plate or dish.

PASTRY: Mix flour, salt and baking powder; rub in lard; make into a dry, stiff paste with cold water; roll out thinly and cut into 8 rounds. Put a portion of the mixture on each round, wet edges, fold in half, crimp with finger and thumb, prick with fork. Bake in hot oven ½ hour.

Exeter Stew

1 kg. (2 lb.) mutton or venison
1 litre (1½ pints) water
45 g. (1½ oz.) dripping
45 g. (1½ oz.) flour

2 or 3 onions
2 tablespoons vinegar
salt and pepper

For the Savoury Balls

125 g. (4 oz.) flour
45 g. (1½ oz.) finely chopped suet
1 tablespoon finely chopped
  parsley
½ teaspoon pepper

½ teaspoon powdered mixed
  herbs
1 teaspoon baking powder
½ teaspoon salt

Remove all fat from the meat and cut into 10 pieces. Put in a stewpan with vinegar and put in oven. Heat fat in frying pan. Fry the sliced onions and flour till brown, add the water, boil up and pour it over the meat in the pan. Season, cover closely and cook gently in oven, 3 hours.

Mix the ingredients for savoury balls together. Add water to bind these into a stiff mixture and make 10 balls.

About 40 minutes before serving bring stew to boiling point, drop in balls and simmer for 40 minutes.

To serve, pile the meat in the centre of a hot dish, strain the gravy over and arrange the balls neatly round the meat.

Faggots

500 g. (1 lb.) pig's fry or liver
125 g. (¼ lb.) onions
125 g. (¼ lb.) caul
pepper

125 g. (¼ lb.) bread
1 teaspoon salt
1 teaspoon sage

Soak bread. Scald the fry and mince it. Mince onion and chop the sage. Squeeze bread very dry and crumble it. Add liver, onions, sage, seasoning and mix well. Soak caul in hot water and cut into rounds the size of a saucer. Fill each piece of caul with the mixture and wrap it well round. Put in greased tin and bake 30 minutes in moderate oven. Serve with brown gravy and cooked peas.

Scotch Haggis

(a)

sheep's bag and pluck
250 g. (½ lb.) minced suet
250 g. (½ lb.) oatmeal

4 small onions
1 teaspoon powdered herbs
pepper and salt

Wash bag in cold water; scrape and clean well and let it lie in cold salted water during night. Wash the pluck and boil for 2 hours, letting the windpipe hang out of pot. When cold cut off the windpipe. Mince half the liver, the heart, lights, suet and onions all very small. Add the oatmeal, previously toasted golden-brown, pepper, salt, herbs and a cup of the liquid in which the pluck was boiled.

Mix well. Fill the bag rather more than half with the mixture and sew it up. Place it in a pot of boiling water and boil for 3 hours, pricking occasionally to keep it from bursting.

(b)

Procure a sheep's bag, clean it and lay in salt and water for a night; parboil 1 ox heart, 500 g. (1 lb.) liver, pluck and lights for 1 hour; when cool mince and add 500 g. (1 lb.) minced suet, and 500 g. (1 lb.) oatmeal which has been nicely toasted in the oven (this makes all the difference to the flavour of the haggis), add 2 finely chopped onions, season well with pepper and salt, add 1.25 l. (2 pints) of the water in which the liver, etc., was boiled, mix well, turn the bag with the plain side out, fill it, sew securely, put into a pot of boiling water, keep pricking for 5 minutes then boil briskly for 3 to 4 hours.

Mock Haggis

250 g. (½ lb.) liver   1 medium-sized onion
125 g. (¼ lb.) suet   pepper and salt
1 large breakfast cup oatmeal

Cover liver with water and boil for 20 minutes, having first removed scraggy bits. When cold, mince it. Brown the oatmeal in a little butter, then add finely chopped suet and onion, minced liver and seasoning.

Mix all ingredients with some of the water the liver was boiled in, but do not make too soft. Grease basin, pour in mixture and steam 3 hours.

Heart Stuffed

1 ox heart   little butter or dripping
2 or 3 rashers bacon   flour

Wash heart well in salted water; slash down centre and stuff with following mixture: 1½ cups breadcrumbs, 1 tablespoon butter, salt and pepper, teaspoon of thyme, teaspoon of chopped parsley mixed with slightly beaten egg.

Sew or skewer opening in heart.

Into stewpan put rashers of bacon and a little butter, followed by stuffed heart. Brown all sides, then add ½ teacup of water and close lid tightly; let it simmer about 3 hours, adding a little more water from time to time so that it is never dry. Thicken gravy with a little flour and flavour before serving.

Irish Stew

500 g. (1 lb.) loin chops   ½ cup milk
1 kg. (2 lb.) potatoes   salt and pepper
250 g. (½ lb.) onions

Cover meat with warm water. Peel onions and add to meat. Cook for 2 hours till tender. ½ hour before serving add potatoes cut in halves or quarters. Just before serving, add milk and serve at once otherwise the milk will curdle.

Kidney Hot Pot

1 ox kidney or	flour
4 sheep's kidneys	pepper and salt
1 onion	½ cup stock or
potatoes	1 dessertspoon Bovril

Thoroughly wash kidney in salted water. Remove fat from centre and put in casserole. Cut kidney in small pieces and roll in flour, pepper and salt until well coated. Put in saucepan with melted fat and fry till brown, then slice onion and as many potatoes as required, very finely, on to the top. Add stock and steam slowly with the lid tightly closed for ¾ hour. Shake the pan occasionally without lifting lid, to prevent sticking. The addition of a few fresh mushrooms improves the flavour.

Stuffed Breast of Lamb or Veal

1.25 kg. (2½ lb.) breast of lamb	1 teaspoon chopped parsley
4 heaped tablespoons	¼ teaspoon thyme
white breadcrumbs	salt and pepper
1 tablespoon chopped	1 small onion
suet or lamb fat	milk or beaten egg

Remove the bones from the meat as neatly as possible with a sharp knife. Mix all the dry ingredients for the stuffing, adding sufficient milk to bind. Lay the meat on the board, inside uppermost; spread with the stuffing; roll up tightly and neatly and tie into a good shape. Put on a meat trivet in a baking tin and bake for 15 minutes in a hot oven, then reduce the heat. Allow 20 to 25 minutes to each 500 g. (1 lb.) of stuffed meat and 20 minutes over. Baste frequently. Meanwhile cover the bones with water, add a little salt, simmer gently while the meat is cooking and use for the gravy. Place the meat on a hot dish; remove the string; pour the gravy round and serve with redcurrant jelly.

NOTE:—Loin of lamb or mutton can be used instead of breast for this dish. Either makes a more succulent joint but proves less economical.

Fried Liver and Bacon

250 g. (½ lb.) liver	seasoning
125 g. (¼ lb.) fat bacon	300 ml. (½ pint) water
1 desertspoon flour (browned)	

Cut the bacon into thin rashers. Remove rind. Wash and dry the liver. Cut into slices and coat in the seasoned flour. Fry the bacon and fry the rind to extract the fat. Remove the bacon from pan and place on hot dish. Fry the liver in the bacon fat for about 6 or 8 minutes. Remove the liver. Slightly fry the flour, add the liquid, boil well for 5 minutes and season with pepper and salt. Arrange the liver in the centre of the dish, place the bacon on top and pour the gravy round. Garnish with parsley.

Mutton Boiled

1 to 1.5 kg. (2 or 3 lb.) mutton   1 turnip
   (neck or shoulder)   1 onion
2 carrots   salt

Wash meat and put into boiling salted water, so that it is well covered. Boil quickly for 5 minutes, to seal the outside and keep in the juices. Skim well. Add carrots, turnip and onion, whole or in large pieces. Cook gently till tender. Place the meat in the centre of a dish with the vegetables round it. Serve with caper or parsley sauce (*see* Sauces). The liquid may be used for soup.

Mutton Cutlets

cutlets of mutton   dripping
flour   breadcrumbs

Trim cutlets neatly. Make a little thin batter with flour and water. Dip the cutlets into it, then cover them with breadcrumbs and fry quickly in clarified dripping. Drain them free from fat. Serve hot.

If preferred, dip the cutlets in egg and breadcrumbs instead of batter and fry them. Arrange them standing on end and touching one another, around a mound of mashed potatoes. Be sure to cut the cutlets thin; if they are thick they will be underdone and most people prefer mutton well done.

Mutton Pies

500 g. (1 lb.) flour   300 ml. ($\frac{1}{2}$ pint) water
1 teaspoon salt   750 g. (1$\frac{1}{2}$ lb.) mutton
1 beaten egg   pepper and salt
125 g. ($\frac{1}{4}$ lb.) butter or lard

Put flour in a basin with salt. Bring butter and water to boiling point and pour into flour. Knead until it looks like putty. Take two-thirds of the dough, divide into 8 pieces and shape into pies (moulding them round the end of a bottle is easy). Let them become firm, while preparing meat by cutting into small pieces and seasoning. Fill the cases. Roll out the remaining third of the dough; cut into rounds to fit the pies; cut a hole in the centre of each with a thimble. Brush the inside of the cover with egg, fit on and fasten the edges together, cutting with the back of a knife to ornament. Brush egg all over top and sides and bake in a hot oven for $\frac{3}{4}$ hour. Pour hot stock into pies when cooked.

Steamed Breast of Mutton

breast of mutton   2 onions
2 carrots   salt and pepper
2 turnips

Wipe and trim the meat, removing any gristle, and add just sufficient boiling water to cover. Add salt and pepper to taste, bring to the boil and skim, then add the vegetables previously diced. Stew the mutton slowly for 2$\frac{1}{2}$ hours. Remove the bones; place meat on a hot dish and pour the gravy over and arrange the vegetables round the meat. Serve with onion sauce.

Ox-Tail

1 ox-tail	turnips
onions	pepper and salt
carrots	potatoes

Cut ox-tail in joints; wash in salted water; dust with flour and brown with a few onions in fat in stewpan. Remove fat; add boiling water and stew for four hours, then add carrots, turnips and seasoning, return to fire and cook till vegetables are tender. Thicken the gravy, boil potatoes and add. A little port wine or vinegar improves the flavour.

Pilau of Mutton

1.25 kg. (2½ lb.) lean mutton	15 g. (½ oz.) green ginger
250 g. (½ lb.) rice	(sliced thinly)
250 g. (½ lb.) onions (sliced)	30 g. (1 oz.) pistachio nuts
125 g. (¼ lb.) butter or ghee	(blanched)
30 g. (1 oz.) stoned raisins	¼ teaspoon ground cinnamon
30 g. (1 oz.) blanched almonds	⅛ teaspoon ground cloves
30 g. (1 oz.) dried apricots (sliced)	⅛ teaspoon ground cardamons
6 eggs	⅛ teaspoon cumin seeds
salt	⅛ teaspoon black pepper

Mince a quarter of the meat finely and cut the rest into neat slices convenient for serving. Put the sliced meat into a stewpan, add the onions and ginger and 1 teaspoon of salt. Cover with cold water and cook very gently till the meat is tender, then strain off the stock. Meanwhile the rice should have been well washed, parboiled and drained; now put it into the stewpan with the stock and simmer until the rice is tender and the stock has become evaporated or absorbed. Heat one-third of the butter or ghee in another stewpan, put in the slices of meat, sprinkle over them the ground cloves, cumin seeds, cinnamon and cardamon, stirring well for a few minutes. Spread the prepared rice over the meat, pour on a little melted butter or ghee, cover closely and cook very gently for ½ hour. Heat the remaining butter or ghee in another pan, put in the minced mutton with a little salt and stir until lightly browned. Add the rest of the flavouring ingredients, the raisins, almonds, pistachio nuts, apricots and well-beaten egg and stir over a gentle heat for a few minutes. Serve the slices of meat embedded in the rice, spread the minced preparation on the top and garnish with the remaining eggs, either fried or poached.

Savoury Cutlets

375 g. (¾ lb.) liver	salt and pepper
30 g. (1 oz.) butter	one egg
one small onion	a few pickled anchovies
a few cloves	breadcrumbs

Scald the liver to harden it a little; then grate or chop it. Add salt and pepper, the egg, melted butter and chopped onion. Mix well. Clean and chop the anchovies and add them to mixture with breadcrumbs to form a not too stiff paste. Form into cutlet shape and fry gently.

Savoury Roll Pudding

500 g. (1 lb.) flour
1 teaspoon baking powder
500 g. (1 lb.) minced beef
1 cup water or more

a little chopped onion
250 g. (½ lb.) suet
pepper and salt to taste

Sift flour with baking powder; add suet finely shredded, pepper and salt. Mix to a firm dough with cold water. Roll out as for roly-poly. Break up the mince with cold water till it will spread easily over the paste. Sprinkle with pepper and salt and a little chopped onion. Roll up the paste, put into large pudding basin well greased. Cover with greased paper and steam 2 hours.

Steak and Kidney Pie or Pudding

125 g. (¼ lb.) kidney
500 g. (1 lb.) steak
½ small onion
seasoning

dripping
teaspoon Bovril
250 g. (½ lb.) rough puff or
    short paste
1 tablespoon flour

Cut up the kidneys, remove core and wash in salted water. Cut up steak and onions. Dust all with flour and brown in the oven with a little dripping. Remove fat and add water, put all in saucepan, cover and cook for 1 hour. Add a little Bovril and seasoning. Put into pie dish and cover with rough puff or short crust. For pudding, line a bowl with suet crust; pour in the partly cooked meat, cover with crust and steam 2 hours.

Sweetbreads Stewed

1 set calf's sweetbreads
1 onion
1 cup milk
½ cup water

1 clove
1 tablespoon flour
½ tablespoon butter
salt and parsley

Soak sweetbreads in cold water 1 hour. Then put in cold water and bring to boil. Strain and throw away water. Cut into convenient pieces and remove fat. Place in a saucepan with onion sliced, milk, water and seasoning. Cook very gently for 1½ hours. Blend flour with a little gravy and stir into boiling liquid. Add the butter and cook for 5 minutes. Pour into dish and garnish with parsley.

Sweetbreads Fried

sweetbreads
egg

flour
breadcrumbs

Prepare sweetbreads as above recipe. After simmering 2 hours, drain, separate sections and flour well. Dip in egg, coat with breadcrumbs and fry. Serve on mashed potatoes with tomato sauce.

Toad-in-the-hole

125 g. (¼ lb.) flour
½ teaspoon salt
¼ teaspoon pepper

300 ml. (½ pint) milk
1 large egg or 2 small eggs
250 g. (½ lb.) sausages

Put flour into large basin; mix in salt and pepper; break egg; put in the centre of flour; stir with wooden spoon. Add a little of the milk gradually, working down flour from the sides of the basin. When stiff, beat very well for 10 minutes. Skin sausages and cut in pieces; lay in pie dish and add remainder of the milk to the batter. Pour over sausages and bake for ¾ to 1 hour in a moderate oven.

Tripe and Onions

500 g. (1 lb.) tripe (cleaned and prepared)	marrow bone
	300 g. (½ pint) milk
1 onion	flour
water	salt

Put tripe into water, bring to boil and strain. Put it back in the pan with sufficient fresh water to cover it and also marrow bone and onion. Bring to the boil and continue to boil the tripe slowly until very tender. Remove the tripe and cut into small pieces. Make a sauce with part of the water in which it has been boiled, the milk, seasoning and flour to thicken. Stew for ½ hour. A little cream added to the sauce, just before serving, is desirable but not necessary. The remainder of the stock is a good foundation for soup.

Should it be impossible to get prepared tripe, it should first be blanched by pouring 2.5 litres (2 quarts) boiling water in which 1 dessertspoon of bicarbonate of soda has been dissolved over the tripe and leaving to soak for 5 minutes. The water should then be poured away and the tripe simmered in fresh water for 4 or 5 hours.

CURRY DISHES

Curry Powder

30 g. (1 oz.) cayenne pepper	60 g. (2 oz.) mustard
60 g. (2 oz.) ginger	125 g. (4 oz.) fenugreek seed
250 g. (8 oz.) coriander seed	125 g. (4 oz.) cinnamon
250 g. (8 oz.) turmeric	

pound, bottle and cork well.

Boiled Rice for Curry

1 cup rice	a little salt
1.25 l. (1 quart) boiling water	

Wash the rice thoroughly, then put it into the boiling water with a little salt. Boil quickly until grains are soft but not pulpy. Pour into colander and place under running water till each grain is separate; drain well and return to pan till thoroughly hot, shaking the pan repeatedly so that the rice will not stick to saucepan. When dry, serve hot.

Indian Curry

3 fair-sized onions
3 heaped tablespoons fat
2 tablespoons curry powder
2 tablespoons vinegar
meat, fresh or cooked

1 breakfast cup gravy or soup
1 tablespoon good chutney
2 full tablespoons milk
1 tablespoon apricot or peach
jam

Cut onions finely; brown in boiling-hot fat, then add curry powder. Stir constantly, to prevent the powder burning, for 10 minutes (this prevents the raw taste that is sometimes found in curries when the powder is not well cooked). Add gravy or soup—if neither is available use the same quantity of hot water; cook for 5 minutes; stir constantly, then add chutney, apricot or peach jam, vinegar and a little sugar. When the curry is suited to taste, add milk; cook all together for 10 minutes, then put in the meat, cut up in small pieces and allow the curry to simmer on side of stove till required for the table. The longer the curry simmers the better it is, but care must be taken not to let it burn.

If fresh meat is used for the curry, the meat must be fried till half-cooked before it is added to the curry gravy. Just before serving curry add 1 tablespoon of milk; this gives the curry a soft taste, which all good Indian curries ought to have. If coconut cream is to be had, it is better than fresh milk.

Coconut Cream (Tui ya Nazi)

Get a fresh coconut, grate all the nut out of the shell and place in a basin and cover with boiling water. Let it stand for 10 to 15 minutes, strain. The resulting liquid is the coconut cream that is used by Indian cooks.

Curry Balls

200 g. (6 oz.) minced cold meat
200 g. (6 oz.) boiled rice
curry powder

a squeeze of lemon juice
1 egg
breadcrumbs

Flavour meat and rice with curry powder and lemon juice. Bind with egg. Form into balls: dip in egg, then in breadcrumbs and fry a golden-brown. Serve with rice and a curry sauce and chutney.

Curried Brinjal or Egg Plant

Cut up and fry 3 or 4 onions in 1 tablespoon butter till golden-brown. Add 1 tablespoon curry powder and 2 cups stock or milk. Peel egg plant thinly and cut into dice, then add to the sauce. Just before serving, add a dessertspoon of flour mixed to a smooth paste with a little cold water. Serve with rice.

Curried Cucumber

2 large cucumbers of even size
125 g. ($\frac{1}{4}$ lb.) cooked cold meat
$\frac{1}{2}$ slice white bread soaked
  in milk

1 egg
1 dessertspoon curry powder
pepper and salt

Peel cucumbers; cut in halves and scoop out seeds so as to form hollowed shells; slice the bottoms level so that cucumbers will stand upright. Mince the meat, add bread, egg, curry powder, pepper and salt. Mix well and fill cucumber shell with the mixture. Make a sauce as follows:—

1 cup of stock or gravy	1 teaspoon sugar
2 large sliced onions	1 tablespoon butter
25 g. (1 oz.) curry powder	

Fry onions in a little butter until brown. Make a sauce from the stock or gravy, the fried onions, curry powder and sugar; add butter if gravy is not rich enough. Arrange stuffed cucumbers in sauce, cover closely and simmer gently for 1 hour. Serve with boiled rice.

Dry Curry

500 g. (1 lb.) cooked chicken, rabbit or other white meat	1 tablespoon curry powder a pinch of salt
1 minced onion	1 tablespoon cream or milk
butter	

Fry onion in butter until light brown in colour. Cut into very small pieces the chicken, rabbit or other white meat and mix with the onion and stir together over the fire until the meat is thoroughly hot; then sprinkle over the meat the curry powder and salt. Thoroughly mix meat and powder and then pour into pan cream or milk. Stir again thoroughly over the fire till moisture has evaporated and serve piping hot with rice.

Any or all of the following should be served with curry, etc.:—

boiled rice	grated coconut
chilli butter (creamed butter with finely chopped green chillies)	sliced banana chipatties strawberry jam
chutney	nuts (browned and finely minced)
bombay duck	
cucumbers in coconut milk	sliced ripe tomatoes
raisins (stoned and heated)	papadoms

Curried Eggs

4 or 5 hard-boiled eggs	1 level tablespoon flour
butter	1 level tablespoon finely chopped sour apple or banana
1 teaspoon finely chopped onion	1 teacup gravy or milk
1 tablespoon (level) curry powder	

Halve hard-boiled eggs across. Fry the onion in a little hot butter. When lightly browned stir in curry powder and flour, adding as much more butter as may be necessary to slightly moisten the whole. Allow it to cook very gently for at least 20 minutes, stirring occasionally; then add sour apple or banana. 10 minutes later mix in gravy or milk; stir and boil for a few minutes, then strain. Reheat, season to taste and put in the eggs. Cover, and keep the pan warm for 10 minutes before serving. Boiled rice may be served separately or may form a border round the dish on which the eggs are sent to table.

Curried Fish

some uncooked fresh fish
salt and pepper
1 egg

flour or breadcrumbs
olive oil, butter or dripping

Divide fish into pieces suitable for serving; sprinkle with salt and pepper; dip into well-beaten egg, flour or crumbs and fry in olive oil, butter or dripping. When cooked, put into the oven in a deep dish. While fish is frying prepare curry sauce as follows:—

1 cup vinegar
2 medium finely sliced
  onions
1 tablespoon curry powder

1 tablespoon flour
a little cold water
pepper and salt

Put vinegar into a small enamelled saucepan and when boiling add onions and allow to continue boiling. Mix curry powder and flour into a paste with a little cold water and add to the boiling vinegar and onions; add pepper and salt and pour over the fish. A few lemon leaves laid among the fish before sauce is added improve the flavour.

Curried Tinned Salmon

curry sauce
1 tin salmon

pepper and salt
boiled rice

Prepare a curry sauce as indicated above. Place the salmon, including the liquid, in the sauce; cover closely; simmer for a few minutes; add pepper and salt and serve very hot with boiled rice.

Curried Kidneys

4 or 6 sheep's kidneys

Prepare the kidneys; split them and skewer the two halves of each. flat; grill for 6 to 8 minutes. Prepare a curry sauce as follows:—

30 g. (1 oz.) butter
1 heaped dessertspoon
  curry powder
1 heaped dessertspoon flour

salt to taste
1 thinly sliced onion
1 breakfast cup gravy or
  Bovril

Melt butter in a saucepan; add curry powder and flour mixed, salt and onion, lastly the gravy. Allow this to simmer until it thickens, then add the kidneys and cook slowly for $\frac{1}{2}$ hour.

Minced Curry

1 kg. (2 lb.) cold mutton
2 onions
30 g. (1 oz.) butter
1 slice bread soaked
  in milk

2 tablespoons curry powder
2 tablespoons vinegar
a little salt
2 eggs
milk

Mince mutton; fry onions in the butter; then add curry powder, vinegar, sugar and salt and fry all for a few minutes. Put together the meat, onions, etc., bread soaked in milk and squeezed dry and 1 egg. Mix thoroughly and put into a buttered pie dish or into several small buttered cups. When meat is all arranged, beat up the other egg with a little milk and pour over the top. Bake. If liked, sweet blanched almonds may be chopped finely and mixed with the meat.

Curry and Rice

Curry:-

cooked vegetables, meat or fish	curry powder
a few onions	some *"tui ya nazi"*
butter or dripping	lemon juice
	a little unripe mango if in season

Fry onions in butter or dripping. Then add curry powder and some *"tui ya nazi"* and cook very thoroughly. (To this may be added a little lemon juice and when in season a little unripe mango.) Complete by adding any cooked vegetables, meat or fish that may be on hand.

Rice:-

rice   tui ya nazi

Before the rice is quite cooked add a little *tui ya nazi*. This being a form of fat makes the rice both appetising and nutritious.

Curried Vegetables

3 large potatoes	600 ml. (1 pint) good stock or Bovril
1 sliced onion	
125 g. (4 oz.) butter	1 sliced uncooked onion
1 tablespoon curry powder	½ peeled vegetable marrow
250 g. (½ pint) shelled green peas	juice of ½ lemon or
250 g. (½ pint) haricot beans soaked overnight	1 tablespoon vinegar
a little browned flour	salt and pepper
	a few slices of cucumber

Peel potatoes; cut into small strips and fry with 1 onion in half the butter till golden-brown. Put into a saucepan with stock, onion, vegetable marrow, peas, haricot beans, slices of cucumber, lemon juice or vinegar and curry powder. Simmer very slowly; if necessary, stir occasionally but not so as to mash the vegetables. When vegetables are nearly cooked add the remaining butter and flour to thicken the gravy. Season with salt and pepper and cook till vegetables are soft but not broken.

Samosas

Pastry:—

250 g. (8 oz.) plain flour	a little oil and flour
½ teaspoon salt	about 300 ml. (½ pint) warm water

Filling:—

250 g. (8 oz.) minced beef	1 clove garlic, crushed
½ teaspoon crushed fresh ginger	1–2 green chillies, seeded and chopped
salt	
¼ teaspoon cinnamon powder	¼ teaspoon powdered cloves
2 tablespoons water	½ teacup chopped onion
2 tablespoons roughly chopped green	dhania (Chinese parsley)

Paste:—

2 tablespoons plain flour	3–4 tablespoons warm water
oil for deep fat frying	lemon wedges

(*Continued*)

Method:—

PASTRY:—Sift the flour with the salt and bind with water. Knead the dough well on a floured board. Take walnut sized balls of dough at a time and roll each out about 8 cm. (3 in.) in diameter. Brush each circle of dough with oil and flour. Sandwich both the circles together sealing in the oil and flour. Roll out again as thin as possible to about 20 to 25 cm. (8 in. to 10 in.) in diameter. Dry the pastry on both sides in a hot large frying pan. Separate the layers and keep in a damp tea towel. Proceed in the same manner with the rest of the dough. Cut the circles of pastry into 3 equal sections. Each section of pastry will make 1 samosa. Fold the pastry and fill with about 1 dessertspoon of the filling and seal the ends with the paste. Fry in hot oil until golden brown in colour, drain on absorbent paper and serve hot with lemon wedges.

FILLING:—Wash the beef and put into a pan and cook until well browned. Add the garlic, ginger, chillies, salt, cinnamon, cloves and water. Simmer for about 5–7 minutes. Remove from heat and stir in the onions and the green dhania. Cool and use to fill the samosas.

PASTE:—Mix the flour with the water to make a sticky paste. Use to stick the samosa ends.

ROASTING AND ACCOMPANIMENTS FOR ROAST MEAT

Roast or Baked Meat

Wash or wipe meat well. In hot weather use 1 teaspoon vinegar in the water. Place the joint in a tin and put dripping over it. Put in the hottest part of the oven for first 15 minutes; this seals or hardens the outer layer of meat and so keeps the juices in. After the first 15 minutes move to a cooler part of the oven and cook till tender. Baste the meat every 10 or 15 minutes to keep the joint moist. The usual time allowed for cooking is 20 minutes to each 500 g. (pound) of meat, and about 20 minutes over. Pork and veal require longer cooking than beef or mutton and thick joints require a longer time than thinner ones.

Thickened Gravy (to serve with roasted meats and poultry)

After roasting the meat pour off the fat carefully, leaving about a tablespoon of fat at the bottom of the meat tin, with the brown sediment from the meat; the latter is required to make the gravy rich and good. Add 1 tablespoon flour and brown over a gentle heat. Add 1½ cups water or stock and salt and pepper. Allow to boil and add a few drops of gravy browning if necessary.

Beef. Yorkshire Pudding (*see* below). Horseradish Sauce (*see* Sauces).

Mutton. Redcurrant Jelly. Onion Sauce (*see* Sauces).

Lamb. Mint Sauce (*see* Sauces).

Veal. Parsley Stuffing (*see* below). Small rolls of bacon. Lemon.

Pork. Sage and Onion Stuffing (*see* below). Apple Sauce (*see* Sauces).

Browning

1 cup sugar   1 cup cold water
½ cup warm water

Put sugar and cold water in a saucepan and allow the sugar to dissolve. Boil until it turns a dark brown. Cool slightly and add warm water. Stir till sugar is quite dissolved, then bottle.

Pot Roast

Pot roasting is roasting in a stewpan. To heat an oven for the sole purpose of cooking a very small joint is extravagant and unnecessary. Small joints—rump, steak, loin and best end of neck and small birds—may be roasted in a stewpan with a well-fitted lid.

1. Place enough fat in the saucepan to cover about 4 cm. (1½) inches and make hot.
2. Tie the meat into a neat shape and put into the hot fat.
3. Cook for a few minutes on each side to coagulate the surface albumen.
4. Cover with the lid, place the pan over moderate heat, baste occasionally and turn the meat from time to time.
5. Cook until tender and make the gravy in the usual way.

Parsley Stuffing

4 tablespoons breadcrumbs or   grated rind of ½ lemon
   1 cup soaked bread   ½ teaspoon mixed herbs
1 large spoon chopped suet or   beaten egg or a little milk
   melted fat   pepper and salt
2 small spoons chopped parsley

Mix all ingredients together and bind with egg or milk. If soaked bread is used care should be taken that it is squeezed dry before being added to the other ingredients and that it is not lumpy.

Sage and Onion Stuffing

2 large onions   3 tablespoons breadcrumbs
1 small spoon powdered sage   1 tablespoon butter
pepper and salt

Boil onions 15 minutes, then chop them and add to all the other ingredients.

Yorkshire Pudding

4 large spoons flour   2 eggs
1 cup milk   ¼ small spoon salt
2 large spoons dripping

Put flour and salt into a large basin. Make a hole in the centre of the flour and put eggs into it and some of the milk. Stir with a wooden spoon, gradually working in the flour. Add milk as required, till half is used, keeping the mixture like thick cream. Beat for 10 minutes, then stir the rest of the milk in gently. Stand for 1 hour in a cool place. Heat the dripping in a tin and pour in the batter. Cook in a very hot oven till well risen, brown and crisp. Cut into squares and serve around joint of roast beef.

POULTRY, GAME AND JOINTS

ACCOMPANIMENTS FOR POULTRY

Fowl. Parsley Stuffing (*see* Roasted Meat section). Small rolls of bacon. Bread sauce (*see* Sauces).

Turkey. Chestnut Stuffing (*see* below). Sausages. Bread Sauce.

Duck or Goose. Sage and Onion Stuffing (*see* Roasted Meats section). Apple Sauce (*see* Sauces).

GENERAL RULES FOR ROASTING POULTRY OR JOINTS

Time depends on size of bird. Weigh and allow 20 minutes to every 500 g. (1 lb.) and 20 minutes over.

Singe and truss the bird, then stuff it. Put in baking pan, dredge with flour, pour fat over and bake, basting frequently. When cooked, pour off fat and put the bird on another dish. Pour boiling water into brown flour in pan and stir well. Replace on the stove and simmer. Strain gravy before sending to table.

Roasting with water instead of fat, or half and half, is quite satisfactory, while the double roaster or baking pot is also satisfactory and does not require so much basting.

The Best Way of Plucking Fowls

As soon as the bird is killed, plunge it into a bucket of boiling water for one minute. Every feather will come out easily, the flesh will not tear and all insects which infest the bird will be destroyed.

Chicken à la Maryland

slice of ham (thick)	1 cup thick tomato sauce
2 tablespoons fat	1½ cups maize grains or rice
1 spring chicken cut into	(cooked)
pieces	¼ teaspoon sugar
½ cup buttered breadcrumbs	1 cup thick cream

Cut the ham into pieces for serving and fry in fat until delicately browned. Arrange the ham in a heavy baking dish. Brown the pieces of chicken (floured) in the fat the ham was cooked in. Sprinkle the chicken with pepper and salt and arrange on top of the ham. Pour the tomato sauce over, cover and cook in a moderate oven for 45 minutes. Remove and add the maize or rice, then the sugar and cream and top with the buttered crumbs. Place in a hot oven until the crumbs are nicely brown and the mixture is cooked through. Serve with fried bread and a salad of fresh vegetables.

Chicken and Mushrooms

1 chicken	lard
flour	mushrooms tinned or fresh
salt and pepper	

Clean, singe and cut up the chicken. Sprinkle with salt and pepper, dredge with flour and fry in lard. Put in a stewpan and cover with stock previously made from the giblets and trimmings of the fowl. Cover closely and simmer till the meat is tender. Add the mushrooms and cook together for 5 minutes.

Chicken Au Gratin

Make a smooth foundation sauce from 60 g. (2 oz.) butter, 30 g. (1 oz.) flour and 1 breakfast cup milk. The butter should be melted in a pan, after which the flour must be stirred in and the paste cooked for 5 minutes, before the milk is added gradually while the mixture is constantly stirred. Mix into the sauce 45 g. (1½ oz.) grated cheese and boil slowly for 5 minutes, finally stirring in seasonings of salt and pepper.

Cut the cold chicken meat into small pieces, having removed all skin. Arrange in a buttered fireproof dish, pour over it the sauce and add a good layer of breadcrumbs mixed with more grated cheese. Pour over all 30 g. (1 oz.) melted butter and brown in a hot oven.

Chicken with Rice

1 fowl	2 turnips or swedes
2 onions	2 carrots
1 leek	1 teacup rice

Cut up vegetables into small pieces and place in pan along with fowl. Add 1.75 litres (3 pints) boiling water. Place pot inside oven and simmer 2 to 3 hours.

Half an hour before serving add 1 teacup washed rice to stock. Season. Serve chicken surrounded with cooked rice.

Chicken Creams

125 g. (4 oz.) raw chicken meat	75 ml. (½ gill) milk
1 tablespoon white	75 ml. (½ gill) cream
breadcrumbs	1 white of egg
45 g. (1½ oz.) butter	pepper and salt

Warm the milk and butter, then add the chicken finely minced and the breadcrumbs and afterwards mix in the cream and the white of egg, stiffly whipped. Put into a well-greased basin and steam ¾ hour. Turn out and serve with egg or parsley sauce (*see* Sauces).

Chicken Patties

1 cold chicken	chopped parsley
salt and pepper	

Chop meat of chicken finely and season well. Make a large cupful rich white sauce, add a little chopped parsley, then chicken meat. Bring nearly to the boil. Have ready some patty-cases baked quickly to light brown. Slip from pans while hot, fill with mixure and set into oven to heat. Arrange upon dish and serve hot.

Chicken Pie

Prepare as for Salmi of duck or chicken, add 2 hardboiled eggs cut in slices and cover with pastry.

Chicken Pilau

1 chicken
2 litres (3 pints) stock or water
150 g. (5 oz.) rice
100 g. (3 oz.) butter
6 peppercorns
30 g. (1 oz.) stoned raisins
salt and pepper

2 large onions
2 small onions
hard-boiled eggs
1 carrot
1 blade mace
30 g. (1 oz.) blanched almonds

Cut chicken into pieces; remove skin. Stew backbone, giblets, neck, trimmings, etc., in the stock together with the outside layer of large onions, carrot, mace and peppercorns. Boil for 2½ hours, then strain. Heat half the butter in a frying-pan, cut up the remainder of the large onions and fry till slightly brown, add rice, 1 litre (1½ pints) of stock, salt and pepper and cook gently. Take remaining half of the butter, fry the chicken until well browned. When rice has absorbed the greater part of the stock put the fried chicken and curry powder into the saucepan and mix well together. Cook until chicken and rice are quite tender. Before serving, fry the small onions (sliced), the raisins and almonds; pile the pilau in the middle of a hot dish and arrange them round and on top with sliced hard-boiled egg.

NOTE: Curry powder may be added if desired or the pilau may be served with a curry sauce (*see* Sauces).

Chicken, Supreme of

1 or 2 chickens
4 eggs
⅓ cup thick cream, or
½ cup good milk

salt
pepper
1 tablespoon butter

Mince the uncooked meat, using about 1.5 kg. (3½ lb.) of meat. Beat 4 eggs till thick and creamy and add to the minced chicken. Then add cream, or milk and butter, salt and pepper.

Turn into buttered mould, set the mould in a pan half-filled with hot water, put buttered paper over the mould and bake in a hot oven for 20 minutes. Serve with white sauce.

Duck, Stewed

1 duck
2 onions
sage

butter or dripping
thyme
flour

pepper, salt
beef gravy

Sprinkle duck with flour, and brown. Fry onions until transparent. Pour out dripping, put in beef gravy, water or stock to cover duck; add herbs minced and simmer till tender. Serve cooked green peas round duck.

Duck, Wild Roast

1 wild duck
2 slices of fat bacon
60 g. (2 oz.) dripping
1 wineglass port

juice of 1 lemon
300 ml. (½ pint) gravy
watercress
potato straws

When duck is drawn and trussed, spread it with dripping; lay the two slices of bacon across it and place the rest of the dripping in the tin. Bake in rather a quick oven for one hour, basting frequently. Untruss; arrange on hot dish and keep warm while making 300 ml. ($\frac{1}{2}$ pint) of nice brown gravy. Before serving, slit breast in three or four places; squeeze the lemon juice and pour the port wine over it. Garnish with watercress and serve with potato straws and slices of orange.

Fowl Boiled

1 fowl	1 teaspoon salt
1 onion	a bunch of parsley
1 carrot	1 bay leaf
1 turnip	

Prepare fowl and place in well-buttered paper or muslin cloth. Place in boiling water with onion, carrot, turnip, salt, parsley and bay leaf. Simmer gently according to size—a chicken about $1\frac{1}{2}$ hours, a full-sized fowl 3 hours.

For sauce which is poured over fowl, melt 30 g. (1 oz.) butter, stir in gradually 30 g. (1 oz.) flour, add 300 ml. ($\frac{1}{2}$ pint) milk. Thicken and add the chopped-up whites of two hard-boiled eggs. Grate the yolks over sauce on top of fowl and garnish round with rolls of fried bacon and parsley.

Chicken Salad

2 young tender lettuces	boiled beetroot or tomato
the remains of cold fowls	white of hard-boiled eggs
a good salad dressing	cucumber

Wash, dry and slice finely the lettuces and arrange in the centre of a salad bowl. Trim and cut the fowl into neat pieces and place on the lettuce; pour a good salad dressing over the whole. Garnish with alternate slices of cucumber and boiled beetroot or cucumber and tomato and among them arrange little mounds of the white of hard-boiled eggs chopped finely.

Fowl or Chicken Fricassée

(a)

1 fowl (cooked)	1 bunch herbs
lemon peel	pepper and salt
1 blade mace	yolks of 2 eggs
1 sliced onion	

Cut the fowl into neat joints. Make a gravy from all trimmings by stewing them in 1 l. ($1\frac{3}{4}$ pints) water with a strip of lemon-peel, a blade of mace, onion, herbs, pepper and salt. Reduce the gravy by boiling until just enough is left to warm up the meat thoroughly, the quantity of liquid required depending on the quantity of meat. Strain the gravy, return it to the saucepan and put in the fowl. Do not let it boil but get the meat properly hot and then thicken the gravy with a little flour. Beat the yolks of eggs until creamy and add to the gravy but do not permit the latter to boil, for, if it does so, it will curdle.

91

(b)

remains of roast or boiled chicken	300 ml. (½ pint) stock or water
white sauce (*see* Coating sauce, page 64)	1 chopped onion
	seasoning

Cut fowl into neat joints; place in saucepan with onion and stock. Cook gently till onion is tender. Make sauce, using part liquid in which chicken has been cooked and part milk. Place chicken in centre of hot dish and pour sauce over. Garnish with hard-boiled egg.

Fowl (Old)

Skin the fowl and cut it up. Place in Pyrex dish with 1 cup of water, a blade of mace, 1½ tablespoons butter, 1 chopped onion, pepper and salt to taste, a little allspice and 1 tablespoon sago or vermicelli. Cover and place dish in the oven for 4 or 5 hours, adding stock or water when required. Just before serving add 1 beaten egg and a little lemon juice. The fowl should be served with a nice quantity of gravy but not enough to make it sloppy.

Forcemeat Balls

1 large cup breadcrumbs	1 teaspoon chopped onion
1 dessertspoon butter	1 raw egg
1 teaspoon thyme	pepper and salt
1 teaspoon chopped parsley	

Mix ingredients. If too stiff add milk. Make into balls as large as pigeon's eggs.

Forcemeat Stuffing

2 cups raw minced meat (the giblets from poultry can be used)	1 spoon of vinegar or juice of ½ lemon
salt and pepper	1 egg
¼ teaspoon ground cloves	a little minced ham or bacon
1 teaspoon ground coriander	1 large slice of white bread soaked in milk
	a little nutmeg

Mix all ingredients thoroughly.

When using up scraps of stale bread for stuffing, soak in cold water, for if boiling water is used the bread gets slimy.

NOTE: Sausage meat mixed with breadcrumbs and a little egg can be used in place of above for stuffing turkey.

Fritot of Chicken or Partridge

1 bird	1 tablespoon vinegar
3 tablespoons salad oil	60 g. (2 oz.) butter
1 beaten egg	½ lemon
breadcrumbs	salt and pepper

Cut bird into small joints; lay on a plate with the oil and vinegar, sprinkle with salt and pepper and leave for 3 hours. Brush thoroughly with egg and dip in breadcrumbs. Melt butter, brush it over the

breadcrumbed joints, then dip them in crumbs again. Fry slowly in the
butter in a frying pan till tender. Serve with green peas and potatoes.

Goose Roast

When roasting goose use butter, not dripping or lard, as there is
much natural oil about a goose.

Use the same stuffing as for ducks (*see* Stuffings).

Serve with apple sauce or cut-up orange.

If not very young, roast first till brown, then place in a saucepan.
Strain off fat, make a good quantity of gravy. Pour over goose and
simmer slowly for 1 hour more.

Guinea-Fowl Roast

guinea-fowl   watercress
60 g. (2 oz.) dripping   bread sauce

Draw, truss and lard guinea-fowl; put in meat tin with dripping.
Cook in hot oven for 10 minutes and then a moderate oven for 40
minutes, basting frequently. Place in hot dish, garnish with watercress
and serve with bread sauce (*see* Sauces). Garnish with watercress and
serve with potato straws and slices of orange.

Pepper Pot

fat pork, cut in dice   cold meat, poultry, browning,
game   chillies or capsicums

Fry pork till brown, then put in a casserole with the melted fat.
Add cold meat, poultry or game, cut up without any stuffing or vegetables and add enough cold water to cover the meat. To every 500 ml.
(1 pint) of water add 1 tablespoon browning and chillies or capsicums to
taste. The materials should be kept in the casserole and boiled up
every morning. Always be careful to remove the fat on the surface
before heating and serve in the casserole.

Pigeon Pie

2 or more pigeons   250 g. ($\frac{1}{2}$ lb.) beefsteak
pepper and salt   30 g. (1 oz.) butter
chopped parsley   1 onion
1 or 2 hard-boiled eggs   300 ml. ($\frac{1}{2}$ pint) brown stock
1 egg   puff paste

Cut up pigeons by dividing them down the centre of the back
and breast and then cut each half in two. Season them with pepper,
salt and chopped parsley if liked. Treat beefsteak cut in thin slices
in the same way. Melt butter in a frying-pan. Fry onion finely chopped
in it, then put in the pigeons and beef and fry for a few minutes to set
the juices. Sprinkle them with a little flour and brown them, add
the brown stock made from cooked meat bones and quite free from
fat, stir it till all boils, then arrange the pigeons and meat in a pie dish
with some sliced hard-boiled eggs. Pour in the gravy and cover in the
usual way with a good puff paste. Brush this over with whole beaten-up
egg. Stand the dish in a tin containing a little hot water and bake the
pie in a hot oven according to size.

Poultry Braised

Roast according to General Rules (*see* above) till brown; strain off fat; make a good gravy with water or stock; put all in a pot and simmer with a few onions cut up, for 1 hour. Thicken gravy before serving.

Rabbit, Casserole of

1 young rabbit
  (cleaned and jointed)
125 g. (¼ lb.) streaky bacon

breadcrumbs
milk
salt and pepper

Place a layer of rabbit in the bottom of the casserole. Cover with breadcrumbs and season with salt and pepper; then cover with a layer of bacon. Over this lay more rabbit, then breadcrumbs seasoning and bacon and finish with a layer of breadcrumbs. Pour over sufficient milk to cover the mixture. Place the covered casserole in a pan of boiling water. Cook in the oven for 3 hours or until required. Just before serving, brown the breadcrumbs. This is an excellent dish to serve when there is a possibility of delay, as it will not spoil with over-cooking.

Rabbit Pie

1 young rabbit
125 g. (4 oz.) bacon
short pastry

flour
pepper and salt

Wash rabbit carefully and allow to lie for 1 hour in clean salted water. Remove; dry carefully with clean towel and cut into neat joints. Dip in a mixture of flour, pepper and salt. Fry bacon in saucepan; remove when cooked and brown rabbit in the fat. This will absorb all the fat. Return bacon to saucepan; add a small cup of water; stir well; close the lid and simmer carefully for 2 hours. Put into a pie dish and pour round a little stock or water. One or two hard-boiled eggs may be added or a few forcemeat balls (*see* page 92). Cover with a short crust (*see* Pastry Section) and bake in a hot oven.

Ragoût of Chicken or Turkey

200 g. (6 oz.) cold cooked
  turkey or chicken
50 g. (2 oz.) cooked ham
300 ml. (½ pint) milk
a dust of nutmeg
salt and pepper

125 g. (4 oz.) spaghetti
30 g. (1 oz.) flour
30 g. (1 oz.) butter
parsley
lemon rind

Chop the turkey or chicken and cooked ham. Boil the spaghetti in salted water until soft and then drain it and cut it in small pieces. Make a sauce with the flour, butter and milk; season it with salt, pepper and nutmeg. Add the minced turkey or chicken and ham to the sauce. Add a teaspoon chopped parsley and a little grated lemon rind. Grease some scallop shells, put in a layer of the spaghetti and then fill in with the turkey mixture. Sprinkle the top thickly with breadcrumbs; put a small piece of butter on each and bake in a moderate oven till brown.

Salmi of Duck or Chicken

1 duck or chicken	bay leaf
dripping	small onion
1 rasher of bacon	rind and juice of 1 orange
600 ml. (1 pint) gravy or well-flavoured brown sauce	1 wineglass of red wine (if desired)
thyme	

Spread duck or chicken with dripping and tie rasher over its breast. Bake in quick oven for 20 minutes. Cut into small joints and place in a casserole. Break up carcass and put into gravy or brown sauce with thyme, bay leaf, small onion, rind and juice of orange. Simmer this gently for 1 hour. Strain the sauce over the duck joints in the casserole. Add red wine and simmer for another 30 minutes. Serve in the casserole.

Bread Stuffing

2 teacups breadcrumbs	grated rind of lemon if liked
1 tablespoon butter or chopped suet	1 egg
	pepper and salt
thyme, parsley or mixed herbs	

Rub fat into breadcrumbs and seasonings and bind with beaten egg. Double the quantity for a turkey. Add sage instead of thyme, parsley and cooked chopped onion for duck or goose.

Chestnut Stuffing

1 kg. (2 lb.) chestnuts	30 g. (1 oz.) butter
300 ml. (½ pint) stock or water	salt, pepper and pinch sugar

Slit the skin of the chestnuts and bake them for 20 minutes. Remove both outer and inner skins and put chestnuts into a stewpan, adding just enough stock or water to cover them. Simmer till tender, then rub through a sieve. Add melted butter, sugar, salt and pepper. If liked, 500 g. (1 lb.) sausage meat may be mixed with the chestnuts when cooked, *or* the following mixture, which makes a nice stuffing:—

1 cup breadcrumbs	½ tablespoon minced onion
1 tablespoon parsley	milk or cream to bind

COOKED MEAT DISHES

Ideas with Leftovers

Care for leftovers just as you would fresh meats. Don't let them go to waste. Store them in the refrigerator, covered closely to prevent drying. To save space, cut meat from bones and store in a covered container or wrap tightly in waxed paper or tinfoil.

Ways to use Leftovers

Slice and use for hot or cold sandwiches. Heat slices in gravy or sauces.

Cube and use in casseroles with noodles, spaghetti, macaroni or mixed vegetables.

Mince and mix with mayonnaise and relishes for sandwich fillings. Use with fresh meat in a meat loaf.

Use in stuffed green peppers, stuffed tomatoes or cabbage rolls. Serve with tomato sauce.

Use in meat croquettes, fritters, meat patties or spaghetti sauce. Use for curries.

Reheating Meat

Some of the daintiest and most tasty dishes may be made from the remains of cold meat if the process of reheating is carefully carried out and the meat not rendered tough and indigestible by being recooked instead of being merely reheated.

Cover Shepherd's pie, macaroni cheese or similar dishes, with a plate or greased paper till the cooking is nearly finished, removing this in time to let the top brown attractively; otherwise the top layer of potato or macaroni will bake hard and dry.

Try rolling rissoles of fish or meat into semolina instead of breadcrumbs before frying. Semolina takes on a delightful brown and fries easily.

Casserole of Cold Meat

500 g. (1 lb.) potatoes
15 g. (½ oz.) butter
salt and pepper
1 teaspoon Bovril
1 cup of water

250 g. (½ lb.) cold meat (minced finely)
parsley or other garnish
browned crumbs
1 egg

Boil the potatoes; dry well; then pass through a potato masher. Add the butter, seasoning and egg, reserving a very little of the egg for brushing over the casserole. Have a plain mould well greased and lined with browned crumbs. Spread the potato smoothly over the bottom and sides of the mould, leaving a hollow to contain the meat; brush over the egg and bake in a quick oven till firm and brown at the edge. Mince the meat, melt Bovril in hot water and add to meat. Turn the casserole on to a dish, then reverse it and fill with the prepared meat. Garnish. If veal is used, garnish with bacon rolls.

96

Cold Meat and Tomatoes

cold meat
tomatoes
potatoes (parboiled)
salt and pepper

onions (parboiled)
500 ml. (1 pint) milk or beef
    extract
breadcrumbs

Cut meat into slices. Place in a dish alternate layers of meat, sliced and peeled tomato, slices of potato and chopped onion, with seasoning between each. Continue the layers until the dish is full. Add milk or stock; sprinkle breadcrumbs on top. Bake ½ hour.

Cottage Pie

1 kg. (2 lb.) potatoes
250 g. (½ lb.) meat (cold)
15 g. (½ oz.) dripping
1 small onion

1 teaspoon flour
150 ml. (¼ pint) water or stock
1 teaspoon salt
½ teaspoon pepper

Boil, dry and mash potatoes; mix with salt, pepper, a little milk and butter. Take all skin and gristle from meat and cut in very small dice.

Heat dripping; fry onion; add flour, water and seasoning. Boil well and strain. Grease a pie dish and mix meat and gravy in it. Pile potatoes on top, decorate and brush with a little milk. Brown top and serve very hot.

Darioles of Cold Meat

500 g. (1 lb.) minced meat
300 ml. (½ pint) thick
    brown gravy

yolks of 2 eggs
seasoning

Mix the meat with half the gravy and eggs, season well. Pour into small buttered pans and cover with a greased paper. Steam till set, not allowing the water to boil. Turn out on a hot dish; heat the rest of the gravy and pour round.

Duck, Mock

2 cups scraps of cold meat
½ cup breadcrumbs or
    cold boiled rice
1 teaspoon powdered sage

pepper and salt
1 raw egg
3 hard-boiled eggs

Mince the meat, add breadcrumbs or cold boiled rice, sage, pepper, salt and raw egg. Mix well and spread half the mixture in a Pyrex dish. Cut the hard-boiled eggs into slices; put these on the first layer, then put the rest of the mixture on the top of the eggs and bake for ½ hour. Turn out when cold. Serve with salad.

Kromeskies

125 g. (¼ lb.) cooked veal or
    beef
60 g. (2 oz.) cold ham
1 teaspoon chopped
    parsley
1 teaspoon onion juice
salt and pepper

30 g. (1 oz.) butter
30 g. (1 oz.) flour
150 ml. (¼ pint) milk
8 thin fat rashers of bacon
deep fat for frying

(Continued)

For the Batter:—

125 g. (¼ lb.) flour	½ level teaspoon castor
a pinch of salt	sugar
1 teaspoon of yeast	150/200 ml. (1 to 1¼ gills) warm milk

Put the veal and ham through the mincer.

Melt the butter in a saucepan. Stir in the flour and when well blended add the milk and bring the mixture to the boil. Boil gently for a minute or two, keeping it well stirred, then draw the pan aside and mix in the minced veal and ham, chopped parsley, onion juice and seasoning to taste. Spread this on a plate and leave until it is cold.

Meanwhile you can prepare the batter. Sift the flour and salt into a basin. Put the yeast and sugar into a cup and mix until they liquefy, then add the milk, which should be lukewarm. Strain this into the flour and mix to a smooth batter, then beat it well and let it stand in a warm place to rise, for about ¾ hour.

Divide the meat mixture into 16 portions and form each into a thin roll and remove the rind from the rashers. Rather fat, wide rashers are the best for this purpose and they should be cut thinly. Cut the rashers in halves or into pieces large enough to enclose the veal rolls, then take each roll and wrap it in a piece of bacon.

Heat a deep pan of fat and when it begins to smoke faintly dip the rolls into the prepared batter and coat them evenly. Then place the rolls in the hot fat and dry gently until golden, by which time the bacon should be cooked. Drain them on paper and serve.

Meat and Vegetable Pie Cold

potatoes, boiled	2 hard-boiled eggs
pieces of cold meat	good gravy or Bovril
fried tomatoes	Worcester sauce
fried onions	pastry

Put a layer of potatoes in the bottom of a pie dish, then a layer of cold meat, then a layer of fried tomatoes and onions. Continue this until the dish is full. Add hard-boiled eggs, sliced, and gravy or Bovril in which put a little Worcester sauce; then cover with pastry and bake.

Meat Gâteau Cold or Hot

thick slice stale bread	pepper and salt
milk	a little stock or sauce
375 g. (¾ lb.) finely minced meat	1 egg
	slices hard-boiled egg
chopped parsley	
breadcrumbs	

Cut bread into small pieces and soak in milk. Beat up well and mix with minced meat. Add chopped parsley, pepper and salt and moisten with stock and beaten egg, or a little sauce will do. Sprinkle a greased pie dish with breadcrumbs and line it with slices of hard-boiled egg. Add carefully the meat mixture and bake for 30 minutes. Turn out and shape on a hot dish. Pour some hot brown sauce round it and serve hot.

If served cold, the sauce should be omitted and a well-seasoned green salad placed around.

Mince au Gratin

sauce or gravy	3 tablespoons grated cheese
cold meat	3 tablespoons breadcrumbs
butter	salt and pepper

First prepare meat by removing all skin, gristle and discoloured parts from the remains of a joint and either chopping the meat or putting it through a mincer. Mix together the breadcrumbs and grated cheese. Grease a casserole and put in some of the crumbs and cheese: then put in a layer of meat and a little seasoning and moisten with a few spoons of well-made sauce or gravy. Repeat the layers until the casserole is almost full, with gravy or sauce last. Sprinkle grated cheese and breadcrumbs on top and a few pats of butter. Bake in a good oven until nicely browned.

Mince Roll

1 cup minced cooked beef	2 eggs
1 chopped onion	1 slice bacon
1 cup breadcrumbs or cold cooked potatoes	a little chopped parsley or dried mixed herbs
	salt and pepper

Mix the ingredients with 2 raw beaten eggs. Boil in cloth (dipped in hot water, squeezed and floured) for 1½ hours. Serve with brown gravy. A round 500 g. (1 lb.) tin can be used if well greased and covered with a little buttered paper and lid securely fastened. Cold mashed potatoes may be added instead of breadcrumbs.

Patties

any boiled poultry, mutton or game	30 g. (1 oz.) flour
	a little milk
30 g. (1 oz.) butter	chopped parsley
seasoning	

Cut meat up into small pieces and add to a good sauce made as follows: to the butter add flour and enough milk to make the sauce, add chopped parsley and seasoning to taste. Fill hot patty casings and serve.

If game is being used a little stock instead of milk and a tablespoon of port wine greatly add to the flavour.

Potato Bridies

flour	minced meat
a few boiled potatoes	

Mix potatoes with a little flour and form into scones. Spread the minced meat on half the scone; turn over the other half on the meat and pinch all round. Fry in smoking-hot fat and serve hot.

Rissoles

125 g. (¼ lb.) scraps of cold meat   salt and pepper
2 cooked potatoes   1 tablespoon parsley
½ teacup white breadcrumbs   a little nutmeg
some gravy or sauce   1 egg
browned crumbs

Chop and mince the meat finely; add the potatoes mashed and also the white breadcrumbs, salt, pepper, nutmeg and any left-over gravy to moisten the mixture. Mix all thoroughly together with half the egg. Form into round pieces or into cutlet shapes, using a little flour on the hands and board to prevent the mixture sticking. Coat these with the rest of the egg, to which add a little milk and finally roll the rissole in crushed brown crumbs, of which one should always have a supply on hand. Fry in deep fat until a golden colour and drain thoroughly. Dish daintily, garnished with tiny springs of parsley.

Sausage Potatoes

250 g. (½ lb.) sausages   salt and pepper
1 kg. (2 lb.) cooked potatoes   a few sprigs of parsley
yolk of 1 egg   dripping
milk

Prick the sausages and steam or simmer them in (150 ml. ¼ pint) boiling water about 20 minutes; then skin them and cut in two. Mash the potatoes (which are better warm) and beat with a wooden spoon until very light; add yolk of egg and enough milk to moisten. Take a spoonful of the potato, lay a piece of sausage on it, cover with potato (leaving it quite rough), put in a greased baking tin and bake about 20 minutes until nicely browned; then put a sprig of parsley on each one. Serve with Piquante sauce (*see* page 69).

Savoury Cold Meat

cold lean mutton or pork   1 egg
parsley   1 tablespoon grated cheese
½ an onion   breadcrumbs
a little sage

Cut meat into neat slices, with as little fat as possible, making the slices the same thickness. Chop a little parsley and onion finely and add sage. Break egg on a plate, beat it well and put in the herbs and grated cheese. Have ready a frying pan half full of smoking-hot fat. Dip meat into mixture so as to cover both sides and cover with breadcrumbs. Fry the slices for 3 minutes in the boiling fat, drain them on a piece of clean paper on a hot plate and serve on a mound of mashed potatoes. Place some fried tomatoes round dish.

Shepherd's Pie

cold mutton   onion
salt and pepper   milk and water or stock
dried herbs   potatoes
butter   some boiling milk

Chop or mince mutton and season with a small quantity of salt, pepper and dried herbs. Into a buttered pie dish put a layer of the cold meat; sprinkle over it cooked sliced onion and pour over enough milk and water (or stock) to cover. Bake for 20 to 30 minutes. Boil some potatoes, mash and add a little butter and boiling milk to moisten; spread on top of pie and smooth potatoes with knife dipped in milk. Return to oven to brown and serve.

MEATS TO BE EATEN COLD

Aberdeen Sausage

500 g. (1 lb.) stewing steak
125 g. (¼ lb.) fat bacon
1 egg
¼ teaspoon each pepper and salt

2 teaspoons Worcester sauce
   or Bovril
½ cup breadcrumbs
thyme

Mince the steak and bacon; add salt, pepper and sauce. Soak the bread in water and when well soaked squeeze out all the water. Bind all together with the egg. Roll in flour and bake; or place in a floured cloth, plunge in boiling water and boil for 2 hours. When ready, take out and roll in brown breadcrumbs.

Aspic Jelly

2.5 l. (2 quarts) jellied veal
   stock
60 g. (2 oz.) gelatine
150 ml. (¼ pint) sherry
150 ml. (¼ pint) vinegar (white)

shells and whites of 2 eggs
bouquet-garni (parsley, thyme,
   bay leaf)
2 strips of celery

Let the stock become quite cold and remove every particle of fat. Put into a saucepan with the gelatine, herbs, celery cut into large pieces, the eggshells and the whites previously slightly beaten. Whisk till nearly boiling, then add the sherry and vinegar. Continue the whisking till quite boiling, then draw the saucepan aside. Let the contents simmer for 10 minutes. Strain till clear and use as required.

Beef Loaf

1 kg. (2 lb.) minced beef
2 cups breadcrumbs
1 onion minced
1 teaspoon salt

½ teaspoon ground pimento
pepper to taste
1 or 2 eggs
1 cup milk

Mix all the ingredients in a bowl, adding the milk until fairly moist. Bake in a moderate oven for 1½ hours. Turn out when cold.

Brawn

sheep's trotters
a little cold mutton
1 tablespoon vinegar
a few coriander seeds
hard-boiled eggs, parsley and slices of lemon

1 red chilli
1 teaspoon ground allspice
4 or 5 peppercorns
1 bay leaf

After the sheep's trotters are thoroughly cleaned and blanched, put them into a saucepan and boil until quite tender. Set aside to get cold and then remove the bones and any fat that may be on the surface; put what remains into a saucepan with the vinegar, chilli, allspice, peppercorns, coriander seed and bay leaf. Tie all the spices loosely in a little muslin bag so that they may be removed when the brawn is flavoured sufficiently. Cut up into the brawn a little cold mutton or sheep's tongue. Boil for 1 hour and then pour into a mould. Garnish with slices of hard-boiled eggs, thin slices of lemon and small sprigs of parsley.

Pig's feet and half chap may be used instead of the trotters and mutton.

Chicken Mould

1 fowl
15 g. ($\frac{1}{2}$ oz.) gelatine
pepper, salt, pinch of cloves
water

1 dessertspoon lemon juice
2 hard-boiled eggs
chopped parsley

Barely cover a fowl with water and simmer till tender. Take it out, skin and remove the bones. Mince the meat and return to the stock. Soak gelatine in a little cold water for 1 hour; add this to the meat mixture with the seasonings and stir well. Remove from the fire and add the lemon juice. Slice the eggs and decorate a mould with them and the parsley. Pour a little of the liquid on the eggs and parsley and when set add the rest of the mixture. Serve on a bed of lettuce.

Salt or Corned Beef

Take salt or pickled beef and put in a pot with warm water. Bring to the boil and simmer till quite tender. Leave it in the stock in which it was cooked until cold.

Galantine of Veal, Beef, Mutton or Boned Chicken

500 g. (1 lb.) raw beef, veal,
  mutton or boned chicken
500 g. (1 lb.) bacon
3 or 4 eggs
200 g. (6 oz.) breadcrumbs

salt
rind and juice of 1 lemon
1 teacup stock or gravy
pinch of nutmeg
pepper

Mince meat with breadcrumbs; add bacon, cut into dice. Add seasoning and bind with 2 eggs. Spread all in a floured cloth and put 2 hard-boiled eggs cut in halves in the mixture and some whole pickles (if liked). Roll in cloth tightly and boil for 2 hours. Take out and place in a pie dish, in the cloth, with a little of the liquid it has boiled in, to cool. Place a plate on top with a heavy weight to press the galantine flat. Remove cloth, sprinkle with dry breadcrumbs or glaze.

For mutton or chicken galantine take half the quantity of mince-meat and spread this on 1.5 kg. (3 lb.) of flank of mutton boned or chicken boned. Roll in cloth and proceed as above.

GLAZE FOR GALANTINE:—

2 teaspoons Bovril	3 sheets gelatine
250 ml. (½ pint) hot water	

Dissolve the gelatine in a little cold water. Mix beef extract with hot water, add the gelatine and stir well.

Garnish for Cold Meat

15 g. (½ oz.) gelatine	1 cup beetroot (diced)
1 cup cold water	3 teaspoons sugar
1 tablespoon lemon juice	1 tablespoon horseradish
1 cup cooked peas or	1 teaspoon Bovril
sliced carrots	boiling water

Soak the gelatine in the cold water. Add the boiling water in which Bovril has been dissolved, lemon juice and sugar. Allow this to cool a little and then stir in the horseradish. Leave again until it begins to set, when the peas or carrots and beetroot are added. When cold and set, cut in squares.

To Boil a Ham

Soak the ham in quantity of cold water for 12 hours, changing the water several times, scrape it clean and place in a large stewpan with more than sufficient cold water to cover it. Let it come to the boil, remove the scum as it rises and keep it boiling very gently, until tender, for 4 or 5 hours according to size. Now take the pot from the heat and let the ham get cold in the water in which it was boiled. Remove the rind and sprinkle it with breadcrumbs.

Baked Ham

Soak in water overnight. Wrap in tinfoil or make a thick paste of flour and water and roll out to 1 cm. (½ ins.) thick and use this to cover the ham. Maize meal and boiling water may also be used for the paste.

Bake the ham in a moderate oven for 40 mins. per kg. (20 mins. per lb.) plus 30 mins. Remove covering, and thick skin.

The juice from a tin of half peaches or pineapple slices may be poured over and the ham returned to the oven for 10 minutes.

Serve hot with the warmed peaches or pineapple, green peas and mashed potatoes.

Boiling bacon may also be cooked in this way after soaking in water.

High Hack

500 g. (1 lb.) freshly minced	1 egg to bind
beef	salt and pepper to taste
1 cup breadcrumbs	

Mix all the ingredients in a bowl. Press into a well-greased pie dish, cover with buttered paper and bake for 2 hours in a warm oven. When cold, turn out with the gravy on top.

Pickle for Preserving Meat

5 litres (16 cups) water   30 g (1 oz.) saltpetre
60 g. (2 oz.) sugar   250 g. ($\frac{1}{2}$ lb.) salt

Boil water and pour over sugar, salt and saltpetre. Let cool, then strain and pour over meat. Stand for 3 or 4 days before using, or less, according to weather.

Potted Hough

1 to 1.5 kg. (2 to 3 lb.)   parsley
   shin of beef   salt and pepper

Take beef, wash and trim off any fat. Put into saucepan with water to cover. Bring to the boil and simmer slowly till the meat is falling from the bone. Strain. Return the stock to the saucepan and simmer until it is reduced to a breakfast cup of liquid. Meanwhile, remove meat from the bone and cut it up finely with a sharp knife. Add salt and pepper to taste and return it to the liquid. Pour all into a bowl and leave until set. Serve garnished with parsley.

Pressed Beef Cold

about 2 kg. (3 to 5 lb.) brisket   1 breakfast cup stock
   of beef (salted)   15 g. ($\frac{1}{2}$ oz.) gelatine
1 turnip   2 l. (3 pints) boiling water
a small bunch sweet herbs

Tie up the meat with tape to keep its shape. Bring the water, to which has been added the turnip and herbs, to boiling point and pour over the meat. Return to saucepan and bring back to boil, removing any scum that rises. Simmer the meat slowly from 6 to 8 hours, then lift it out and press it into a round mould or a saucepan of suitable size. Dissolve the gelatine in a little cold water and add to the stock. Pour it over the beef in the mould and leave till cold.

Russian Loaf

375 g. ($\frac{3}{4}$ lb.) sheep's liver   salt and pepper
125 g. ($\frac{1}{4}$ lb.) very fat bacon   herbs
1 small teacup breadcrumbs   1 egg

Take the liver and bacon and mince very finely. Put the breadcrumbs, pepper, salt and herbs into a basin and mix well. Now add the minced liver and bacon with the egg well beaten. Press firmly into a basin, cover with a greased paper and steam for 1$\frac{1}{2}$ hours. Serve cold, in thin slices.

Sheep's Tongues in Tomato Aspic

4 sheep's tongues   1 teaspoon sugar
1 kg. (2 lb.) tomatoes   salt and pepper
1 bay leaf   30 g. (1 oz.) gelatine
1 small onion   1 cup cold water

Boil salted sheep's tongues till tender. Cut in halves and place in the following aspic: Slice the tomatoes; place in saucepan; add bay leaf, onion, sugar and a little water. Season with pepper and salt. Stew for five minutes, then strain through a sieve. Dissolve the gelatine in the cold water, add to the strained tomato juice and leave in a mould till firm.

Tongue (Dry Pickle)

1 tongue about 1.5 kg. (3 lb.)
Rub into clean tongue a mixture of:

15 g. (½ oz.) saltpetre   7.5 g. (¼ oz.) pepper
125 g. (4 oz.) salt   60 g. (2 oz.) brown sugar

Place in a refrigerator for 4 or 5 days, turn each day, then wash and boil for 3 to 4 hours.

To make rolled or pressed tongue, roll it round, press it tightly, and tie while hot. Press it into a round mould or small saucepan; pour over some of the hot liquor and put a plate, on which is a heavy weight, on top. When wanted, turn out, remove string and serve surrounded with parsley. It may be glazed as for pressed beef.

Veal Mould

250 g. (½ lb.) lean veal   a little grated lemon rind
1 hard-boiled egg   150 ml. (1 gill) jellied white stock
60 g. (2 oz.) bacon   salad to garnish
1 teaspoon chopped parsley   seasoning

Decorate a soufflé tin with egg and parsley. Cut veal and bacon into dice. Mix them with the seasoning and the stock and turn into the decorated tin. Cover with greased paper and bake in a moderate oven for 1½ hours. If the stock is not jellied, dissolve a little gelatine in it. When cold and set, dip the mould in warm water and turn it out. Garnish with salad.

VEGETABLES AND VEGETABLE DISHES

General Rules for Cooking Vegetables

Choose fresh, unbruised vegetables. Do not store indefinitely but try to use straight away. Put directly into boiling water, not cold, and use only the absolute minimum amount of water for cooking.

Spinach requires scarcely any water at all. Never cover with water.

Scotch broth made with fresh vegetables, cut up at the last minute and plunged into the simmering stock, retains a large proportion of Vitamin C.

Adding a little soda to preserve the green colour of vegetables does no harm. Canned fruits and vegetables retain almost all their Vitamin C due largely to the efficiency of canning processes and also because only the best and freshest fruits are used.

The salt should be added when vegetables are nearly cooked. A little sugar and mint added to peas improve the flavour.

To prevent odour from boiling cabbage, put a small piece of white bread (tied in a muslin bag) into the saucepan, which should not be covered during cooking.

When a meal is delayed, vegetables cooked with soda are apt to turn a nasty colour. To prevent this, pour off the soda water and add fresh boiling water and leave on the side of stove. Strain when required.

Do not use aluminium saucepans for vegetables that require soda, as soda discolours the aluminium.

Reheated vegetables have no Vitamin C.

Average Time-table for Boiling Vegetables

Artichokes, French or Globe .	25 to 30 minutes
Artichokes, Jerusalem . .	15 to 25 minutes
Asparagus	15 to 20 minutes
Beans	15 to 20 minutes
Beetroot . . .	1½ to 2 hours
Brussels Sprouts . .	10 to 15 minutes
Cabbage	10 to 15 minutes
Carrots	20 minutes
Cauliflower . . .	20 minutes
Egg Plant . . .	10 to 20 minutes
Endive	10 to 15 minutes
Kale	20 to 30 minutes
Kohlrabi	20 to 40 minutes
Leeks	20 to 35 minutes
Maize	30 minutes
Marrow	20 minutes
Onions	30 minutes
Parsnips	30 minutes
Peas	10 to 15 minutes
Peppers, green . .	10 to 15 minutes
Potatoes	20 to 45 minutes
Pumpkin . . .	20 minutes
Spinach . . .	10 minutes
Swedes . . .	30 minutes
Turnips	30 minutes
Yams	20 to 30 minutes

Vegetables cooked in Pressure Cooker—*see* Instruction Booklet.

Preparation and Cooking of Dried Pulses

Wash dried peas, beans or lentils and to each 500 g. (1 lb.) allow 1.25 litres (1 quart) of cold water. Soak overnight (this helps to break down and soften the cellulose and protein). Next day cook steadily until tender in the water in which they have been soaked. If very old a pinch of soda may be added to the water in which they are boiled.

FRESH VEGETABLES

Conserve Method of Cooking Vegetables

This method may be used either for cooking root or green vegetables. An advantage is that, as there is no water thrown away at the end, no goodness is lost. A disadvantage is that the colour of green vegetables is not retained because no soda is used, but on the other hand, soda neutralises the vegetable acids and destroys the vitamins.

To 500 g. (1 lb.) vegetables allow
¾ teacup cold water (or stock)
30 g. (1 oz.) fat (preferably butter)
1 teaspoon salt (pepper if liked)

Prepare vegetables in the usual way but cut up smaller. Put in saucepan with water, butter and salt. Cover with a very closely fitting lid and cook gently for 1 hour or longer till vegetables are nearly tender. Shake at intervals. When nearly ready remove lid and evaporate the water. Serve very hot.

Artichokes

(1) JERUSALEM. Peel with a fruit knife and cover with cold water or they will discolour. Put into a saucepan of freshly boiling salted water, cover and boil for 20 minutes without removing the lid. Place in a vegetable dish and cover with white sauce.

(2) GLOBE. Wash well and place in salted water, head downwards, to allow the insects to come out. Place in boiling salted water and boil for 20 minutes. Serve with melted butter.

Asparagus

Cut away the ends. Tie the asparagus stalks and stand them in the saucepan with water 4 cm. (1½ in.) deep. Steam for ½ hour or till tender. Add salt to the water. Serve with melted butter, or with Hollandaise sauce poured over.

Bean and Tomato Pie

500 g. (1 lb.) haricot beans   sliced tomatoes
1 onion   grated cheese
cayenne pepper

Soak beans overnight. Cover with salted boiling water, change water twice, each time using boiling water. Cook beans till tender. Butter a pie dish and place beans and onions minced, cayenne, sliced tomato and some grated cheese alternately, till dish is full. Bake in moderate oven and serve very hot.

Beans and Tomato Sauce

1 breakfast cup haricot
  beans

2 tablespoons grated cheese
150 ml. ($\frac{1}{4}$ pint) thick well-
  flavoured sauce (tomato)

Wash and soak beans. Drain and put into a saucepan with plenty of water and a little bicarbonate of soda. Let the beans boil for 1 or 2 hours, when they should be quite tender but unbroken. Drain and return to saucepan, adding the tomato sauce. If desired grated cheese may be added. Heat for 10 minutes.

Beetroot

Select firm round beetroot. Put into a pan of boiling water with a little salt and boil for 1 to 2 hours. Strain and leave to cool, then peel. If not required for immediate use, pickle in vinegar (*see* Pickle section). If used as a hot vegetable, cut into convenient pieces and reheat with a little butter.

Brinjal or Egg Plant Baked

The secret of preparing this vegetable is to slice it thinly and pepper it. Bake in the oven until crisp and brown. If fried, it absorbs too much fat and is rather rich for the average palate. When cooked, put salt on and a pinch of curry may be sprinkled if liked. This is a nice accompaniment at breakfast with bacon and eggs.

Cabbage Farcie

cabbage leaves
tomato sauce
1 sausage

1 tablespoon breadcrumbs or
  mashed potato
seasoning

Skin the sausage, add the breadcrumbs or mashed potatoes and seasoning, form into little rolls, wrap in whole cabbage leaves, previously blanched in boiling water to which a pinch of bicarbonate of soda has been added, tie with thread and stew in brown or tomato sauce for $\frac{1}{2}$ hour. Remove thread, dish on a hot dish, strain the sauce over and garnish with parsley.

Cabbage Red

small to medium red cabbage
2 tablespoons lemon juice
  or vinegar

1 large tablespoon lard
salt

Cut or shred cabbage very fine; place in colander and pour over boiling water; melt lard in a pan; add cabbage, pour over lemon juice or vinegar; add salt; cook slowly, stirring frequently.

Cabbage Red (Boiled)

Shred and wash cabbage. Place in boiling water with a good handful of salt and boil gently for $1\frac{1}{2}$ to 2 hours. Strain. Serve with fried sliced onions and butter and seasoning to taste.

Casserole of Vegetables

125 g. (¼ lb.) haricot beans   240 ml. (1½ gills)   2 small onions
2 medium carrots   vegetable stock,   2 tomatoes
2 sticks of celery   gravy or milk & water   salt and pepper
1 teaspoon chopped   60 g. (2 oz.) dripping
   parsley
125 g. (¼ lb.) minced meat (if desired)

Soak the beans for 24 hours, then boil until tender. Cut the onions into rings; fry in smoking-hot dripping until golden-brown. Add the carrots and celery and stir until all the dripping is absorbed. Place in casserole. Add the liquid, then the sliced tomatoes, meat if any, chopped parsley and lastly the beans. Season each layer; cover and stew gently for 40 minutes.

Cauliflower or Marrow au Gratin

1 cauliflower or vegetable   ½ tablespoon grated cheese
   marrow   cayenne pepper
3 tablespoons grated cheese added   brown crumbs
   to 300 ml. (½ pint) thick coating
   sauce

Cook the cauliflower and trim off all the leaves except the very small ones next to the flower. Add the cheese and cayenne to the sauce. Place the cauliflower in a fireproof dish and coat with the sauce. Sprinkle the top with grated cheese and brown crumbs. Place under the griller or in a very hot oven till lightly browned. Vegetable marrow is cooked in the same way.

Chowchows (Stuffed)

chowchows   parsley
some cold meat   tomatoes
salt and pepper   brown breadcrumbs
                        butter

Cut chowchows in two. Boil till tender, then scrape out the pulp, taking care not to break the skin. Mince some cold meat and add to the pulp. Season well with salt, pepper, parsley, tomato, etc. Put into the skins, sprinkle with brown breadcrumbs and add dabs of butter. Put in baking tin; bake slightly. Serve very hot.

Game Salad

the remains of any kind of   mayonnaise sauce
   cold game   beetroot for garnish
1 hard-boiled egg   pepper and salt
lettuce

Remove the bones and cut the flesh into dice of medium size. Wash, trim and dry the lettuce and tear it into shreds. Stamp out some fancy shaped pieces of white of egg, chop up the remainder of the egg and mix it with the meat. Arrange the meat, lettuce and mayonnaise in alternate layers in a salad bowl, raising the centre in pyramid form, and add a sprinkling of salt and pepper to each layer. Cover the surface with a thin layer of mayonnaise sauce, garnish with stars or fancy shapes of sliced beetroot, hard-boiled yolk of egg and serve.

Haricot Savoury

1 cup haricot beans	butter
2 onions	sage
2 tomatoes	salt and pepper
white sauce	breadcrumbs
grated cheese	

Soak the beans overnight or longer. Peel the onions and tomatoes, slice them and fry in butter. Put all into a pie dish with a flavouring of sage, salt and pepper and moisten with white sauce. Cover with breadcrumbs mixed with grated cheese; put small pieces of butter on the top and bake for 1 hour.

Lentil Rissoles

500 g. (1 lb.) lentils	1 chopped fried onion
500 g. (1 lb.) mashed potatoes	pepper and salt
white of 1 egg	parsley chopped finely

Soak lentils. Cook in a little water till tender. Add other ingredients to lentils and mix well together. Roll in flour and form into rissoles or sausages. Coat with white of egg and fry till golden brown colour. (Breadcrumbs are not necessary for coating these rissoles.)

Onions (Stuffed)

1 kg. (2 lb.) onions	60 g. (2 oz.) butter
250 g. (½ lb.) carrots	250 g. (½ lb.) cooked peas
30 g. (1 oz.) cheese	seasoning

Choose good, even-shaped onions weighing about 6 to one kilogram (3 to the pound). Peel them and boil gently in a saucepan with enough water to cover and some salt to flavour for about ¾ to 1 hour, then lift them out and drain.

Meanwhile, scrape and wash the carrots and cut into small dice. Cook them in boiling water (slightly salted), then drain. Drain off some tinned peas and mix with an equal quantity of diced carrot, seasoning them with pepper.

When the onions have cooled, remove the outer layer and scoop out some of the centre part, being careful to keep them whole.

Season the inside of the onions and fill with carrots and peas, adding also a little finely grated cheese to each and a final sprinkling of cheese on top.

Place them in a tin with the butter and bake till tender, keeping them basted.

Heat up the remainder of the diced carrot and peas, tossing them in butter, and serve the onions on a hot dish with an extra heap of vegetable on top of each and the remainder round the dish. Serve with cheese and onion sauce (*see* Sauces).

Potato Chips

Scrub and peel the potatoes and cut them into thin slices or strips. Wash and dry well. Fry a few at a time in a pan of smoking-hot fat until they are tender. Remove from the pan and bring the fat to smoking heat again. Then fry the potatoes a second time to make them crisp and brown. Drain on paper to remove all fat. Sprinkle with salt and pepper and serve on a hot dish.

Potato Croquettes

500 g. (1 lb.) potatoes	½ teaspoon chopped parsley
30 g. (1 oz.) butter	seasoning
1 yolk of egg	a little milk
breadcrumbs	

Boil the potatoes. Dry them well, then mash them. Add the butter, parsley and seasoning, then the yolk of egg and beat over a gentle heat till smooth. If too dry, add a little milk or extra yolk of egg. Turn on to a plate to cool. Divide into equal sized pieces and form into balls. Coat the balls twice with egg and crumbs. Fry in deep fat, drain well and serve garnished with fried parsley.

Potato Pie

potatoes	a few dabs butter
onions	flour
salt and pepper	1 cup of milk

Put alternate layers of sliced potato and onion in a dish with a close-fitting lid. Season each layer with a dust of pepper and salt and a few dabs of butter. On the last layer sprinkle a little flour and more butter. Add milk and bake slowly for 2 hours. The lid of the dish must fit closely.

Grated cheese may be added to this dish if desired.

Potato Salad

potatoes	good mayonnaise sauce
spring onion	hard-boiled egg
parsley	salt and pepper

Boil quantity of potatoes required in jackets. Peel when cold, and cut in slices. Sprinkle with salt and pepper. Add finely chopped spring onion and parsley. Cover with mayonnaise sauce and sprinkle mashed hard-boiled egg on top.

Potato Turnovers

500 g. (1 pint) boiled and mashed potatoes	minced meat
1 egg	onions
1 tablespoon flour	thyme

Mix potatoes with egg and flour. Roll out and cut into circles the size of a saucer. Place on each a large spoonful of mince, seasoned with onions and thyme. Double over and pinch together like a turnover. Place on a greased sheet of paper in a pan; brown in a hot oven and serve with gravy or tomato sauce.

Rhondda Pie (for using up cold vegetables)

cold potatoes
cauliflower or cabbage
carrots or green beans
salt and pepper

peas
1 cup white sauce left over
  or freshly made
grated cheese

Cut up potatoes, cauliflower or cabbage, carrots or green beans and peas. Mix well with white sauce and a little salt and pepper to taste. Place in a pie dish and cover well with grated cheese. Bake ½ hour in a moderate oven. Any cold vegetable not mentioned above may be added as desired.

Russian Salad

1 l. (1½ pint) mayonnaise sauce
1 small cauliflower
125 g. (1 gill) cooked green peas
125 g. (1 gill) mixed vegetables
  (dice of carrot, turnip
  and French beans)

3 new potatoes
2 tomatoes
2 gherkins
1 truffle
salt and pepper

For garnishing:
shredded salmon
diced hard-boiled
  white of egg
shredded beetroot

stoned olives
fillets of anchovy
capers

Divide the cauliflower into small sprays, boil them and the peas, carrot, turnip and beans separately and drain well. Boil the potatoes and when cold cut into neat strips. Cut the tomatoes into moderately thin slices and shred the gherkins and truffle finely. When all the cooked ingredients are cold and well drained, arrange them with the tomatoes, gherkins and truffle in distinct layers in a salad bowl. Season each layer with a little salt and pepper and cover lightly with mayonnaise sauce. Pile the salad high in the centre and cover the surface lightly with mayonnaise. Decorate with small portions of shredded salmon, shredded beetroot, dice of white of egg, olives, capers and fillets of anchovy. Serve the remainder of the mayonnaise sauce separately.

This salad is frequently prepared in a cylindrical shaped mould with suitable border. First mask the mould with aspic and tastefully decorate with the available vegetables.

Salad American

1 white cabbage very
  finely shredded
60 g. (2 oz.) butter
160 ml. (1 gill) vinegar

1 teaspoon sugar
1 teaspoon salt
pepper to taste
150 ml. (¼ pint) of sour cream

Bring the butter, vinegar, sugar, salt and pepper just to boiling point. Pour over the cabbage and when quite cold stir in the cream and serve or moisten the cabbage with salad dressing and serve at once.

Salad Mixed

lettuce, fresh
cold cooked peas
cold chopped French beans
small quantity chopped
    avocado pear (sprinkled
    with lemon juice)

sliced tomato
beetroot
finely chopped parsley
a cold hard-boiled egg
salad dressing

On a bed of lettuce arrange very neatly equal quantities (separately) of peas, French beans, tomato, beetroot, avocado pear and celery. Garnish with egg. When all are arranged nicely, add salad dressing.

Spanish Rice

1 large onion
250 g. (½ lb.) tomatoes
1 cup stock

pepper and salt
2 cups boiled rice
1 tablespoon butter

Chop the onion and fry it in the butter with the tomatoes. Add stock or meat extract, salt and pepper. Cover and let simmer for about 10 minutes, then add rice. Mix well together. Stir in butter and serve very hot.

Spanish Sardine Salad

12 or 14 sardines
2 tablespoons capers
1 crisp lettuce
stoned Spanish olives

anchovy butter
vinegar
salt and pepper

Remove the skin and bones from the sardines and divide them into short pieces. Wash and dry the lettuce thoroughly, tear it into fine shreds and put it into a basin with the sardine and capers. Arrange the salad in a salad bowl, piling it high in the centre. Garnish with the olives filled with anchovy butter and serve.

Anchovy butter is made by mixing butter and anchovy paste together.

Spinach

750 g. (1½ lb.) spinach
15 g. (½ oz.) butter

salt and pepper

Wash spinach in several waters. Pick well over, removing coarse stalks. While the spinach is still wet pack into a saucepan, put on the lid and cook till tender, stirring occasionally. Strain through a colander, chop well or rub through a sieve and press out the water carefully. Add melted butter or 1 teacup of thick white sauce to the spinach and seasoning and reheat. Pile in a vegetable dish or serve with poached eggs on top or slices of hard-boiled egg as garnish and small pieces of French toast.

Sweet Potatoes

Peel and cook like ordinary potatoes.

Sweet Potatoes (Boiled)

Boil the potatoes in water with their jackets on, peel and cut in slices before serving. Alternatively, half boil the potatoes, remove the skin, put into the oven or before the fire until brown. Cut in slices and serve hot.

Sweet Potato Rissoles

Boil and mash the potatoes, add pepper and salt and, if liked, a little chopped parsley. Shape the rissoles, cover them with egg and breadcrumbs and fry until a light brown.

Sweet Potatoes—Rechauffé

Mash cold boiled sweet potatoes until free from lumps. Stir into every pound of potatoes 2 tablespoons flour, 2 tablespoons chopped onion and 30 g. (1 oz.) butter. Add sufficient milk to moisten, press into a mould, turn out and bake in a moderate oven until nicely browned.

Sweet Potato Bread

1 cup mashed potatoes 1 cup maize meal
1 cup flour 2 teaspoons baking powder
milk

Mix all ingredients, using sufficient milk to bring to a stiff consistency, and bake in a hot oven.

Sweet Potatoes (Fried)

Cut cold boiled potatoes into thin slices. Season with salt, put in a frying basket and cook in lard for 5 minutes.

Sweet Potatoes (Glazed)

Cut cold boiled potatoes in slices about 2·5 cm. (1 inch) thick and season well with pepper and salt. For 1 kg. (2 lbs.) potatoes melt ½ cup of butter and add to it 2 tablespoons of sugar. Dip the slices in this liquid and lay them in a pan and cook for 12 minutes in a very hot oven, in which time the potatoes should turn a rich glossy brown. Serve hot.

Tomato Pie

thin slices of bacon salt and pepper
sliced tomatoes mashed potatoes
Bovril

Lay slices of bacon in a pie dish and cover with tomatoes. Repeat layers till the dish is full. Make a brown gravy sauce with Bovril, add salt and pepper to taste. Pour this into the dish, cover all with mashed potatoes and bake in a moderate oven. Serve hot with green peas or cabbage.

Tomatoes (Stuffed)

4 tomatoes	15 g. (½ oz.) butter
2 tablespoons fresh breadcrumbs	½ teaspoon chopped parsley
	seasoning
½ tablespoon chopped cooked ham or meat	sauce to bind
	brown crumbs
1 teaspoon cooked onion chopped	4 rings fried bread

Cut a small round from the top of each tomato and scoop a hole in the centre. Sauté the ham and onion in the butter. Add the crumbs, parsley, seasoning and the inside part of the tomatoes. Then add sauce to bind. Fill the tomatoes and pile the mixture on top. Bake in a slow oven for about 15 minutes. Sprinkle brown crumbs over and serve on the fried bread. Garnish with parsley.

Turnips Creamed

turnips	1 tablespoon butter
salt and pepper	½ cup milk

Peel and slice the turnips needed. Cook until tender, then drain off all the water. Add salt and pepper, butter and milk. Mash, replace and heat thoroughly before serving.

Vegetable Marrow or Cucumber Savoury

vegetable marrow or cucumber	grated cheese
dripping	breadcrumbs
salt and pepper	butter

Peel vegetable marrow or cucumber; steep in salted water for ½ hour and then drain. Cut as many slices as you require to fill the dish you are using. Melt a little dripping in a pan, put in the slices, season with pepper and salt and fry for a few minutes, stirring constantly. Place on a buttered dish. Scatter thickly with grated cheese and over this breadcrumbs seasoned with pepper and salt and a few bits of butter on the top. Bake for ¼ hour and serve hot.

Vegetable Marrow (Spanish)

1 vegetable marrow	30 g. (1 oz.) butter or clarified
1 large onion	dripping
2 tomatoes	pepper and salt
a little stock	

Fry sliced onion and tomatoes in the butter or clarified dripping. Cut vegetable marrow into cubes, after peeling and removing the seeds. Add the marrow to the onion and tomato, stock, pepper and salt. Let all simmer gently till the marrow is cooked, then serve very hot, garnished with small pieces of toast.

115

Vegetable Marrow (Stuffed)

1 vegetable marrow
60 g. (2 oz.) cold meat
60 g. (2 oz.) breadcrumbs
seasoning

1 tablespoon chopped parsley
and thyme
a little stock or milk

Peel marrow. Cut in half lengthways and take out seeds. Mince meat and mix with soaked bread, parsley, thyme and seasoning. Fill one half of marrow with mixture and tie the two halves together. Sprinkle with flour and bake and serve with brown sauce; or steam and serve with white sauce.

Viennese Carrots

500 g. (1 lb.) carrots
500 g. (1 lb.) fresh peas
1 small onion
1 teacup of hot cream
or milk

2 teaspoons cornflour
1 yolk of egg
1 teaspoon finely chopped
parsley
pepper

Leave the carrots whole if very small, otherwise halve or quarter them lengthwise and put them into boiling salted water. When they have cooked about 10 minutes add peas and onion chopped to a pulp. Mix with the yolk of egg the cornflour, parsley, pepper and finally the hot cream or milk. As soon as the peas are ready, drain off the water, stir in the cream, etc., and shake the pan gently for 2 or 3 minutes before serving. With thin slices of meat, coated with egg and breadcrumbs, crisply fried and piled on top, this makes a good luncheon dish.

To preserve French Beans for use during shortage of Vegetables

Wash and cut beans as for immediate use. Cover the bottom of an earthenware jar with salt, put in a layer of beans, then salt again, then beans and so on until it is full, seeing to it that the last layer is salt. Cover with plate or lid and tie down to keep dust out. When required for use, shake off salt and wash in cold water. Place in fresh water for a few hours, changing the water. Boil in boiling water with small pinch of soda bicarbonate. These will be found as nice as fresh beans.

Dried Bananas

Bananas should be just ripe. Peel and slice longways, put on trays to dry in the sun, cover with butter muslin. When quite dry, store. Soak in water before cooking.

Dried Herbs

Collect parsley, sage and thyme just before they flower, wash well, keeping the different varieties separate. Place on a paper in a cool oven and dry thoroughly until brittle to touch. Rub leaves off stalk and bottle.

MAIZE AND MAIZE MEAL RECIPES

Maize Escalloped

1 cup maize
1½ tablespoons butter
salt and pepper

2 eggs
2 cups milk

Cook cobs and remove grains when cooked. Beat eggs and milk. Add butter, pepper and salt. Mix with cooked grains, place in a buttered pie dish and bake in a moderate oven till set and brown.

Maize Meal Puffs

1.25 ml. (1 quart) milk
2 cups maize meal
½ cup fine sugar
1 cup white flour
½ tablespoon mixed spices

4 eggs
1 tablespoon butter .
½ teaspoon soda bicarbonate
1 teaspoon cream of tartar

Boil the milk and stir carefully into meal and flour to avoid lumps. Boil for 10 or 15 minutes, stirring all the time to prevent scorching, and then add the butter. Remove from heat and beat well. When cool, add eggs, one at a time, beating thoroughly. Add sugar, spices, soda and cream of tartar. Bake in well-greased small tins. Serve with any pudding sauce (*see* Sauces).

Maize Sponge Muffins

1 cup flour
½ cup maize meal
½ teaspoon bicarbonate
of soda
½ cup sugar

2 yolks of eggs
1 white of egg
1 tablespoon melted butter
1 cup sour milk

Mix all dry ingredients together. Stir in melted butter, sour milk, yolks of eggs well beaten, and mix thoroughly. Lastly, add the white of 1 egg, stiffly beaten to a froth. Pour into well-greased muffin or sandwich tins and bake in a hot oven.

Maize Baked and Tomatoes

2 cups green cooked
maize grains
3 or 4 tomatoes
salt and pepper

½ cup breadcrumbs
a little butter

Pour boiling water over the tomatoes and remove the skins. Butter a pie dish. Put a layer of tomatoes and then a layer of mashed maize grains alternately in the dish and sprinkle with salt and pepper. When pie dish is full, cover with breadcrumbs. Put small pieces of butter on top and bake in a hot oven for ½ hour.

Maize Meal Biscuits

375 g. (12 oz.) maize meal
310 g. (10 oz.) flour
125 g. (4 oz.) butter or dripping
250 g. (8 oz.) sugar

1 egg
1 level teaspoon bicarbonate of soda
cold water

Melt butter and mix with maize meal flour, sugar and soda. Add eggs slightly beaten and enough boiling water to make a stiff dough. Roll out on a floured board, cut into shapes and cook in a slow oven.

Brown Maize Meal Bread

600 ml. (1 pint) buttermilk
½ cup maize meal
½ cup sugar
½ teaspoon bicarbonate of soda

2 cups coarse brown meal
1 cup flour
½ cup syrup or treacle

Mix all dry ingredients. Warm the syrup or treacle and add the buttermilk mixed with soda. Stir into dry ingredients. Bake in a moderate oven in a well-greased breadpan for 1½ hours.

Green Maize and Creamed Chicken

3 cups raw green maize cut from cob
1 cup minced cooked chicken
30 g. (1 oz.) ham or bacon

1 cup white sauce (see Sauces)
2 teaspoons cream
2 eggs, salt and pepper

Mince the raw grain, the chicken and ham separately and add to grain. Have a cupful of white sauce ready, to which add cream, the yolks of eggs and the well-beaten whites. Season and pour all into a well-greased pie dish and bake till firm. Serve with hot tomato sauce.

Green Maize

5 or 6 cobs
1½ cups milk
small lump of butter

1 heaped teaspoon flour
enough water to cover

Cut the grains off the cobs and put them in a pot with a little water to cover and boil about 20 minutes with the lid closely shut. Mix flour with milk, butter and seasoning; bring again to the boil and cook a further 10 minutes. Serve as entrée or vegetable.

Green Maize au Gratin

Add a little grated cheese to the above recipe. Place in a pudding dish with more grated cheese on top and small pieces of butter and bake in a moderate oven.

Green Maize à l'Oeuf

Place the above mixture in a pie dish and make a few holes in the surface. Break an egg into each hole and bake in a slow oven until eggs are set but not hard.

Boiled Green Maize Cobs

Remove husks and silk from cob and cook from 20 to 30 minutes in boiling water. Salt must not be added, as this hardens the maize. Maize cobs are best cooked directly they are picked, otherwise they lose their sweetness. Serve with melted butter and a stick at either end of the cob, to hold it by.

Green Maize Custard

1 cup cooked green maize	3 eggs
1 breakfast cup milk	a little finely chopped onion
pepper and salt to taste	

Cut grains from as many cobs as will make a cupful. Boil for 20 minutes. Take off fire to cool. Add 3 eggs slightly beaten, salt and pepper to taste, onion and 1 cup of milk. Mix well together and pour into buttered mould. Bake in a moderate oven; when set, turn out and serve with tomato sauce (*see* Sauces).

Green Maize Omelette

1½ cups cooked	butter
green maize grains	2 tablespoons milk
3 eggs	salt and pepper
1 white of egg	

Mince the grains; add eggs well beaten, also milk and seasoning. Lastly, add white of another egg well beaten to a froth. Fry in pan with butter (size of walnut), browning both sides. Fold over and serve on a hot dish.

Green Maize Soup

4 or 5 green maize cobs	1 large onion
1 turnip	2 large cups of white sauce
2 l. (1½ quarts) boiling water	(*see* Sauces)

Cut grain off cobs and pass through mincer with the onion and turnip. Collect all milky juice and put in a saucepan with boiling water and cook for 1½ hours.

Strain and add white sauce and a little cream if you have it to spare. Garnish with chopped parsley.

Maize Meal and Rice Waffles

½ cup maize meal	1 tablespoon melted butter
½ cup cold boiled rice	½ teaspoon bicarbonate of
2 eggs	soda
150 ml. (1 pint) sour milk	½ teaspoon salt

Mix dry ingredients. Add eggs well beaten and sour milk. Beat mixture well, adding soda dissolved in hot water last. Grease waffle irons well, as rice is apt to stick; heat and pour in mixture.

Maize Meal Cake

1 cup maize meal	¼ cup butter
1 cup flour	¼ cup sugar
2 teaspoons baking powder	¼ cup milk
3 eggs	pinch of salt

Mix and sift dry ingredients. Add well-beaten eggs and melted butter and just enough milk to make a good cake mixture. Bake in a buttered tin for ¾ hour.

Maize Meal Sandwich Cake

4 eggs	1 teaspoon baking powder
their weight in butter and sugar	pinch salt
	milk if needed
½ their weight in flour	any flavouring desired
½ their weight in maize meal	

Beat eggs, yolks and whites separately. Beat butter and sugar to a cream. Add beaten eggs, the yolks and whites separately. Add baking powder to flour and maize meal. Stir in gradually, with pinch of salt and flavouring. If too stiff a mixture, add a little milk. Put into 2 greased sandwich tins and bake in a hot oven (about 20 minutes). When cold spread jam or icing between.

Maize Meal Doughnuts

2 cups flour	2 teaspoons cream of tartar
1 cup maize meal	1 teaspoon soda bicarbonate
1 cup sugar	milk, pinch salt
2 eggs	1 or 2 teaspoons mixed spice

Mix ingredients well together, using only enough milk to make a stiff batter. Fry in deep smoking fat, a spoonful at a time. Should sour milk be used omit cream of tartar. When cooked, roll in fine sifted sugar.

Maize Meal Drop Scones

125 g. (4 oz.) flour	2 tablespoons sugar
60 g. (2 oz.) maize meal	1 egg
1 teaspoon baking powder	milk if needed

Mix the maize meal with the flour. Add sugar, baking powder and butter, lastly egg, well beaten, and if necessary milk. Mix well and drop in dessertspoonfuls on to a hot greased girdle or electric hotplate on top of the stove. When brown, turn and brown other side. Pile on a clean cloth and keep covered till cool.

Maize Meal Fritters

3 cups milk	4 eggs
2 cups maize meal	½ teaspoon soda bicarbonate
1 cup flour	1 teaspoon cream of tartar
pinch of salt	1 tablespoon sugar
1 tablespoon melted butter	

Mix dry ingredients, omitting soda. Stir in well-beaten yolks of eggs, melted butter, soda dissolved in hot water, milk and lastly well-beaten whites of eggs. Mix all thoroughly. Drop into boiling fat in spoonfuls and place when cooked on several layers of soft paper to absorb fat.

Serve with a sauce made as follows:—

1 large tablespoon butter	1½ cups brown sugar
2 large tablespoons flour	1 teaspoon ground cinnamon
1½ cups boiling water	(or ½ grated nutmeg)
lemon juice	

Rub flour and butter together. Add slowly the water, put in a pan, bring to boil and cook for 5 minutes. Add the sugar and spices and lemon juice. Stir till the sugar is thoroughly melted and serve very hot.

Maize Meal Rock Cakes

90 g. (3 oz.) flour	90 g. (3 oz.) sugar
90 g. (3 oz.) maize meal	30 g. (1 oz.) currants
60 g. (2 oz.) butter	nutmeg and spices
a teaspoon baking powder	1 egg, and milk if needed

Mix maize meal and flour and rub in butter; add sugar, baking powder, spices and currants. Mix well, add egg and perhaps a very little milk, but mixture must not be soft. Have ready a greased, hot, oven shelf and put on in rough lumps. Bake in a hot oven for 15 minutes.

Maize Meal Rolls

375 g. (¾ lb.) maize meal	4 teaspoons baking powder
2 tablespoons sugar	½ teaspoon salt
1¼ large cups flour	2 tablespoons butter
1 teacup milk	1 egg

Sieve maize meal, flour, baking powder, salt and sugar. Add milk, melted butter, and egg, well beaten. Mix all well together. Bake in small greased tins (putting a tablespoonful of batter in each tin) for 35 minutes. Split and butter. Must be eaten while hot.

Maize Pancakes

2 cups green maize grains	½ cup cream or
2 tablespoons flour	1 tablespoon melted butter and
4 eggs	milk
1 pinch of salt	2 tablespoons sugar

Mince the raw grains. Add beaten yolks of eggs, then flour and cream and lastly beaten whites of eggs. Drop from spoon on to a hot frying pan; turn; serve with sugar mixed with cinnamon or golden syrup. If desired to serve with meat omit the sugar.

Maize Pie

5 or 6 maize cobs	2 eggs
1 tablespoon butter	500 ml. (1 pint) milk
1 heaped tablespoon flour	salt to taste

Cut grains off cobs (about 2 teacups) and pass through a mincer. Heat butter and flour in saucepan until smooth. Very gradually add the milk and bring to boil. Cool and add eggs well beaten and a pinch of salt. Add the minced grains, pour all into a greased pie dish and bake for about ½ hour in a moderately hot oven or until golden-brown.

Maize and Tomato Salad

As many tomatoes as people to be served
mayonnaise dressing

1 cup cooked maize grains
butter
seasoning

Pour boiling water over some large, firm, tomatoes. Scoop out the centre of each tomato and remove the skin. Leave in a cool place to firm, then fill cavities with the cooked grains to which have been added seasoning, butter and mayonnaise dressing. Serve on a bed of cut lettuce and sprinkle with hard-boiled egg. The tomatoes when filled may be coated with aspic jelly.

Should tomatoes not be procurable, firm baked potatoes may be substituted.

Ugali

1.25 l. (2½ pints) water
375 g. (12 oz.) maize meal
125 g. (4 oz.) butter
chopped parsley

Boil the water, add the maize meal, stirring well. When the mixture forms a dough add in the butter. Stir well and then cover for 5–8 minutes, stir again and cover again. Cook in this way for 30–45 minutes. Put the dough on a clean board, roll it out 2 cm. (¾ in.) thick and cut into shapes with biscuit cutters. Serve on a plate with parsley and tomatoes.

Ugali biscuits may be served sandwiched together with mashed sweet potatoes or arrowroot.

Ugali Balls

Ugali can be rolled into small balls and deep fried in salad oil.

Irio

4 green maize cobs
½ kg. (1 lb.) peas or beans
salt

1 kg. (2 lb.) potatoes
1 or 2 bunches green pumpkin leaves

Take the maize grains off the cobs and boil with peas until soft. Add the potatoes and green leaves and boil until the potatoes are cooked, about 20 minutes. Drain, add salt and mash. Sufficient for 4 people.

Curried Irio

Irio as above
½ kg. (1 lb.) onions

60 g. (2 oz.) fat
1 tablespoon curry powder

Fry onions until brown, then add curry powder and stir in well. If the irio has become hard add a little water and allow it to boil. Add irio to the curry and onions and mix well together. Serve with a ripe tomato.

PUDDINGS

Hints for Puddings and Pies

Prepare the oven or saucepan. With the exception of puddings which have to stand before they are cooked, the method of cooking should always be considered before a pudding is mixed, as some puddings would spoil if not cooked immediately. Therefore, in the case of a boiled or steamed pudding, the first thing to do, always, is to put a saucepan of water on to boil.

If you are going to make a baked pudding, ensure that the oven is sufficiently hot.

Boiled and steamed puddings must always be covered with greased paper or a pudding cloth, in order to keep out the water which collects on the inside of the saucepan lid.

Puddings can be steamed over boiling water or in a saucepan of boiling water, the latter not coming more than half-way up the outside of the basin.

For both steamed and boiled puddings the water must boil before the pudding is put in; should it boil away, only boiling water must be added or the pudding will be heavy.

A baked custard should always be cooked very slowly in a moderate oven. A hot oven will cause milk to boil and evaporate. Water in custard may be caused by using boiled milk but is more likely caused by custard being cooked too quickly.

As a general rule, dry ingredients are all mixed together, then wet ingredients added, but there are exceptions. Puddings containing much fruit must not be made too wet or the fruit will sink to the bottom.

Egg Whites. White of egg is a marvellous medium for giving dishes a lightness that converts a very ordinary sweet into one of the party persuasion. For example, when making a jelly, try adding the white of an egg well beaten and mix well with a fork. When cold, the mixture will be the lightest of jelly sponges and the aeration brought about by the whipped egg will increase the quantity. In the same way it is economical to add a whipped egg white to cream before serving it with a sweet. One egg will be sufficient for about 500 ml. (one pint) of cream.

Amateur efforts to make a frothy meringue top to a pudding are often disappointing because a pinch of cream of tartar has been omitted. The tartar helps to make the meringue stiff and to keep it from "flopping" in the oven.

Use of Baking Powder

The action of baking powder takes place directly it is moistened; therefore a pudding containing this must be cooked directly it is mixed. Bicarbonate of soda requires warmth before it acts, so that a pudding containing soda need not be cooked immediately after mixing unless a warm ingredient has been added.

General Proportions for Milk Puddings
60 g. (2 oz.) grain   60 g. (2 oz.) sugar to
                                   600 ml. (1 pint) milk

Angel's Food
grated coconut   sliced oranges
whipped cream   guava jelly
sugar (if desired)

Place grated coconut and sliced oranges in alternate layers, sprinkling sugar on the oranges if desired and finishing with a layer of the coconut. Decorate with alternate lumps of whipped cream and guava jelly.

Angel Frappé
$\frac{3}{4}$ cup chopped fruit $\frac{1}{2}$ cup cold water
$\frac{1}{2}$ cup sugar   3 tablespoons fruit syrup
1 teaspoon powdered gelatine   3 tablespoons cold water
1$\frac{1}{2}$ cups whipped cream   3 egg whites

Dissolve gelatine in a little cold water. Boil sugar in $\frac{1}{2}$ cup water until it threads; pour slowly on beaten egg whites; beat constantly. Add gelatine and fruit syrup and cool. Fold in cream and chopped fruit. Chill in freezer.

Apple Cake Pudding

Pastry	Filling	Mixture
250 g. (8 oz.) butter	1 kg. (2 lb.) sour	3 eggs
125 g. (4 oz.) sugar	apples	60 g. (2 oz.) sugar
1 egg	2 tablespoons of	125 g. (4 oz.) flour
500 g. (16 oz.) flour	sugar	1 teacup milk
	60 g. (2 oz.) currants	
	a good pinch of	
	ground cinnamon	

Make a short paste of the above and line a cake tin, prick bottom gently then cover with sour apples, peeled and cored, and cut into thin slices. Sprinkle with currants, previously cleaned and stalked, sugar and spice. Put into a hot oven to bake. Make the mixture by beating 3 egg yolks with the sugar, add the sieved flour and milk. Beat whites to a stiff froth and fold in. When the pastry is partly baked, pour mixture on top of apples and cook in hot oven for about 30 minutes.

Apple or Cape Gooseberry Pie
1 cup flour   1 teaspoon ginger
$\frac{1}{2}$ cup butter   1 teaspoon baking powder
1 cup sugar   fruit

Rub butter amongst flour and baking powder until like bread-crumbs. Add ginger and sugar. Put fruit in a pie dish, cover with the above mixture and bake in a medium oven.

Apples (Ginger)

1 kg. (2 lb.) cooking apples   80 g. (2½ oz.) root ginger
300 ml. (½ pint) water to each
   500 g. (1 pound) of sugar

Peel and core apples and place them in cold water. Take the weight of the apples in their weight of sugar and allow 300 ml. (½ pint) of water to each 500 g. (1 pound) of sugar. Put the sugar and water into a stewpan and when boiling put in apples and root ginger. Let them simmer until transparent. (The apples should be whole.) Serve cold with custard.

Apples in Rice

4 apples   500 g. (½ lb.) rice
4 cloves   ¼ cup water
4 teaspoons castor sugar   2 tablespoons jam

Wash the rice well, place in a saucepan of boiling salted water and boil 10 minutes. Strain and wash with cold water. Grease 4 teacups. Put rice about half-way up each cup, pressing sides and bottom. Peel and core the apples and put one in each cup, with 1 teaspoonful sugar and a clove. Cover with remainder of rice and press well down. Place greased paper on the top of each cup and steam an hour. Turn carefully on to a hot dish and serve with apricot or other jam, dissolved in water.

Apple Snowballs

4 apples   whites of 3 eggs
2 tablespoons sugar   1½ dessertspoons castor sugar
4 cloves

Peel apples, core and place on a sheet of greased paper. Put ½ teaspoon sugar and 1 clove in centre of each; bake till soft but not broken. Whisk the whites of eggs and castor sugar till stiff. Put apples on fireproof dish. Surround and cover with white of egg and return to oven for 15 minutes to set the meringue. Serve with cream.

Apple Trifle

500 g. (1 lb.) cooking apples   whites of 2 eggs
sugar to taste   sponge fingers
whipped cream   a little lemon juice

Stew apples till tender, with sugar to taste and a little lemon juice. Beat stiffly the whites of eggs. Mix lightly into the apples and put in a glass dish lined with sponge fingers. Have ready some custard and pour it round the fruit. Cover with whipped cream and set aside till cold.

Apricot Bavarian

1 cup cooked apricots (dried)   ½ cup cold water
½ cup sugar   1 cup cream (whipped)
2 tablespoons gelatine

Soak gelatine in cold water, heat apricot pulp, add sugar, then gelatine, and stir until dissolved. Keep stirring until mixture begins to thicken; add to whipped cream; pour into wet mould. Serve with sweetened flavoured whipped cream.

Apricot Cream

300 ml. (½ pint) apricot purée   45 g. (1½ oz.) castor sugar
300 ml. (½ pint) cream   25 g. (¾ oz) gelatine
1 teaspoon lemon juice   150 ml. (¼ pint) apricot syrup
few drops cochineal

Tinned or bottled apricots may be used and the purée is made by passing them through a fine sieve.

Whip the cream stiffly and stir it lightly into the purée. Dissolve the gelatine in a little water and put with the syrup. Add the sugar and lemon juice and let it cool, then strain into the cream, etc., and add cochineal drop by drop until the desired colour is obtained. Pour the mixture into a prepared mould and chill.

Apricot Delight

1 tin of apricots   185 g. (6 oz.) sugar
3 eggs   300 ml. (½ pint) milk

Rub sufficient apricots through a sieve to make 300 ml. (½ pint) of pulp. Add 125 g. (4 oz.) of sugar and heat in a saucepan. Whip the whites of the eggs stiffly and fold into the warm purée. Grease small soufflé moulds and dredge with sugar; three parts fill with purée, stand in a baking tin containing a little water and cook in a quick oven for about 30 minutes. Serve with custard made from the yolks of the eggs, 300 ml. (½ pint) of milk and the remaining 60 g. (2 oz.) of sugar. Serve immediately.

Apricot Soufflé

300 ml. (½ pint) apricot purée   1 tablespoon lemon
90 g. (3 oz.) sugar   juice
4 eggs   cochineal
150 ml. (1 gill) cream   75 ml. (½ gill) water
15 g. (½ oz.) gelatine   8 pistachio nuts

Prepare the soufflé cases. Separate the whites and yolks of eggs. Put the yolks into a bowl with the sugar and cream them together with a wooden spoon for a few minutes. Add the purée and stir over hot water until thick and hot. Leave until quite cold. Dissolve the gelatine in the water. Whip the cream, also egg whites, very stiffly, add the lemon juice and the dissolved gelatine to the purée, then mix lightly the cream and whites of eggs. Pour into soufflé cases or a large soufflé dish and leave until set. Decorate with chopped pistachio nuts.

Apricot Snow

1 tin apricots   1 teacup cold water
a little sugar   3 eggs
1 tablespoon strained   15 g. (½ oz.) gelatine
    lemon juice

Put apricots into a saucepan. Add a little sugar, boil up, strain off the juice but do not break the fruit. Spread the latter out on a dish. Return the juice to the saucepan with more sugar, lemon juice, and gelatine which has been soaked in the cold water. Stir over the heat until the gelatine is dissolved, then pour it into a bowl. Whip the whites of eggs to a froth. As the mixture cools and thickens add the whites of eggs; then whip all until too stiff to beat any more. Pour into a mould and when firm turn out on a glass dish. Garnish with the apricots laid on to the snow. Pour round the snow a custard made with the yolks of the eggs, or some whipped cream.

Arrowroot Cream

1 tablespoon arrowroot	2 tablespoons water
1 litre (1½ pints) milk	1 dessertspoon sugar
1 bay leaf or the rind of 1 lemon, cut thin	

Mix arrowroot with water; boil milk with bay leaf or lemon rind; add sugar, pour on to arrowroot, stirring frequently until cool; then pour into a glass dish. This may be used with tarts and stewed fruits.

Arrowroot Custard

500 to 600 ml. (1 pint) milk	1 tablespoon arrowroot
2 eggs beaten	sugar
flavouring	

Mix arrowroot with a little of the milk, add eggs, sweeten and flavour to taste. Pour all into the rest of the milk while stirring it. Boil about 3 minutes.

Arrowroot Gruel

Dissolve 1 tablespoon arrowroot in a little cold water, mix well, then add boiling milk or water; keep stirring. Sweeten and flavour to taste. A little rum or other spirit may be added if desired.

Bananas

The banana is essentially the friend of the vegetarian.

Bananas Baked

(a) Cut about 6 mm. (¼ in.) from each end of the required number of bananas but do not peel. Lay them in a baking dish and bake in a hot oven for about 15 minutes. When ready, the skin should burst open like that of a baked apple. Turn over and bake for 5 minutes on the other side. Serve very hot.

(b) Remove a strip of skin from the required quantity of fruit, cutting off ends as in (a). Place in a shallow pan with the exposed side up. Mix 2 tablespoons sugar, 2 tablespoons melted butter, 2 tablespoons lemon juice and a pinch of salt. Baste the bananas with this while they are baking, for about 15 to 20 minutes or till soft. Heat the remainder of the dressing and pour over the bananas. Serve very hot.

Bananas à la Jamaica

1 cup bananas, cut fine
1 cup sugar
juice of 1 lemon
a little milk

1 cup grated breadcrumbs
1 cup suet, free from skin
a pinch of soda bicarbonate

Mix bananas, breadcrumbs, sugar and suet. Stir in juice of lemon and bicarbonate, dissolved in a little milk. Grease pudding bowl. Pour in mixture, cover with greased paper and steam 4 hours.

Bananas à la Trinidad

bananas
castor sugar
60 g. (2 oz.) sugar
thin rind of a lemon

flour (sifted)
3 glasses sherry
½ nutmeg (grated)
1 teaspoon cloves (pounded)

Skin bananas. Place them in a pie dish and soak in a sauce made from the sherry, sugar, nutmeg, lemon rind and cloves. Roll each banana in sifted flour and fry in boiling lard; drain and serve in castor sugar.

Banana Cream

½ teacup tapioca
sugar
sliced bananas

1 breakfast cup water
some strawberry jam
whipped cream

Boil tapioca in water until clear; sweeten to taste. Put a layer of this into a glass dish; over it put a thick layer of sliced bananas, then some strawberry jam, then more tapioca and bananas. Cover all with whipped cream.

Bananas (Fried)

Steam the bananas, then fry lightly in boiling lard; take out carefully so that no grease remains. Serve hot with castor sugar.

Banana Fritters

1 egg
4 teaspoons milk

2 bananas
1 teaspoon flour

Soak bananas in warm water till soft. Lift out, drain and mash. Add other ingredients; mix well and fry.

Banana and Lemon Pudding

1 cup flour
1 tablespoon lemon juice
½ cup cornflour
2 eggs
grated rind of lemon

½ cup sugar
4 tablespoons butter
¾ cup milk
4 bananas
1 teaspoon baking powder

Separate yolks from whites of eggs. Mix flour, cornflour and baking powder together; add grated rind of lemon. Beat sugar and butter to a cream; add yolks of eggs well beaten. Mash bananas;

add to butter and sugar mixture; add milk and stir in slowly the flour mixture. Lastly fold in the whites of eggs well beaten. Put all into a greased pudding dish and bake in a moderate oven $1\frac{1}{2}$ hours or steam at least 2 hours.

Banana Pancakes

bananas   sugar to taste
grated lemon peel

Stew bananas with other ingredients; mash and spread the mixture over pancakes. Roll up: serve with sifted sugar.

Banana Pudding

(*a*)

6 large bananas   1 dessertspoon sugar
3 eggs   500 to 600 ml. (1 pint) milk
apricot jam   thin slices bread and butter

Butter a pie dish and cover the bottom with thin slices of banana. Place over them some thin slices of bread and butter spread with apricot jam (buttered side downwards). Repeat these layers until the dish is three-quarters full. Make a boiled custard and pour over slowly, so that the custard may be absorbed by the bread. Soak for $\frac{1}{2}$ hour. Bake very slowly in a moderate oven until lightly browned. Place dish in a deep tin of water while cooking, the water coming half-way up the outside of the dish, so that the pudding will not burn or dry up.

(*b*)

some bananas   whipped cream

Peel the bananas and beat the fruit until snow-white. Put into small glass dishes and pile with whipped cream before serving.

Banana Pudding Boiled

60 g. (2 oz.) bananas, cut small   185 g. (6 oz.) breadcrumbs
250 g. (8 oz.) castor sugar   125 g. (4 oz.) chopped suet
4 eggs   300 ml. ($\frac{1}{2}$ pint) milk

Mix all ingredients and beat with a wooden spoon for 10 minutes. Boil in a mould for 4 hours, serve plain or with sweet sauce.

Banana Sponge

4 or 5 bananas   150 ml. (1 gill) cream (sweetened)
300 ml. ($\frac{1}{2}$ pint) lemon jelly   apricot colouring, if desired
   previously prepared

Mash bananas with a fork, mix jelly and then add to the pulp. Whisk until white and frothy. Mix in the whipped cream, which has been sweetened, and pile up on a glass dish.

Bananas (stewed)

Take 2 bananas for each person, their weight in sugar, and steam until they swell and become soft. Fry lightly in butter. When brown add the sugar and by degrees warm water to make a syrup. Keep them simmering in the thickening syrup until cooked.

Banana Trifle

sponge cake	castor sugar
bananas	ground almonds
milk	2 egg yolks
a little sherry	300 ml. ($\frac{1}{2}$ pint) milk
a few drops lemon juice	1 tablespoon sugar

Line a glass dish with slices of sponge cake dipped in milk and sprinkled with a little sherry. Now put in a layer of sliced bananas; sprinkle them with castor sugar, a few drops lemon juice and some ground almonds. Put in another layer of sponge cake slices treated as the first and pour over them a custard made of the egg yolks, the milk and the tablespoon of sugar. Decorate with the whites of the eggs stiffly beaten.

Black Cap Pudding

60 g. (2 oz.) currants	1 teaspoon baking powder
185 g. (6 oz.) flour	90 g. (3 oz.) sugar
300 ml. ($\frac{1}{2}$ pint) milk (cold)	2 eggs
$\frac{1}{2}$ teaspoon nutmeg	$\frac{1}{2}$ teaspoon salt

Mix the dry ingredients, then drop in the eggs, not beaten. Add the milk gradually and beat well. Butter a basin, sprinkle the currants in the bottom and pour in the batter. Steam 2 hours and serve with sweet sauce.

Bread and Butter Pudding

2 or 3 slices bread and butter (not very thick)	300 ml. ($\frac{1}{2}$ pint) milk
	1 egg
30 g. (1 oz.) currants	30 g. (1 oz.) raisins
lemon or vanilla essence	1$\frac{1}{2}$ tablespoonfuls sugar

Butter a pie dish, put in slices of bread and butter with currants and raisins sprinkled in between. Beat egg, mix with the milk, essence and sugar, pour over the bread and bake in a moderate oven for about an hour.

Brown Betty

3 cups tart apples, chopped	$\frac{1}{4}$ teaspoon ground cinnamon
2 cups fine fresh breadcrumbs	$\frac{1}{4}$ teaspoon grated nutmeg
$\frac{1}{2}$ cup sugar	1 lemon
2 tablespoons butter	$\frac{1}{2}$ orange
$\frac{1}{4}$ cup water	

Melt the butter in a double boiler over hot water; add the crumbs. Mix castor sugar, grated rind of lemon, cinnamon and nutmeg together. Put half of the buttered crumbs in the bottom of a buttered pie dish, spread lightly with half the apples and sprinkle with half of the sugar and spices. Add another quarter of the crumbs, lay in remainder of the apples and sprinkle with remainder of sugar and spices. Strain the juice of the lemon and half orange over, sprinkle with the water and lay remainder of crumbs on top. Cover closely. Cook ¾ hour in oven; uncover and brown quickly on top. Serve with milk or cream.

Butterscotch Rice Pudding

1.25 l. (1 quart) milk	1 tablespoon butter
2 tablespoons brown sugar	2 tablespoons crushed
¼ teaspoon salt	butterscotch
2 heaped tablespoons rice	1 teaspoon vanilla essence

Place rice in a large, buttered baking-dish with sugar, milk, butter and salt. Put dish in a very slow oven and as soon as a skin appears stir in a little milk to break it. Keep stirring like this occasionally till the rice is nearly cooked and the milk creamy. Then stir in one teaspoon vanilla essence. Dust pudding lightly with grated nutmeg and cover gently with 2 tablespoons of crushed butterscotch. Put back in oven till butterscotch is melted; then serve with milk or cream.

California Lemon Pudding

4 eggs	2 tablespoons boiling water
4 tablespoons sugar	juice and grated rind of a lemon

Beat yolks of eggs lightly, then beat with two tablespoons of the sugar. Add the juice and rind of 1 lemon and the boiling water. Cook all in a double boiler, stirring occasionally, until like thick cream. Beat the egg whites stiffly with the other 2 tablespoons of sugar. When this looks like a meringue, fold it into the hot mixture which cooks it sufficiently to prevent it falling. Pour into a dish and brown in the oven. Serve cold with sponge cake.

Cape Gooseberry Cream

Cook the gooseberries till they are tender with 125 g. sugar for each 600 ml. (¼ lb. sugar for each pint) and just a little water to prevent them catching. Pass them through a sieve and mix the pulp with 15 g. (½ oz.) leaf gelatine dissolved in very little hot water, 300 ml. (½ pint) of cream whipped stiffly with sugar to sweeten and a wineglassful of brandy or curacao, though this can be omitted if preferred.

Pour into a mould and keep in a cool place or on ice until set. Turn into a glass dish and serve with cream.

Caramel Custard

300 ml. (½ pint) milk	a few drops vanilla essence
2 eggs	60 g. (2 oz.) loaf sugar
1 tablespoon castor sugar	2 tablespoons cold water

Boil the loaf sugar and the cold water together till the liquid acquires a light-brown colour. Then pour it into a mould and turn the mould slowly round and round until every part is coated with caramel. Beat the eggs, add the sugar, flavouring and milk. Stir till the sugar is dissolved. Strain this into the mould. Cover with buttered paper and steam very slowly for 40 minutes. Cool and turn out.

Castle Puddings

1 egg
its weight in butter,
   flour and castor sugar

a little grated lemon rind
150 ml. (1 gill) jam sauce (*see* Sauces)
¼ teaspoon baking powder

Butter five dariole moulds or greased teacups. Cream butter and sugar and beat in egg; sieve flour and add lightly to the other ingredients. Add baking powder with the last teaspoon of flour. Half fill the cups with the mixture. Bake in a moderate oven for 20 minutes. Turn out and pour jam sauce round. These puddings may also be steamed.

Charlotte Russe

300 ml. (½ pint) cream
150 ml. (¼ pint) milk
1 dessertspoon castor sugar
Savoy or finger biscuits
jelly

cherries and angelica
10 g. (¼ oz.) gelatine
1 tablespoon brandy or sherry

Cover the bottom of a charlotte-mould thinly with jelly and when set garnish with cherries and angelica. Cover with jelly for 1/1.5 cm. (½ in.) and allow to set. Line the sides of the mould with biscuits. Dissolve the gelatine and sugar in the milk, then strain it and add the brandy and vanilla to taste. When cool stir into stiffly whipped cream. Pour into the prepared mould and set on ice.

Chocolate Bread Pudding

¾ cup stale breadcrumbs
2 cups hot milk
½ teaspoon vanilla essence
½ cup castor sugar

1 egg
1 oz. unsweetened chocolate
1 saltspoon salt

Put the breadcrumbs in a basin, heat 1¾ cups milk and pour over. Cover basin and stand for ½ hour, then melt chocolate over hot water, add sugar and stir in ¼ cup milk gradually, when you should get a smooth paste. Add chocolate sauce to bread. Stir in salt, vanilla and slightly beaten egg. Turn into a buttered pie dish. Bake 30 minutes till set. Serve with milk or cream or Velour sauce (*see* page 67).

Chocolate Pudding

125 g. (¼ lb.) chocolate
90 g. (3 oz.) butter
220 g. (7 oz.) breadcrumbs
vanilla essence

150 ml. (¼ pint) milk
90 g. (3 oz.) sugar
3 eggs

Grate chocolate and dissolve it in the milk. Cream the butter and sugar and add yolks of eggs one by one; add the chocolate, vanilla and the breadcrumbs. Whip whites of the eggs stiffly; stir them in also. Turn into a well-greased fancy mould and steam 1½ hours. Serve with custard sauce.

Chocolate Soufflé (Hot)

150 ml. (1 gill) milk
60 g. (2 oz.) sugar
30 g. (1 oz.) butter

2 heaped tablespoons flour
60 g. (2 oz.) grated chocolate
3 eggs

Melt the butter, mix in dry flour till smooth, then add sugar, chocolate and boiling milk. Let the mixture cool, then add the beaten yolks of eggs and lastly the stiffly beaten whites. Pour into buttered dish and bake in a hot oven for 25 minutes. Serve at once with whipped cream.

Chocolate Soufflé (Cold)

(a)

2 eggs	45 g. (1½ oz.) castor sugar
10 g. (¼ oz.) gelatine	2 dessertspoons cocoa
125 g. (4 oz.) whipped cream	(or chocolate)

Beat yolks and sugar till creamy, mix cocoa and gelatine in a cup, add 80 ml. (½ gill) of boiling water and blend thoroughly. Add sugar and egg mixture and set aside until it is beginning to set. Beat up egg whites till stiff and fold into mixture. Then add cream. Pour into glass dish to set and grate slab chocolate on top.

(b)

1½ tablespoons cornflour	45 g. (1½ oz.) chocolate or cocoa
½ cup sugar	2 whites of eggs
⅓ cup cold milk	vanilla essence
3 tablespoons hot water	pinch of salt
2 cups boiling milk	

Mix cornflour, sugar and salt with the cold milk. Add this mixture to the boiling milk and cook till thick, stirring constantly. Melt the chocolate or cocoa with hot water. Stir till smooth, then add to cornflour mixture. Fold in the stiffly beaten whites of the eggs and a teaspoon of vanilla. Pour into a mould and set aside to cool. Serve with cream or custard made with yolks of eggs.

Chocolate Trifle

125 g. (¼ lb.) chocolate sponge roll	3 dessertspoons sugar
1 l. (1¾ pints) milk	30 g. (1 oz.) almonds
2 eggs (or 3 small eggs)	vanilla flavouring
2 dessertspoons cocoa	cream and a few glacé cherries

Boil the milk. Put the roll into an oval dish and soak it with 300 ml. (½ pint) of the milk, pricking it with a fork so as to get it well soaked. Mix the cocoa with a little cold milk and stir the rest of the boiling milk into it. Return to the pan and boil up for a minute, then cool slightly. Beat up the eggs, pour the hot milk and cocoa on to them. Add the sugar and pour all into a jug. Stand it in a saucepan of hot water and cook until the custard thickens, being careful not to curdle it. When cooked, remove from the heat add the vanilla and leave to cool. Blanch, skin and split the almonds and stick into the roll. Pour the custard over and leave until thoroughly cold. Decorate the top with whipped cream and a few glacé cherries.

Cocoa Rice Pudding

1½ cups boiled rice	¼ teaspoon cinnamon
5 tablespoons sugar	1 square chocolate
2 eggs	2 cups boiling milk

Beat slightly the eggs, sugar and cinnamon. Then slowly pour on them the boiling milk. Add the melted chocolate and the rice. Bake in a dish with hot water till set. Serve with cream.

Coffee Cream

1 cup thick custard	3 tablespoons sugar
15 g. (½ oz.) gelatine	1 cup cream
½ cup very strong coffee	

Soak the gelatine in the cold coffee for an hour, then heat till dissolved. Remove from heat, add the sugar, then the custard, and when beginning to set, whip the cream stiffly and fold in. Pour into a wet mould and leave to set.

Coffee Caramel Fluff

1 large tablespoon gelatine	½ cup cold water
½ cup sugar	½ cup cream
¼ cup very strong coffee	3 eggs

Soften the gelatine in the cold water. Cook the sugar until brown and thick in the coffee. Add the gelatine; when it is dissolved, remove from the heat and beat until cool. Now add the cream, previously whipped stiffly, and the stiffly beaten whites of the eggs. Put aside but before it sets completely, pour into a mould. Serve with a custard made with the egg yolks.

Coronation Pudding

1 tin pears or peaches	2 teaspoons cornflour
15 g. (½ oz.) gelatine	rum to taste
1 tablespoon sugar	white of 2 eggs
300 ml. (½ pint) cream	

Press fruit through a sieve with juice. Add sugar, gelatine and rum. Heat on stove and stir in cornflour mixed with a little cold water and boil till it thickens. Allow to cool and when nearly set stir in the cream, whipped, and the white of eggs, beaten. Put in moulds to set and serve with boiled custard.

Custard Baked

300 ml. (½ pint) milk	vanilla essence and nutmeg
2 eggs	1 tablespoon sugar

Heat the milk. Beat the eggs and add the milk to them little by little till all is well mixed. Add the sugar. Strain into a small buttered pie dish, add a little vanilla essence and grate the nutmeg on the top. Place the pie dish in a roasting pan with a little cold water. Bake in a slow oven for ½ hour.

Custard Boiled
(a)

1 breakfast cup milk	sugar to taste
1 large or 2 small eggs	a little nutmeg

Boil milk with sugar. Let it cool a little. Beat up the egg and add the milk to it, stirring well. Place in a jug in a saucepan of boiling water and stir till it thickens, then remove from the fire. Serve with a little nutmeg (grated) on top.

(b)

2½ cups milk	1½ tablespoons sugar
2 eggs	1 tablespoon cornflour
almond essence	

Boil milk and add sugar. Mix cornflour with a little cold milk and stir into the boiling milk. Beat eggs and pour the mixture on to them. Return to saucepan. Stir and just bring to boil. Cool and add essence.

(c)

raw yolks of 2 eggs	2 tablespoons sugar
4 tablespoons sherry	

Beat yolks, add sugar and sherry. Whisk over heat until mixture is nothing but froth. Must not be allowed to boil or custard will curdle.

Dandy Pudding

300 ml. (1 pint) milk	60 g. (2 oz.) butter
2 eggs	60 g. (2 oz.) sugar
90 g. (3 oz.) flour	1 teaspoon vanilla essence

Boil milk. Put flour in a basin and pour on boiling milk (the flour will naturally go lumpy). Add butter and sugar. When fairly cold, stir in eggs beaten. Put in a greased pie dish and cook in a moderate oven ½ to ¼ hour.

Eve's Pudding

375 g. (¾ lb.) apples	2 eggs, their weight in flour,
2 tablespoons sugar	butter and sugar
2 cloves	¼ teaspoon baking powder

Peel and cut up apples in small thick pieces and cook till tender. Put in a pie dish with sugar and cloves and make flat. Put butter and sugar in a basin and beat with a spoon till quite light and white. Add the eggs, which should be beaten well, and mix thoroughly. Stir in flour and baking powder and beat up well. Pour the mixture smoothly over apples, covering all. Bake to a pale brown in a moderate oven.

Floating Island

1.25 ml. (1 quart) milk	4 tablespoons sugar
¼ teaspoon salt	2 teaspoons vanilla or almond
½ cup currant jelly	essence
4 eggs	

Scald milk. Beat egg yolks and stir in sugar and salt. Add hot milk gradually, mixing well. Cook slowly in saucepan until mixture begins to thicken, stirring continually. Cool, flavour and put into dish. Make a meringue of whites whipped until dry and into which jelly has been beaten, a teaspoon at a time, and heap on top; or drop meringue by spoonfuls on top of custard and put small pieces of jelly in centre of each. Chill and serve.

Fresh Fruit Pudding

slices of bread and butter   fresh fruit
2 or 3 eggs   1 tablespoon sifted sugar for
cream   each white of egg

Butter a deep pie dish, line it with slices of bread and butter and fill it with alternate layers of strawberries (wineberries or any other small fresh fruit), sugar and butter sprinkled with lemon juice. The top layer must be of bread buttered on both sides. Cover with buttered paper or plate and bake for 1½ hours, setting the pie dish in a pan of hot water. When baked, cover the pudding with a meringue, made by beating the whites of the eggs to a stiff froth and lightly stirring in sifted sugar, allowing a tablespoon for each white of egg. Pile the meringue on the top and slightly brown it in the oven. Serve hot with wine sauce or a jug of good cream.

Fruit Blancmange

3 cups milk   1 teaspoon vanilla essence
2 tablespoons cornflour   2 eggs
2 tablespoons sugar   bananas, or any fruit desired

Mix the cornflour with a little milk and put the rest on to boil. Add the cornflour paste to the boiling milk and cook till it will leave the sides of the pan. Add sugar and egg yolks and at once remove from the heat. Add flavouring and stiffly beaten whites of eggs. Mix in sliced bananas or any fruit desired and pour into a wetted mould. Serve with cream or a boiled custard sauce.

Fruit Fools

Add a little cornflour to all fruits, except bananas, if too liquid. When cold, add the whites of one or two eggs stiffly beaten. Serve in individual glass dishes, with a custard or whipped cream on top. Garnish with cherries and chopped almonds.

APPLE. Peel, cut up and bake till soft with a few cloves and sugar.

BANANA. Mash, add sugar and a little lemon juice.

PINEAPPLE. Mince, catching the juice in a bowl held under the mincer. Add sugar to taste and cook till tender.

PRUNE. Stew prunes till tender. Remove skins and stones. Mash prunes, adding sugar to taste and a little of the juice in which they were boiled and a squeeze of lemon juice. Serve with cream.

CAPE GOOSEBERRY. Wash well and stew in a little water till tender. Strain and add sugar to taste. Serve with cream or custard.

GRENADILLA. Scoop out the seeds, add a very little water and sugar to taste; boil a little time, then strain.

GUAVA. Peel and cut in half, stew in a little water till tender. Put through a coarse sieve and add sugar to taste.

MANGO. Peel, cut off flesh in small pieces, steam and add sugar when nearly done. Put through a coarse sieve.

Fruit Fritters

2 tablespoons flour
1 tablespoon salad oil
   or melted butter

1 dessertspoon sugar
bananas or other fruit
whites of 2 eggs

Mix the flour with the sugar, oil and ½ teacup of warm water, making it into a smooth batter. Leave it for an hour and add the whites of the eggs beaten to a froth. Split the banana and divide each half in two or three pieces. Dip in batter and fry in hot fat. Oranges, apples or pineapples may also be cooked this way. Divide the oranges into sections and slice the apples across, about 1 cm. (⅓ inch) in thickness.

Fruit Salad

mixed fruits (fresh or tinned)
a few almonds
juice of ½ a lemon
125 g. (4 oz.) loaf sugar

1 dessertspoon maraschino
1 dessertspoon brandy or
   sherry, if liked

Take 300 ml. (½ pint) of juice from tinned fruit or 300 ml. (½ pint) of water. Boil this with the sugar for 5 minutes to form a syrup. Peel the fruit and remove seeds or stones. Cut into neat pieces and put in a basin with some chopped almonds. Pour hot syrup over fruit, add lemon juice, maraschino and brandy. When the salad is cold, serve in a glass dish and decorate the top with almonds and cherries. *See* recipe for Grenadilla Juice for Fruit Salads.

Ginger Cream

150 ml. (1 gill) custard
75 ml. (½ gill) water
30 g. (1 oz.) ginger cut in dice
30 g. (1 oz.) castor sugar
2 or 3 drops ginger essence if necessary

150 ml. (1 gill) cream
150 ml. (1 gill) ginger syrup
10 g. (¼ oz.) powdered
   gelatine

Dissolve the gelatine in the water and add the ginger syrup. Half whip the cream, add custard, sugar and diced ginger. Strain in the gelatine, add essence if necessary. Stir gently till beginning to set. Pour into mould. When set, dip in warm water. Turn out and decorate with chopped jelly.

Golden Delight

1 very thick slice of
   bread
2 tablespoons milk

60 g. (2 oz.) butter
1 tablespoon golden syrup
vanilla flavouring

Remove the crust from the bread and round the corners. Put the milk flavoured with vanilla over the bread to soak it without making it sloppy. Melt butter and golden syrup together in a frying pan. When melted, put in the bread and baste it well. Serve hot.

Grenadilla Juice for Fruit Salads

Take 6 or 8 grenadillas. Cut open and scoop out the fruit. Put this into a small saucepan with as little water as possible and the juice of a lemon. Bring to the boil slowly. Strain and return to the saucepan, with sugar to taste. Reheat to dissolve the sugar. Cool and pour over the other fruit. If preferred, the juice of an orange may be used instead of the lemon.

Grenadilla Sponge

300 ml. (½ pint) water	juice of 2 oranges
3 dessertspoons sugar	12 grenadillas
2 eggs	2 dessertspoons gelatine

Scrape out the fruit from the grenadillas and cook in the water. Press through a sieve and add the orange juice, sugar and gelatine previously soaked in a little cold water. Put all into a saucepan and heat until the gelatine is dissolved. Then beat in the egg yolks, continuing to beat until the mixture has cooled. When it begins to set, add the well-beaten whites of the eggs. Mould and set aside to set thoroughly.

Ground Rice Snow

3 level tablespoons ground rice	2 eggs
	2 tablespoons sugar
570 ml. (1 pint) boiling milk	½ tablespoon butter
flavouring	

Moisten the ground rice with a little cold milk and mix it with the boiling milk. Boil until it thickens, stirring all the while. Add sugar, stir in butter and, when cooling, flavour. Just before serving, fold in the stiffly beaten whites of the eggs. Pile in the centre of a deep glass dish and pour round a custard, made with the egg yolks and a little custard powder.

Hasty Pudding

500 g. (1 lb.) flour	1 cup sugar
4 tablespoons butter	1 teaspoon baking powder
grated rind of a lemon	300 ml. (½ pint) milk
or lemon essence	1 egg

Put flour, sugar and baking powder into a dish, grate over it some lemon rind and rub in the butter. Beat up milk and eggs and add to the mixture. Bake in a pudding dish in a quick oven for 20 minutes and when ready heap on some jam. Variety can be given to this pudding by adding to the flour ½ teacup grated coconut or 1 large tablespoon cocoa.

Honeycomb Mould

2 eggs	15 g. (½ oz.) gelatine
600 ml. (1 pint) milk	flavouring
2 tablespoons sugar	colouring if desired

Put the gelatine into the cold milk. Separate the yolks from the whites of the eggs. Beat yolks and add them to the cold milk and gelatine. Cook and let this just boil up once to make the custard curdle and so divide the pudding into jelly and custard when cold. Add sugar and flavouring. Fold in the egg whites stiffly beaten and pour into a wet mould. Turn out when set.

Italian Cream

60 g. (2 oz.) gelatine
125 g. (4 oz.) ratafias
8 eggs
grated rind of orange
180 g. (6 oz.) sugar
60 g. (2 oz.) dried cherries
250 ml. ($\frac{1}{2}$ pint) cream
1 wineglass curaçao
1 stick cinnamon
600 ml. (1 pint) boiled milk
60 g. (2 oz.) preserved ginger
60 g. (2 oz.) candied peel

Put ratafias in a pan with the egg yolks, curaçao, cinnamon, sugar and milk. Stir over the stove until it thickens, then rub through a hair sieve into a basin. Add the gelatine previously dissolved, the cream whipped and the fruit cut into small pieces. Mix all well and pour into a mould. Chill and turn out when set.

Italian Pears

1 tin pears
2 dessertspoons sugar
a little butter
2 eggs
lemon juice

Strain the juice from a tin of pears. Butter the bottom of a shallow pie dish and put in the pears, sprinkling each with lemon juice, and place a small piece of butter on top. Bake in a moderate oven until pale brown in colour. Top with a meringue made with the stiffly beaten whites of the eggs and the sugar. Serve with either cream or a boiled custard made with the yolks of eggs.

Jam Pudding Baked

500 g. (1 lb.) flour
250 g. ($\frac{1}{2}$ lb.) butter
500 g. (1 lb.) blackcurrant jam
   (or syrup)
1 cup water
large pinch salt

Put the flour and salt into a basin and rub the butter into it till it is like fine breadcrumbs; add water and mix to a dry paste. Flour a board lightly and roll the paste until it is about 6 mm. ($\frac{1}{4}$ inch) thick. Grease a pie dish, stand it on the rolled-out pastry and cut a piece large enough to line the bottom and sides of the pie dish. Line pie dish with this pastry. Put layers of jam and pastry alternately until the dish is full. Place a piece of pastry on the top and fold the top of the lining from the four sides of the pie dish to the centre. Press well together. Brush over with milk. Bake in a moderate oven from 1 to $1\frac{1}{2}$ hours.

Jelly Cream

250 ml. (½ pint) cream or custard   1 packet jelly

Make the jelly according to the instructions on the packet. Pour into a basin and allow to cool. Before it sets at all, add the cream; stir well and pour into a mould. Be careful the jelly is quite cool before adding the cream or it may curdle.

Jellied Foam

Make a jelly according to the instructions on the packet and when it begins to set add the white of an egg; beat all together until fairly stiff, then turn into a mould or arrange piled up in a glass dish. Jelly may be whipped alone but white of egg increases the quantity.

Jellied Fruits

1 packet jelly   any variety of fruit except
a little sherry if desired   raw pineapple

Make the jelly according to the instructions on the packet and add a little sherry if desired. Have ready a wet mould and pour in half the jelly. When this has set, place in the prepared fruit and carefully pour in a little more jelly. Allow this to set again and add the rest of the jelly. Unless this is done, the fruit will be at the top of the mould. Turn out and serve with whipped cream or custard.

Jellied Sponge

1 packet jelly   some sponge cake

Make the jelly according to the instructions on the packet. Fill a mould with small pieces of sponge cake, pour the jelly over them and leave to set. Turn out and serve with cream or custard.

Kabete Soufflé

4 eggs   jam
1 tablespoon of sugar   300 ml. (½ pint) milk
vanilla essence

Separate white from yolks. Beat whites to a stiff froth. Have ready fairly large saucepan half full of boiling water. When whites of eggs are beaten stiff, add sugar and a drop or two of essence. Take saucepan off stove and put white of egg mixture on top of boiling water, spreading it over evenly with a spoon. Stand aside until cold. Take the 4 yolks, 300 ml. (½ pint) milk, a little sugar, place in another saucepan and stir until it thickens, about 20 minutes, to make custard. Allow to get cold. When whites are perfectly cold, cut into sections, place in dish, pour cold custard round and decorate with spots of jam.

King Edward Pudding

2 eggs   their weight in flour
250 g. (½ lb.) jam or syrup   sugar, butter
1 flat teaspoon baking powder   vanilla essence
1 tablespoon milk

Beat the butter and sugar together until it resembles thick cream. Separate the whites from the yolks of the eggs. Whisk whites to a stiff froth. Beat the yolks and add the butter and sugar. Beat all these thoroughly for a few minutes. Add the flour, baking powder, essence and milk. Lastly, very lightly mix in the whites of the eggs. Put the mixture into a greased pie dish and bake in a moderate oven for over an hour. Turn on to a hot dish. Serve with hot jam or golden syrup. If preferred this pudding may be put into a basin and steamed.

Lemon Pudding

(a)

½ cup flour	1 cup breadcrumbs
½ cup chopped suet	1 egg
½ cup sugar	1 lemon
½ teaspoon soda	a little milk and a pinch of salt

Mix dry ingredients with the exception of the soda. Add grated rind of lemon and strained juice, well-beaten egg and milk. Lastly, add the soda dissolved in a little milk. Pour into a buttered mould and cover with buttered paper. Steam 3 hours. Serve with white sauce flavoured with lemon.

(b)

1 lemon	2 teacups water
2 eggs	1 large tablespoon
1 teacup sugar	cornflour

Grate rind of lemon into saucepan and squeeze in the lemon juice, then add water, sugar and cornflour beaten up with the yolks of eggs. Stir the mixture and boil 5 minutes. Set aside for a little to cool, then stir the whites of eggs, well beaten, into the mixture. Pour into a mould or glass dish and serve cold.

Lemon Solid

300 ml. (½ pint) milk	185 g. (6 oz.) sugar
15 g. (½ oz.) gelatine	2 lemons

Peel lemons very thinly and put the rind in a saucepan with the gelatine, sugar and half of the milk. Heat for a few minutes till dissolved, stirring all the time. Do not allow to become very hot. Strain to remove rind. Add remainder of milk and allow to cool. When nearly cold stir in the strained juice of the lemons. Put into a damp mould and allow to stand till set. Serve with sugar and cream.

Marmalade Pudding

60 g. (2 oz.) flour	1 tablespoon marmalade
60 g. (2 oz.) sugar	1 small teaspoon bicarbonate
60 g. (2 oz.) butter	of soda
2 eggs	

Cream the butter and sugar, add the yolks of eggs, then add the flour with the soda and lastly the marmalade. Mix these well together, then whip the whites of eggs to a stiff froth and add to the mixture, stirring all well together. Pour into a buttered mould and steam for 1 hour. Serve with sweet sauce.

Marmalade Bread Pudding

Take as many thin slices of bread as required. Spread thinly each slice with marmalade.

Arrange in a pie dish. Beat 2 eggs and 500 ml. (1 pint) of milk together, pour half over pie dish and stand for ½ hour. Gently pour over remaining eggs and milk and bake slowly. Serve hot or cold.

Meringues

2 large or 3 small eggs
150 ml. (1 gill) cream
½ teaspoon cream of tartar

125 g. (4 oz.) castor sugar
pistachio nuts
vanilla essence

Cover a board or tin with paper. Put whites of eggs into a cold china basin; add a pinch of salt and whisk till eggs are stiff. Add 1 teaspoon sugar and whisk for 2 or 3 minutes. Add rest of sugar and stir very lightly. Put mixture in forcing bag, fitted with a screw or meringue pipe, and force on to prepared board in small pyramids. Bake in a cool oven for ½ hour or until set.

Mocha Cream

1 cup strong coffee
¾ cup sugar
1 cup whipped cream

1 tablespoon gelatine
¼ cup cold water
vanilla essence

Soak the gelatine in the cold water. Mix it into the hot coffee and add the sugar. When it begins to set, stir in the essence and add to the whipped cream. Fold it well in. Mould and turn out when set.

Mosaic Cream

220 ml. (1½ gills) milk (hot)
30 g. (1 oz.) gelatine
coffee essence
2 eggs

a little sugar
flavouring
cochineal

Dissolve the gelatine in the milk, add sugar and flavouring. Divide into 3 parts and colour with cochineal, coffee essence and 2 egg yolks respectively. Put these mixtures into 3 soup plates and when cold cut into rounds and line a mould with them. Fill the centre with the following cream:

15 g. (½ oz.) gelatine
150 ml. (¼ pint) milk (hot)
2 tablespoons sherry

a little lemon juice and vanilla
1 tablespoon castor sugar
250 g. (½ pint) cream

Melt the gelatine in the hot milk. Whip the cream, add the flavourings and mix with the gelatine. Put into the centre of the decorated mould and, when set, turn out carefully.

Moulded Cream

30 g. (1 oz.) gelatine
1 cup boiling milk
4 tablespoons apricot or
strawberry jam

500 ml. (1 pint) cream
2 tablespoons sugar
2 tablespoons brandy

Soak the gelatine in cold water. Add the boiling milk and stir till dissolved. When nearly cold, add the jam, the sugar and the cream, stirring until smooth. If liked, brandy can be added. Pour into a mould and turn out when firm.

Neapolitan Blancmange

30 g. (1 oz.) gelatine	10 drops almond essence
4 cups milk	60 g. (2 oz.) chocolate or
150 g. (5 oz.) sugar	1 dessertspoon cocoa
1 tablespoon brandy	1 egg yolk
cochineal	

Soak the gelatine in a little milk for 1 hour. Boil the rest of the milk and stir in the sugar and soaked gelatine. Add the almond essence. Divide into 4 equal portions and pour into soup plates. To one, add the brandy; to the second, the beaten egg yolk; to the third, the dissolved chocolate or cocoa; and to the fourth enough cochineal to make it rose-pink. Now wet a mould and pour in the white jelly; as soon as it will bear it, gently pour on the pink, then the yellow and lastly the brown. Turn out carefully next day and serve with cream or custard.

Nougat Pudding

1 lemon jelly	6 ratafias
10 marshmallows	150 ml. (1 gill) cream
30 g. (1 oz.) almonds	juice of ½ lemon
15 g. (½ oz.) pistachio nuts	16 glacé cherries

Make jelly according to the instructions on the packet. Cut up cherries, ratafias, marshmallows and pistachios. When the jelly is almost cold whisk until it is stiff and frothy. Stir in the other ingredients adding the whipped cream, sugar and lemon juice at the end. Pour into a mould and turn out when set.

Orange Blancmange

4 oranges	2 tablespoons cornflour
2 cups milk	3 tablespoons sugar

Mix the cornflour with the juice and the grated rind of the oranges. Heat the milk and sugar and pour over the cornflour mixture, stirring all the time. Return to the pan and boil for 3 minutes. Turn into a wetted mould and serve cold with cream or custard.

Orange Custard

some large juicy oranges	500 ml. (1 pint) milk
3 eggs	3 tablespoons sugar

Peel the oranges, cut into thin slices, removing the pips, and place them in custard cups in layers with a little sugar sifted between them. Make a custard with the eggs, milk and 2 tablespoons sugar. Pour this over the slices of orange. Whip the whites stiffly, add a little sugar and cover each cup with meringue. They may be placed in a moderate oven to set the meringue or eaten uncooked.

Orange Ficat

6 oranges
rind and juice of 1 lemon
500 ml. (1 pint) water

2 tablespoons cornflour
½ teacup sugar

Put the water in a double boiler, add the lemon rind tied in a piece of muslin, cover closely and bring to the boil. Remove rind, add sugar and the lemon juice. When it boils, stir in the cornflour which has been mixed in cold water and boil 5 minutes, stirring constantly. Peel and slice the oranges, removing the pips. Place the slices in a glass dish, sprinkle with a little sugar, pour over the custard and serve as cold as possible with cream whipped stiffly spread over the top.

Orange Pudding

300 ml. (½ pint) milk
2 eggs

90 g. (3 oz.) sponge cake crumbs
grated rind and juice of 3
oranges

Boil the milk and pour over the sponge cake crumbs. Leave to soak for a few minutes; add a little grated rind and the juice of 3 oranges. Sugar to taste. Beat up the eggs and mix well into the pudding. Butter a mould and pour in the mixture. Cover with a piece of buttered paper and bake for ½ hour. Serve hot with sifted sugar on top.

Orange Salad

oranges
sugar

small glass brandy
grated coconut

Peel fruit and cut into slices, removing the pips. Sprinkle with sugar and pour over a small glass of brandy. Garnish with grated coconut. Serve with cream.

Pancakes

3 large eggs
1 tablespoon butter (melted)
600 ml. (1 pint) of milk

a little salt
½ teacup hot water
125 g. (¼ lb.) flour

Whip the whites and yolks of eggs separately. Stir in the melted butter and flour gradually, then the milk and water. Mix smoothly. Let stand for 1 hour, then fry in butter. Cook one side and when brown turn or toss over and cook on the other. Sprinkle with sugar, and roll. Serve on hot dish, garnished with slices of lemon.

Pawpaws

May be eaten sliced sprinkled with lemon juice and sugar for breakfast, dessert or added to fruit salad. Recommended for vegetarians. A very good digestive. Unripe pawpaws if stewed with sugar and a little ginger or cloves are a good substitute for stewed apple.

Pawpaw "Peke Yake"

pawpaw   lemon juice   sugar

Take a ripe pawpaw. Cut in halves and remove skin and seeds.

Cut into neat pieces; place in a dish; squeeze lemon juice over and sprinkle with sugar. Cover with a damp cloth and leave for ½ hour before serving.

Pawpaw and Cream

pawpaw   cream
pineapple, strawberries or raspberries
    Cut a ripe pawpaw in half. Take off the skin and remove the seeds. Prepare a mixture of minced pineapple sweetened with a little cream or mashed strawberries or raspberries similarly treated. Put the mixture in the space from which the seeds were removed and cover with a damp cloth and chill.

Pawpaw Ginger

    Pawpaws not quite ripe. Cut and weigh and have same amount of sugar. First boil pawpaws in water to soften, with rind of lemon, then put into pan with sugar and lemon juice and as much ginger as required and boil sufficiently.

Pineapple Cream

300 ml. (½ pint) cream   45 g. (1½ oz.) castor sugar
150 ml. (1 gill) water   15 g. (½ oz.) gelatine
200 ml. (⅓ pint) pineapple purée   1 teaspoon lemon juice
2 tablespoons pineapple cut into dice
    Whip the cream stiffly, add lightly the pineapple purée and the pineapple dice. Dissolve the gelatine and sugar in the water, add the lemon juice and when sufficiently cool stir it lightly into the cream and pineapple mixture. Pour into a prepared mould and put in a cool place until firm.

Pineapple and Cornflour Meringue

600 ml. (1 pint) of milk   tinned pineapple
2 tablespoons cornflour   2 or 3 eggs
castor sugar   pinch of salt
30 g. (1 oz.) butter   vanilla essence
    Put milk, butter and salt into a lined saucepan and heat. Mix the cornflour smoothly with a little of the syrup of the pineapple. Add to the hot milk. Stir until boiling and simmer for 5 minutes. Remove the saucepan and stir in the yolks of the eggs, sugar to taste and add a few drops of vanilla. Cut some tinned or freshly cooked pineapple in small pieces and lay it in a greased pie dish. Pour the cornflour mixture over it and bake in a moderate oven until lightly browned. Whip the whites of eggs to a stiff froth, add to them a good tablespoonful of castor sugar and pile this meringue on the top of the pudding. Return to very cool oven to set and become delicately brown and serve hot or cold. A fruit sauce or cream may be served separately. Time to bake, 20 minutes. Time to cook meringue, 15 minutes.

Pineapple Pudding

60 g. (2 oz.) butter
60 g. (2 oz.) sugar
2 eggs
milk

60 g. (2 oz.) flour
fresh or tinned
pineapple

Melt butter in a pan and gradually stir in the flour till smooth. Add milk and stir briskly till it boils, then allow to boil for 3 minutes. Beat the yolks of eggs with the sugar, then add to contents of pan, mixing all well together. Have ready in a pie dish the pineapple, pour custard over and place in the oven to set. Whip whites of eggs and decorate pudding. Place in oven to brown, then serve cold.

Pineapple, grated

Grate a pineapple, add sugar, and a little salt if desired. Serve well chilled.

Pineapple Tapioca

1½ cups water
1 cup sugar
2½ cups water

1 pineapple
1 cup tapioca

Soak the tapioca in 1½ cups water overnight. In the morning add 2½ cups water and cook till transparent. Add the sugar and pineapple peeled, cored and finely minced. Turn into wet custard cups or glasses and serve cold with cream.

Plum Pudding

(a)

500 g. (1 lb.) beef suet
500 g. (1 lb.) raisins
500 g. (1 lb.) currants
500 g. (1 lb.) sultanas
500 g. (1 lb.) breadcrumbs
8 eggs
250 g. (½ lb.) apples
2 wineglasses brandy

250 g. (½ lb.) flour
125 g. (¼ lb.) almonds
250 g. (½ lb.) sugar
250 g. (½ lb.) mixed candied peel
1 teaspoon nutmeg
1 teaspoon cinnamon
1 teaspoon mixed spice

Fruit must be well washed and cleaned and thoroughly dried. Blanch and chop almonds finely. Shred and mince suet; add the dry ingredients, the fruit having been previously minced (by hand for preference). Stir in beaten eggs and sufficient milk to make mixture moist. Add the brandy and thoroughly mix before putting into bowls. The above quantities make one large-sized pudding and two smaller ones. Boil the large bowl for 6 hours, the smaller ones for 4. Place greased paper over top of each bowl, then place bowl in a square of cloth, tie securely round rim of bowl, bring the 4 ends of the cloth together and tie on top. This enables one to lift the bowls easily out of the water.

(b)

125 g. (¼ lb.) flour	250 g. (½ lb.) suet
375 g. (¾ lb.) breadcrumbs	250 g. (½ lb.) sultanas
125 g. (¼ lb.) brown sugar	250 g. (½ lb.) raisins
125 g. (¼ lb.) currants	rind and juice of 1 lemon
185 g. (6 oz.) mixed candied peel	3 large (3) eggs
1 heaped teaspoon	60 g. (2 oz.) blanched almonds
baking powder	125 g. (¼ lb.) apples
milk	

Mix well all dry ingredients. Stir in beaten eggs and sufficient milk to make mixture rather moist. A wineglass of brandy may be added if liked. Boil in one or two basins for 4 hours.

Prune Shape

500 g. (1 lb.) prunes	90 g. (3 oz.) sugar
25 g. (¾ oz.) gelatine	1 lemon
2 drops cochineal	

Soak the prunes overnight, then stone and stew till quite soft. Add the gelatine (which has been soaked in cold water till soft) the sugar and the juice of the lemon. Mix well and pour into a wet mould to set. When turned out, decorate with blanched almonds and serve with whipped cream.

A little lemon rind cooked with the prunes improves their flavour.

Prune Soufflé

125 g. (¼ lb.) prunes	pinch of cream of tartar
5 eggs	600 ml. (1 pint) milk
6 tablespoons sugar	½ teaspoon salt
yellow rind of ½ a lemon	

Stew the prunes until they are perfectly tender; then take them out and chop them into small pieces. Beat the whites of the eggs to a stiff froth with the sugar. Add the prunes which should contain as little water or juice as possible. Sprinkle in also a pinch of cream of tartar. Butter a large tin pudding mould and pour in the mixture, which should be as stiff as possible. Bake the pudding for 25 minutes in an oven so moderate that it will do no more than turn the soufflé a delicate brown in that time. Serve with a soft custard sauce made from the yolks of the eggs, with 4 tablespoons sugar, milk, lemon rind and salt. Let the sauce be ice cold when it is served but serve the pudding the moment it comes out of the oven or it will fall.

Queen of Puddings

1 breakfast cup stale	2 tablespoons sugar
breadcrumbs	2 tablespoons jam
2 eggs	½ teaspoon vanilla essence
2 breakfast cups milk	

Butter a pudding dish and put in the breadcrumbs. Beat yolks of eggs with the sugar till creamy and add milk, warmed. Pour this mixture over the breadcrumbs; allow to stand ½ hour; then bake in a moderate oven for about 1 hour till set. Remove from oven and spread with jam. Beat whites of eggs to a stiff froth, spread on top of jam and return pudding to oven for about 5 minutes. Serve with cream.

Ratafia Soufflé Pudding

45 g. (1½ oz.) flour	3 eggs
150 ml. (1 gill) milk	almond or ratafia flavouring
30 g. (1 oz.) butter	45 g. (1½ oz.) sugar
6 ratafia biscuits (crushed)	

Put a saucepan of water on to boil. Grease a soufflé tin. If this is not obtainable, use a small round cake tin that will hold about 1 litre (1½ pints). Grease a piece of paper and tie round the tin so that it comes 5 to 7 cm. (2 or 3 in.) above the top of the tin. Melt the butter in a saucepan, add the flour, mix well together, add the milk and stir quickly for a few minutes; then remove from the stove. This mixture makes the foundation for the soufflé and it must be cooked before the other ingredients are added. When cooked it will easily leave the sides of the saucepan. Separate the yolks of the eggs from the whites. Add the yolks, sugar and ratafia crumbs to the foundation just made and stir round quickly for a few minutes; each yolk should be beaten in separately. Add the flavouring. Whisk the whites to a stiff froth and mix lightly with the other ingredients. Pour into prepared tin and cover with a greased paper. Stand in a covered saucepan of boiling water on a saucer turned upside down. Steam gently for 35 minutes. Take soufflé up directly it is cooked. Turn carefully on to a hot dish. Serve with apricot sauce round the soufflé. (The water in the saucepan must not come more than half-way up the soufflé tin.)

Rhubarb Mould, with Gelatine

rhubarb sufficient to measure	juice of 1 lemon
1.25 l. (1 qt.) after it has been	15 g. (½ oz.) gelatine
cut up	2 tablespoons water
600 ml. (1 pint) water	500 g. (1 lb.) sugar
a few drops cochineal	

Put rhubarb, water, sugar, juice and grated rind of lemon into a pan and simmer till cooked. Sieve if desired. Dissolve gelatine in two tablespoons water and strain into the rhubarb. Colour with a few drops of cochineal. Beat the mixture well and pour into a wet mould. Turn out when cold and serve with custard or cream.

Rhubarb Mould with Cornflour

500 g. (1 lb.) rhubarb	2 tablespoons cornflour
a little water	160 ml. (¼ pint) water
sugar to taste	

Stew the fruit with a little water and sweeten. Put through a sieve and make up to 480 ml. (¾ pint). Blend the cornflour with 160 ml. (¼ pint) water and add to the fruit. Bring to the boil and boil 5 minutes, stirring all the time. Pour into a wetted mould. When cold, turn out and serve with cream or custard.

When the rhubarb is young the skin need not be removed. The white root should only be scraped, as there are medicinal properties in the root. After being well wiped with a damp cloth cut into 2.5 cm.

(1 in.) pieces and scald with boiling water for a few minutes. This removes the astringent taste. Strain and place in a bowl, sprinkling sugar on each layer. Cover with water and steam in oven.

Rice Pudding

2 tablespoons uncooked rice	2 tablespoons sugar
2 cups milk	butter size of walnut
1 egg	½ cup cleaned and picked
pinch of salt	raisins

Wash the rice well and boil in a very little water. Place it and the raisins in the bottom of a pie dish. Beat the egg well, add salt and milk and stir well. Pour this over the rice and raisins. Sprinkle the top with nutmeg and break the butter in small pieces over all. Bake in a slow oven.

Sago Pudding

50 to 60 g. (2 oz.) sago	2 breakfast cups milk
2 tablespoons sugar	1 egg, pinch of salt
a little grated nutmeg	

Wash the sago well and put into a greased pudding dish. Beat egg with sugar till light and creamy, add salt and milk, stir well and pour over sago. Sprinkle nutmeg on top and bake very slowly in oven till the pudding is set and browned on top.

Schoolroom Trifle

sponge or Madeira cake	fruit juice
2 eggs	jam
1 cup milk	1 tablespoon sugar
flavouring essence	

Put the cake in a glass dish, pour over it any kind of fruit juice or fruit syrup and allow to stand. Make a custard of the egg yolks, milk, sugar and flavouring. Put aside to cool. Cover the cake, which will now have absorbed the fruit juice, with strawberry or raspberry jam. Pour the custard over this and, before serving, decorate with the stiffly beaten egg whites. Cherries and angelica may be used for decoration if desired.

Semolina Pudding

1½ tablespoons semolina	1 tablespoon sugar
550 ml. (1 pint) milk	½ teaspoon vanilla essence
2 eggs	

Boil milk and sprinkle in semolina, add salt and stir till boiling. Cool slightly and add sugar and essence with the beaten yolks of eggs. Beat whites to a stiff froth; stir lightly in. Put it buttered dish and bake 20 minutes.

Semolina Snow

2½ breakfast cups water   1 lemon
3 tablespoons semolina   sugar to taste

Put the water in an enamelled pan with the juice of a lemon and sugar to taste. Add the semolina and boil 5 minutes. Put in a large bowl and whisk 15 minutes till it becomes like snow.

A very delicious and economical pudding.

Six Cup Pudding

1 teacup chopped suet   1 teacup flour
1 teacup milk   1 teacup sugar
1 teacup jam   1 teacup breadcrumbs
a pinch of salt   ½ teaspoon soda

Chop suet finely and put in a basin with the breadcrumbs, flour, sugar and salt. Mix these dry ingredients together, make a well in the centre and put in the jam. Heat the milk slightly in a small saucepan, add the soda and mix quickly. Pour this while still frothy on to the top of the jam and mix all together. Put the mixture into a greased mould or basin, cover with greased paper and steam steadily until thoroughly cooked. Serve with arrowroot or white sauce.

A cupful of currants and sultanas mixed may be used instead of the jam, or any other small fruit. Steam 3 hours.

Snow Pudding (Lemon)

2 tablespoons cornflour   2 or 3 lemons or oranges
1 small cup sugar   2 large cups boiling water
2 or 3 eggs

Mix cornflour with juice of 2 or 3 lemons and put lemon skins on to boil with the boiling water. Stir sugar into cornflour mixture. Pour into this the boiling water; return to saucepan and let it boil and thicken. Remove from fire and stir in lightly whites of eggs beaten stiff. Pour into wet mould. Make a custard of yolks of eggs and pour over the pudding when turned out.

Vanilla Soufflé

30 g. (1 oz.) butter   30 g. (1 oz.) sugar
30 g. (1 oz.) flour   3 eggs
150 ml. (¼ pint) milk   ½ teaspoon vanilla essence

Melt the butter in a saucepan and mix in the flour. Add milk and bring to boiling point. Add sugar, after mixture has cooked a few minutes. Allow to cool slightly and add yolks of eggs, beating all thoroughly. Whip the whites of the eggs to a stiff froth and fold into the mixture. Pour into prepared soufflé tin and steam gently 40 minutes.

Stewed Fruits

All dried fruits should be washed well, soaked overnight in cold water, then gently cooked in the water in which they have been soaked, either inside the oven or on top of the stove. Add sugar to taste, when nearly done. A small piece of lemon peel, or cinnamon, adds to the flavour of prunes and peaches, etc. When cooking fresh fruits the syrup should be made first and the fruit added when boiling, to keep the fruit whole. Then cook very gently till tender.

Stirling Pudding

500 g. (1 lb.) stewed fruit, plums, currants or raspberries
30 g. (1 oz.) castor sugar
30 g. (1 oz.) melted butter
90 g. (3 oz.) flour
1 egg
1 teaspoon baking powder
milk if necessary

Put cooked fruit in a pie dish and pour the following mixture on top. Mix flour and sugar in a basin. Stir in egg and butter and lastly baking powder. If too stiff, add a little milk. Bake in a moderate oven.

Strawberry Cream

1 teacup strawberry jam and 1 teacup milk
or 500 g. (1 lb.) fresh strawberries and 60 to 120 g. (2 to 4 oz.) sugar
pink colouring
150 ml. (1 gill) water
15 g. ($\frac{1}{2}$ oz.) gelatine
juice of $\frac{1}{2}$ lemon
250 g. ($\frac{1}{2}$ pint) cream

Rub jam or fruit through a hair sieve. Dissolve gelatine in water over a gentle heat. Add sugar and lemon juice and mix with fruit juice. Whip cream and stir the mixture into the cream. Colour with cochineal. Put into a damp mould. Turn out when set and decorate as desired.

Suet Pudding

125 g. ($\frac{1}{4}$ lb.) flour
125 g. ($\frac{1}{4}$ lb.) breadcrumbs
125 g. ($\frac{1}{4}$ lb.) suet
1 teaspoon baking powder
$\frac{1}{4}$ teaspoon salt
cold water

Shred suet and chop it, using some of the flour to do so. Mix all dry ingredients, then make into a stiff paste with water. Form into a smooth roll and put into a floured cloth or greased pudding bowl. Boil 1$\frac{1}{2}$ to 2 hours. Serve with golden syrup or any kind of hot jam sauce.

Summer Pudding

some slices of bread
fresh fruit (strawberries, raspberries, loganberries, etc.)
sugar

Line a round pudding basin with slices of bread. Cook fruit, with sugar to taste, in a little water. When cooked pour into the lined basin a little of the fruit, add another slice of bread, then more fruit, another slice of bread and so on till the basin is filled, finishing by pouring on the remaining fruit. Put a saucer on top and weight to press the bread together. When required turn out on a glass dish and serve with cream or custard.

Tapioca Custard Pudding

60 g. (2 oz.) tapioca
3 eggs
30 g. (1 oz.) butter
1 pinch salt

60 g. (2 oz.) castor sugar
600 ml. (1 pint) milk
2 teaspoons grated orange rind

Put milk, tapioca and salt in a saucepan. Simmer 25 minutes. Stir in sugar, orange rind, yolks of eggs and butter. Pour into a buttered pie dish. Sweeten stiffly frothed whites of eggs with a tablespoon castor sugar. Pile on top of pudding. Bake very slowly 45 minutes, till whites are firm and golden. If wanted plainer, stir whites of eggs into mixture along with yolks.

Treacle Duff

$\frac{1}{2}$ teaspoon baking powder
$\frac{1}{2}$ teaspoon ground ginger
2 eggs
2 teaspoons treacle

weight of 1 egg in sugar
weight of 2 eggs in flour and
butter

Beat butter and sugar to a cream. Add the flour and well-beaten eggs, alternately, then stir in the treacle, ground ginger and lastly the baking powder. Pour into a greased mould and steam for $1\frac{1}{2}$ hours. Serve with a sweet sauce.

Treacle and Lemon Pudding

1 large cup treacle or
golden syrup

suet crust
juice and rind of 1 large lemon

Make a suet crust and roll out. Mix in a basin the treacle and juice and rind of lemon. Grease pudding basin, put a little of the syrup in the bottom, then a layer of suet crust and fill the basin with alternate layers of pastry and syrup. Cover with a cloth and boil for about 4 hours.

Treacle Pudding

90 g. (3 oz.) flour
90 g. (3 oz.) breadcrumbs
1 tablespoon treacle
1 teaspoon baking powder

80 ml. ($\frac{1}{2}$ gill) milk
30 g. (1 oz.) brown sugar
30 g. (2 oz.) suet
1 teaspoon ground ginger

Chop suet, using a little of the flour to prevent it from sticking to the knife. Add flour, salt, baking powder, and ginger and mix well. Mix treacle and milk, add to dry ingredients mixing all thoroughly. Pour into a well-greased basin and cover with a greased paper. Steam $1\frac{1}{2}$ hours. Turn out and serve with treacle.

Instead of brown sugar and treacle, 90 g. (3 oz.) of jaggery, dissolved in milk, may be used.

Trifle

4 sponge cakes	60 g. (2 oz.) almonds (blanched
6 macaroons	and peeled)
12 ratafias	grated rind of $\frac{1}{2}$ lemon
2 whites of eggs	300 ml. ($\frac{1}{2}$ pint) custard
strawberry jam	250 to 300 ml. ($\frac{1}{2}$ pint) cream
glacé cherries	castor sugar
angelica	4 to 8 tablespoons sherry

Make the custard and let it become quite cold. Cut the cake into rather thick slices, spread half with jam, cover with the remainder and arrange them alternately with macaroons and ratafias in a glass dish. Pour over the sherry adding a little more if necessary to soak them thoroughly. Sprinkle on the lemon rind, add the almonds and cover with the custard. Mix the cream and whites of eggs together, whip stiffly, sweeten to taste with castor sugar and pile lightly on top of the custard. Garnish with halved cherries and strips of angelica.

Urney Pudding

2 eggs	30 g. (1 oz.) sugar
60 g. (2 oz.) flour	jam or marmalade
60 g. (2 oz.) butter	$\frac{1}{2}$ teaspoon baking soda

Put the butter and sugar in a basin and beat to a cream. Add the eggs and beat smooth. Mix the soda with the flour and add to the mixture, blending all thoroughly. Add jam or marmalade. Pour into a buttered mould, cover with greased paper and steam for $1\frac{1}{2}$ hours. Turn out and serve with hot sweet sauce. If marmalade is used more sugar will be required.

Vanilla Cream

250 ml. ($\frac{1}{2}$ pint) thick cream	vanilla flavouring
250 ml. ($\frac{1}{2}$ pint) custard	15 g. ($\frac{1}{2}$ oz.) gelatine
2 tablespoons cold water	cherries and angelica
45 g. ($1\frac{1}{2}$ oz.) castor sugar	

Make custard, add sugar and allow to cool. Dissolve gelatine in the cold water and heat slightly. Add to the custard. Half whip the cream and add custard to it when cold. Add flavouring. Stir until just beginning to set. Decorate a mould with cherries and angelica and pour the mixture in. Turn out when set.

Vermicelli or Macaroni Pudding

1 teacup vermicelli or	1 egg
macaroni broken small	2 tablespoons sugar
2 breakfast cups milk	pinch of salt and nutmeg

Boil vermicelli or macaroni in salted water till soft. Beat egg and sugar together, add milk. Put boiled macaroni or vermicelli, egg, sugar and milk, in greased pudding dish. Sprinkle nutmeg on top and bake in oven till set and brown.

ICED PUDDINGS

Ice Cream

SIX GENERAL HINTS:—

(1) The proportions for making a custard for ice cream should be 1 large egg to every 250 ml. ($\frac{1}{2}$ pint) of milk.

(2) The custard must be made with care and be perfectly smooth.

(3) Be careful about sweetening the custard. If not sweet enough, it takes a long time to freeze; if too sweet, it will not freeze at all.

(4) If cream is too expensive, use unsweetened (condensed) milk as a substitute.

(5) A small quantity of cornflour, i.e. about one teaspoon to each pint, will make the custard more velvety.

(6) Be sparing in the use of colouring matter. The colour deepens during the freezing process.

Coffee Ice Cream

250 ml. ($\frac{1}{2}$ pint) custard (see below)   250 ml. ($\frac{1}{2}$ pint) cream
2.5 (3) teaspoons coffee essence.

Custard for Ice Cream

1 egg   250 ml. ($\frac{1}{2}$ pint) milk   sugar to taste
Bring the milk almost to boiling point and pour it over the well-beaten egg, stirring all the time. Put the mixture back into the saucepan and stir until the mixture thickens. Do not boil; stir in the same direction all the time. Neglect of these precautions may mean curdling of the custard. Now stir in the sugar and strain the mixture before freezing. Sufficient for 4 persons.

Cream Ice (Uncooked)

125 ml. ($\frac{1}{4}$ pt.) cream   1 egg or 2 whites
2 tablespoons sugar (icing   flavouring (vanilla or
   or fine castor)   almond, etc.)

(a) *Using egg yolk and white.*

Beat yolk with sugar till pale and very thick, flavour, half-whip cream, beat white stiff and fold into the other ingredients mixed together, put into tray in refrigerator and leave 2 hours, no stirring required.

154

(b) Using egg whites only (no yolk).

Whip whites till stiff, whip cream till thick but not stiff, add sugar and flavouring required to cream, gradually fold the stiff whites into the cream, freeze for 2 hours.

Pawpaw Ice Cream

250 ml. (½ pint) pawpaw purée   75 g. (3 oz.) sugar
250 ml. (½ pint) cream
    Mix the sugar and purée together and add them to the cream. Put into a freezer and stir once or twice.

Strawberry Ice Cream

250 ml. (½ pint) sieved   75 g. (3 oz.) sugar
  strawberries or strawberry jam   125 ml. (¼ pint) cream
125 ml. (¼ pint) custard
or omit the custard and put in 250 ml. (½ pint) cream

Vanilla Ice Cream

375 ml. (¾ pint) boiled custard   125 ml. (¼ pint) cream
  (as directed above)   vanilla essence

Vanilla Ice Cream Pudding

250 ml. (½ pint) milk   85 g. (3 oz.) sugar
2 eggs   1 teaspoon vanilla essence
250 ml. (½ pint) cream   1 dessertspoon flour
    Boil the milk, add flour blended in a little cold milk and stir 3 minutes till cooked. When off the boil pour over the eggs beaten up, return to saucepan and stir till it thickens but not boils. Add sugar and flavouring. Pour into a bowl to cool. Beat cream and mix well into the custard. Put in the freezer, with ice and salt packed round it, fasten machine and stir till frozen. If wanted moulded, put in a mould and pack tightly to give firmness. Close mould carefully; plunge into a bed of ice and salt. When dishing, dip mould into cold water and turn out like jelly.

WATER ICES

GENERAL HINTS:

(1) Water ices take longer to freeze than cream ices.
(2) Add liqueurs sparingly. Too much flavouring retards freezing.
(3) Be careful in sweetening. Too little sugar makes a water ice rough and too much prevents freezing.

Syrup as Basis for Water Ices:

1.25 l. (2 pints) water   juice of ½ a lemon
500 g. (1 lb.) loaf sugar
    Place the water and sugar in an enamel saucepan. Boil steadily for 10 minutes. Do not stir but take off the scum as it rises with a wooden spoon. When the liquid is syrupy, remove from the stove. Add the lemon juice and strain through muslin.

Mixed Fruit Ice (Tutti Frutti)

500 ml. (1 pint) orange or   1 glass of any liqueur
    lemon ice
250 ml. (½ pint) of any fruits liked, i.e. strawberries, cherries, etc.
    Cut the fruits into dice and soak them in the liqueur. When the orange or lemon ice is nearly frozen, sprinkle in the fruits and finish freezing.

Orange and Lemon Water Ice

250 ml. (½ pint) orange juice   500 ml. (1 pint) of above syrup
250 ml. (½ pint) lemon juice   whites of 2 eggs
    Peel the oranges and lemons thinly and pour the hot syrup over the strips of peel. Squeeze the required amount of juice and when the syrup is cold add it. Strain through muslin and partly freeze. Whisk the egg whites and, when the ice is half frozen, mix them in and finish freezing.

Pineapple Water Ice

1 tin pineapple   250 ml. (½ pint) water
500 ml. (1 pint) syrup as   a dash of lemon juice
    described above
    Cut the pineapple into small pieces and place them, the syrup and the water in an enamel saucepan. Cook till tender, skimming the scum off. Leave till cool, then add lemon juice and freeze.

PASTRY

GENERAL HINTS

The secret of good pastry is to have hard butter and good flour, to handle it lightly, to have a hot oven and to work in a cool place. A marble slab makes the ideal pastry board. The best method is to mix flaky or puff pastry and let it stand in a cool place overnight between two plates and cover the top one with a damp cloth. Roll out and bake next morning. When baking do not open the oven door on any account until the paste has had time to rise. After the crust has set, greaseproof paper may be laid over it to prevent it from colouring too much. When baking meat pies of any kind take care to leave a good hole in the top crust or the pies will be unwholesome to eat.

To Glaze Sweet Pastry. Take the white of an egg and fine sugar. Break the white of egg into a soup plate; beat up till the froth will stand alone. When pastry and pies are nearly baked, remove from the oven, brush them over with the egg froth and sift fine sugar over. Put back into the oven for glazing to dry, taking care it does not darken. Sugar and water also make a glaze for sweet pastries.

Short Crust. Suitable for fruit pie, tarts, flans, etc. Oven temperature: 220°C (425°F).

Puffed Pastry, Flaky Pastry and Rough Puffed Pastry. Suitable for meat pie, sausage rolls, Cornish pasties, etc. Oven temperature: 230°C (450°F).

Another method for glazing is to beat the yolk of an egg and a little warm butter. Brush it over the pastry when nearly baked, powder with sugar and set in the oven to dry.

For meat pies, glaze with the yolk of egg only.

Biscuit or Flan Crust

500 g. (1 lb.) flour
250 g. (½ lb.) butter
250 g. (½ lb.) castor sugar
1 egg

½ teaspoon baking powder
   sifted with flour
2 tablespoons water

Rub butter into flour and work all together into a nice smooth dough. This paste can be used for all kinds of short pastry, small biscuits with icing on top or biscuits brushed over with egg and dipped into coconut before being baked. A small piece of cherry may be placed in centre. A most useful recipe for small pastries, custard tarts and flans.   *Temp. 220°C (425°F).*

Choux Pastry

250 ml. (½ pint) water
75 g. (3 oz.) butter
25 g. (1 oz.) castor sugar
vanilla

a pinch of salt
150 g. (6 oz.) flour
4 eggs

Put water, butter and salt in a pan and bring to the boil. Meanwhile sift the flour on to some paper and when the mixture boils take it off the heat and tip the flour in rapidly. Beat well; when well mixed return to the heat and cook about 5 minutes. Stand aside to cool, then add the whites and yolks of the eggs, beating each thoroughly, and at the same time add vanilla and sugar. Put this mixture into forcing bag and pipe into fingers on a well-greased tin, or drop small spoonfuls on greased tin. Bake in oven fairly quickly.

Temp. 200°C (400°F).

Flaky Pastry

(For Meat and Mince Pies, Sausage Rolls, Veal and Ham Patties, Covered Tarts, etc.)

250 g. (8 oz.) flour
185 g. (6 oz.) butter (or butter and lard)

cold water to mix
¼ teaspoon salt

Place sifted flour and salt in a bowl and rub into it one-quarter of the butter. Mix with water to a stiff paste. Turn out on a floured board and roll lightly into an oblong strip. Divide butter into 3 portions. Put one portion in small dabs on the pastry two-thirds of the way down the strip. Fold in three, with plain part in the centre. Seal edges and give the pastry a half-turn. Roll out again into a strip. Repeat this process twice again till remainder of butter is used up, being careful to fold and turn in the same direction each time. Let the pastry stand in a cool place for some time, overnight if liked, then fold again. Roll out to desired shape and thickness and use as required.

Hot Water Pastry

(For Raised Pies of Pork, Veal or Ham, etc.)

250 g. (8 oz.) flour
60 g. (2 oz.) butter or lard
1 egg yolk if liked

salt
about 475 ml. (¾ gill) water or milk

Sieve flour and salt into a warm basin. Boil water or milk with the butter and add to the flour. Add the egg yolk if using it. Mix well. Then knead with the hand till smooth. Shape, while hot, the amount of pastry necessary to line mould for a meat pie; or, if required for small pies, mould the pastry over a bottle or jam jar. Put in meat and stock. Cover with a lid of the pastry. Seal edges well. Make a hole in centre of cover. Decorate with trimmings of pastry and brush over with yolk of egg.

Puff Pastry

(a)

(For Patties, Puffs, Sausage Rolls, etc.)

500 g. (1 lb.) flour   salt
500 g. (1 lb.) butter   water

Take half the flour and cut 125 g. (¼ lb.) butter into it with a knife, roughly. Then mix with cold water (about a cupful). Take a little more flour and turn out dough on to pastry board or slab. Roll lightly and spread a portion of the butter on, dusting over with flour and then folding and rolling out lightly. Repeat this until all butter and flour is used up. Let it stand for a few hours in a cool place or overnight. Then roll it out very thin, dust with flour and fold as many times as you like. Roll out again lightly about 15 cm. (½ in.) thick and cut as required. Put in a very hot oven to puff it up and later let the oven cool down or remove to lower ledge in oven. A little more flour can be used for rolling out if you have used up the 500 g.

(b)

500 g. (1 lb.) flour   cold water
500 g. (1 lb.) fresh butter   lemon juice

Sift flour on to board. Put lemon juice into centre and some cold water and mix to an elastic dough. Lightly flour the board and roll the paste out. Then place the butter on one side and fold the other part over it. Stand this on a floured plate and put in a cold place for 10 minutes. Replace on board and gently roll out; fold in three and roll again. This process of rolling and standing should be repeated six or seven times, when the paste will be even in colour and ready for use. It may be allowed much longer intervals if convenient.

Orkney Puff Pastry made with Cream

250 g. (½ lb.) butter, ice cold   1 cup cream
2 cups flour   1 teaspoon baking powder
¼ teaspoon salt

Sift flour, salt and baking powder; cut up butter, rub into flour, add cream, put in refrigerator for 1 hour in greaseproof paper. Use as required.

Rough Puff Pastry

(For tartlets, sausage rolls, meat pies, etc.)

375 g. (¾ lb.) butter   500 g. (1 lb.) flour
a pinch of salt   squeeze of lemon juice
cold water

Cut the butter into pieces the size of walnuts. Add to the sifted flour. Mix to an elastic dough with the lemon juice and water. Roll out, fold in three and repeat the process three times. Cut into any shape desired.

Short Pastry

(For fruit tarts and pies, open tarts, Cornish pasties, etc.)

250 g. (8 oz.) flour
pinch of salt
cold water

120 g. (4 oz.) butter (or 60 g. (2 oz.) lard and 60 g. (2 oz.) butter)
½ teaspoon baking powder

Sieve the flour and salt and baking powder. Add butter cut into small pieces, then rub it in with the tips of the fingers till it is like fine breadcrumbs. Add water and mix with knife till the ingredients are bound together and form a stiff paste. Turn out on to a floured board. Knead slightly with the tips of fingers till free from cracks, turn the smooth side up and roll out as required. Bake in a hot oven.

A richer pastry can be made by adding the yolk of an egg to the water used in mixing.

Suet Pastry

(For dumplings for soups or stews, fruit and meat puddings, etc.)

250 g. (8 oz.) flour (or 125 g. (4 oz.) flour and 125 g. (4 oz.) breadcrumbs)
125 g. (4 oz.) suet

¼ (1) teaspoon baking powder
¼ teaspoon salt
water to mix

Mix flour, salt and baking powder in a basin. Skin and chop suet finely, using plenty of the flour from the basin. Mix to a medium dough (not sticky and not too hard). Turn on to a floured board and work in rough edges and cracks. Use as required. Steam or boil.

Swiss Pastry

Use puff or flaky pastry previously cooked in 5 cm. (2 in.) strips. Slit into three layers carefully with a knife and spread raspberry jam. Place one layer of pastry on top, then a layer of thick custard, thick chocolate sauce, or whipped cream. Lay the other piece of pastry on top. Ice with water icing. Cut into neat oblong pieces.

ADDITIONAL PASTRY RECIPES

Apple Amber

short pastry or biscuit crust as above
750 g. (1½ lb.) apples
125 g. (¼ lb.) sugar

2 eggs
a little water
1 tablespoon castor sugar
60 g. (2 oz.) butter or margarine

Line a piedish or tin with pastry and decorate the edge. Stew apples with butter, sugar and water. Rub through a sieve. Add the yolks of the eggs. Pour into a piedish and bake till firm in a hot oven 220°C (425°F). Whip the whites of eggs to a stiff froth and fold in one tablespoon castor sugar. Pile on top of pudding and brown lightly in a moderate oven 150°C (300°F). Serve with cream.

Apple Balls

pastry as required
1 teaspoon apricot jam
for each apple

6 or 8 apples
1 teaspoon brown sugar for
each apple

Roll out pastry and cut into as many squares as there are apples. Peel and core the apples without breaking them. Spread each square with jam. Stand the apple on it. With sugar fill the holes. Close up the pastry round the fruit. Press edges together. Bake apples on a greased tin in a brisk oven till the pastry is nicely browned. They will take about 25 minutes to bake, according to the size of the apples.

Temp. 220°C (425°F)

Apple Pie

6–8 apples
¾ cup white or
½ cup firmly packed brown sugar
2 tablespoons butter

¼ teaspoon salt
½ teaspoon cinnamon or nutmeg
½ teaspoon grated lemon rind
1 tablespoon lemon juice

Line a 25 cm. (9 in.) pie plate with pastry and fill with apples pared and sliced thin; sprinkle with mixture of sugar, salt and spices and lemon rind; then with lemon juice and dot with butter. Moisten edge of pastry, cover with top-pastry and press edges together. Brush pastry with milk; bake in hot oven, 230°C (450°F), for 10 minutes; then reduce heat to 175°C (350°F) and bake 40–50 minutes longer.

Apricot Custard

3 eggs
600 ml. (1 pint) milk
short crust

vanilla essence
tinned apricots
15 g. (½ oz.) castor sugar

Beat up eggs, add milk, sugar and a few drops of vanilla essence. Line a piedish with short crust pastry, pour in the mixture and let it cook very slowly in a medium oven 175°C (350°F.) When custard begins to set, add apricots and return to oven until it is set. When cold, grate ratafias thickly over the top.

Balmoral Cheese Cakes

rich short crust
120 g. (4 oz.) sifted castor sugar
30 g. (1 oz.) stale sponge
cake crumbs
30 g. (1 oz.) candied peel
finely chopped
2 eggs

120 g. (4 oz.) butter
30 g. (1 oz.) glacé cherries
8 g. (¼ oz.) cornflour
1 egg white
1 teaspoon brandy

Cream butter and sugar and add the two well-beaten eggs, crumbs, cornflour, cherries and peel. Then add the brandy and stiffly beaten egg white. Line some patty tins with the short crust pastry, put about a teaspoon of the filling into each. Bake in a fairly hot oven for 15 minutes, temperature 200 to 230°C (400 to 450°F), until well risen and firm to the touch. Turn out and cool on a wire tray.

Banana Fluffy Puffs

flaky or rough puff pastry   egg
bananas of equal size   castor sugar
jam

These are delicious hot or cold, made with flaky or rough puff pastry. Split the bananas lengthwise but not quite in two; then squeeze plenty of lemon juice over the inside and spread with jam. Place the two pieces of banana together and roll in castor sugar. Roll the pastry out till it is about 5 mm. ($\frac{1}{4}$ in.) thick; cut into oblongs (the size naturally depends on the size of the bananas). Place the banana on the pastry, moisten the edges with white of egg, fold over and press the edges together and decorate with a knife. Brush over with white of an egg, sprinkle with castor sugar and bake in hot oven for about 15 minutes.

Temp. 230°C (450°F).

Banana Tart

cup mashed bananas   2 eggs
sugar   2 spoons cream or 1 of butter
lemon juice $\frac{1}{2}$ cup milk
1 tablespoon flour

Line a plate with pastry. Take the fruit, sugar and squeeze of lemon juice. Beat in yolks of eggs, then the cream or butter, add the milk and the flour which has been mixed with a little milk to a smooth paste. Mix all together and lastly whites of eggs (beaten stiff). Sprinkle top with ground cinnamon and sugar and bake.

Temp. 220°C (425°F).

Butterscotch Pie

pastry to line sandwich tin   3 tablespoons flour
1 cup brown sugar   2 yolks of eggs
1 cup milk or water $\frac{1}{4}$ teaspoon salt
$\frac{1}{4}$ cup butter $\frac{1}{2}$ teaspoon vanilla
2 tablespoons powdered sugar   1 cup whipped cream

Melt the butter in saucepan, add half of the brown sugar and stir over the stove till syrupy. Mix in the flour with the rest of the brown sugar and place in a double boiler with the milk or water. Add the other sugar and cook for 15 minutes, stirring occasionally. Beat the egg yolks, mix with a little of the filling and return to boiler. Take off the stove and stir thoroughly. Add vanilla and, when cool, place in baked pastry case. Cover with whipped cream, sweetened, and serve at once.

Canadian Tartlets

Short Crust Pastry   Filling
120 g. (4 oz.) flour   1 teacup cleaned currants
90 g. (3 oz.) butter (or $\frac{3}{4}$ teacup castor sugar
half lard and butter)   1 egg
1 dessertspoon sugar   1 teaspoon vanilla essence
     piece of butter size of an egg

Cream butter and sugar, add egg and other ingredients. Put into patty tins which have been lined with pastry and bake in oven, temperature 200°C (400°F) for 20 minutes. This may be baked in one round sponge cake tin if liked and cut when cold.

Chocolate Shortcake

175 g. (6 oz.) short pastry
raspberry jam
2 small tablespoons butter
3 dessertspoons sugar

2 teaspoons cocoa
1 egg
2 tablespoons flour

Roll out the pastry and line a flan ring or deep sandwich tin with it. Trim and decorate the edge and spread a thin layer of jam in the bottom. Mix the flour and cocoa together. Whisk the sugar and egg together for a few minutes until thick and creamy. Stir in the flour and cocoa and lastly the melted butter. Put this mixture over the jam and spread evenly. Put in a hot oven and bake for about 15 to 20 minutes. Cool on sieve, dust with castor sugar or sieved icing sugar before serving.   *Temp. 230°C (450°F).*

Chocolate Tartlets

about 120 g. (¼ lb.) flaky pastry
2 teaspoons cocoa
75 g. (2½ oz.) castor sugar
jam

90 g. (3 oz.) ground almonds
1 egg
30 g. (1 oz.) butter
flavouring

Roll out the pastry thinly, cut into rounds and line some tartlet tins. Put jam in the bottom of each. Beat the sugar and butter to a cream, add the egg, stir it in quickly and beat the mixture for a few minutes. Mix the cocoa and ground almonds together: stir in with a few drops of vanilla. Put into the prepared tins and about three parts fill them. Place on a baking sheet and bake in hot oven for about 15 to 20 minutes. Leave on a sieve until cold, then dust with sieved castor sugar.   *Temp. 230°C (450°F).*

Cream Puffs and Éclairs

Make Choux Pastry. Put into a forcing bag and pipe into fingers on a well-greased tin, or drop small spoonfuls on greased tin and bake in a fairly quick oven about 25 minutes. Cut with sharp knife near base to admit filling of either cream or custard.

Éclairs may be covered with coffee or chocolate icing (*see* Icings).

Cream Tarts

puff paste
2 eggs (yolks only)
1 white of egg

1 tablespoon of apricot jam
the weight of one egg in butter
and sugar

Line some patty pans with puff paste and fill them with this mixture. Take the jam, yolks of eggs, the white of egg, butter and sugar; whip all to a cream, put into the little tins and bake in a hot oven for 20 minutes.   *Temp. 220 to 230°C (425 to 450°F).*

Date Pie

Short Crust Pastry	Filling
250 g. (½ lb.) flour	3 eggs
6 tablespoons butter	125 g. (¼ lb.) sugar
1 teaspoon baking powder	pinch of salt
water	2 breakfast cups milk
a pinch of salt	2 cups dates
	vanilla essence

Line a piedish with short pastry. For the paste, sift the flour into a basin, rub the butter or dripping finely into it, add the baking powder and salt, then gradually enough cold water to form a stiff paste. Roll out and line a piedish with it. Fill with the following mixture. Beat the eggs with the sugar, a pinch of salt, essence and milk. Add dates which have been cooked in boiling water until tender and pressed through a sieve. Bake in a moderate oven till firm to the touch.

Temp. 220 to 230°C (400 to 425°F).

Devonshire Puffs

apples	sugar to taste
lemon peel	short crust

Peel and bake some apples. When cold, mix the pulp, free from cores, with enough sugar to sweeten and a little lemon peel. Lay the apple on a square of paste and fold it over so as to form a three-cornered puff. Bake in a quick oven for 20 minutes. Sift white sugar over and serve.

Temp. 220°C (425°F).

Eccles Cakes

60 g. (2 oz.) currants	flaky pastry
30 g. (1 oz.) sultanas	¼ teaspoon ground cloves
30 g. (1 oz.) sweet almonds	½ teaspoon ground cinnamon
30 g. (1 oz.) chopped mixed peel	grated rind and juice of lemon
15 g. (½ oz.) sugar	

Clean and pick the fruit, mix all ingredients thoroughly in a small basin. Roll out the pastry until it is about 1 cm. (½ in.) thick, then cut into rounds roughly 8 cm. (3 in.) across. Put about 2 teaspoons of the fruit and spice mixture into the centre of each piece of pastry. Moisten the edges and gather up sufficiently tightly to enclose the contents. Flour the pastry board, place the smooth side of the cake uppermost and roll it lightly. Cut two slits on top and brush over with sugar water. Place in a greased baking sheet and bake in a hot oven for 10 to 15 minutes.

Temp. 230°C (45°F).

Fruit Flan

185 g. (6 oz.) biscuit or short crust	juice of ½ lemon
sweetened stewed fruit, or ½ size tin of fruit	30 g. (1 oz.) sugar
	10 g. (¼ oz.) gelatine
	1 teacup juice or syrup from fruit

Line flan ring or sandwich tin with pastry. Prick the pastry and line with a piece of greased paper (greased side down). Half fill paper with crust or rice to prevent pastry rising in the centre. Bake in a hot oven. Remove the paper, etc., and return pastry to oven till it is crisp and dry. When cold, arrange the fruit daintily in the case. To the fruit syrup add sugar, lemon juice and gelatine. Heat and allow gelatine to dissolve. Let this cool and when just beginning to set pour over the fruit. Serve with cream.

Instead of using gelatine, the syrup may be thickened with 1 teaspoon of blended cornflour, which must be cooked 3 or 4 minutes in the syrup before pouring over the fruit.

Iced Chocolate Tart

180 or 250 g. (6 or 8 oz.)
   short or flaky pastry
1 dessertspoon cocoa
45 g. (1½ oz.) butter
45 g. (1½ oz.) castor sugar

2 sponge cakes (stale)
1 egg
almond flavouring
jam

Roll out the pastry rather thinly, cut out a round and line a sandwich tin. Trim and decorate the edge neatly. Cream the butter and sugar, rub the sponge cakes through a sieve and mix with the cocoa. Separate the eggs and whip the whites to a stiff froth. Add the yolk to the creamed butter and sugar, stir in quickly and beat well, add the sponge cake crumbs, cocoa and a few drops of flavouring. Lastly add the white of egg and fold in lightly. Spread a thin layer of jam in the bottom of the prepared tin and cover with above mixture. Place in a hot oven and bake for about 15 to 20 minutes. When cold, ice the top with white icing, stick a cherry in the centre, with stalks of angelica round it.   *Temp. 220° to 230°C (425° to 450°F).*

Lemon Chiffon Pie

1 tablespoon gelatine
¼ cup water
4 eggs, separated
1 cup sugar
½ teaspoon salt

1½ teaspoons grated lemon rind
6 tablespoons lemon juice
1 baked pastry shell
1 cup whipped cream

Soften gelatine in two tablespoons water; combine slightly beaten egg yolk, ½ cup sugar, salt, lemon rind and juice and remaining two tablespoons water. Cook over boiling water until mixture thickens, stirring constantly. Add softened gelatine, stirring until dissolved. Cool until mixture begins to thicken, then gradually beat remaining ½ cup sugar into stiffly beaten egg-white and fold into lemon-gelatine mixture. Turn into baked pastry shell and chill until firm. When ready to serve, top with whipped cream.

Lemon Curd Tart

short paste or puff paste
500 g. (1 lb.) castor sugar
4 eggs

3 lemons
125 g. (¼ lb.) butter

Cut small rounds of puff or short paste or line a plate. Take the lemons, grated rind and juice, sugar and butter and place in a jar or saucepan in another saucepan of water. Bring to the boil or until all is thoroughly dissolved. Then add the beaten eggs and stir till it thickens. Ready for bottling and keeps well. Put this mixture into the pastry when cooked.

Lemon Custard Pie

250 g. (8 oz.) short pastry   juice of 2 lemons
500 ml. (1 pint) custard   grated rind of 1 lemon
75 g. (2½ oz.) stale cakecrumbs   sugar to taste

Line a pie dish with pastry. Make custard and when cold add other ingredients. Pour into dish and bake in a moderate oven till pastry is crisp.   *Temp. 205°–220°C. (400–425°F).*

Lemon Pie

1¼ cups sugar   a little salt
⅓ cup flour   grated rind and juice of 1 lemon
3 eggs   water
1 tablespoon butter   short crust

Mix the sugar thoroughly with ⅓ cup of flour; add salt. Grate a little rind from the lemon, mix with the juice of a whole lemon and add to sugar. Beat the yolks of eggs well, stir in a small cupful of water and blend carefully with the sugar and lemon mixture. Put all in a dish lined with short crust, add the butter cut into bits and bake in a moderate oven.   *Temp. 220°C (425°F).*

Loquat Pie

4 cups stoned and skinned   2 tablespoons sugar
   loquats   2 tablespoons lemon juice
2 cups water   2 tablespoons butter
3 cups sugar   2 eggs
¼ tablespoon flour   1 tablespoon water

Line a pie dish. Take the stoned and skinned loquats and break in halves. Add the water and sugar and stew till quite soft. Strain the liquid through a colander and cool. Then beat the eggs well, adding to the liquid and the flour mixed with water. Heat until syrup thickens. Now put the loquats on the pastry in the piedish and pour syrup over them. Add sugar, lemon juice and butter. Put on upper crust and bake.

Peaches, plums and other fruits may be used instead of loquats for this pie.   *Temp. 220°C (425°F).*

Milk Tart

1 breakfast cup milk   1 tablespoon flour
sugar to taste   stick of cinnamon
2 eggs

Line a tin plate with short pastry. Take the milk, sugar and cinnamon; bring to the boil and thicken with flour. Beat in the yolks of eggs and remove from the stove or otherwise the eggs might curdle. Beat the whites of eggs stiff and add to the mixture. Pour into pastry and bake in a hot oven.   *Temp. 220°C (425°F).*

Mincemeat (Fruit)

250 g. (½ lb.) apples
125 g. (¼ lb.) currants
125 g. (¼ lb.) cut up raisins
125 g. (¼ lb.) fresh chopped suet
30 g. (1 oz.) ground almonds
½ wineglass brandy
a little ground nutmeg

125 g. (¼ lb.) sultanas
125 g. (¼ lb.) sugar
rind and juice of lemon
1 tablespoon chopped mixed
  peel
10 g. (¼ oz.) mixed spice

Cut the apples into small pieces. Stone and cut up the raisins. The easiest way is to pass fruit through a mincer. Mix all ingredients well and put in glass jars. It is always better if kept a few weeks.

Mince Pies

Line patty tins with flaky pastry and put in mincemeat. Cover with an upper crust, brush over and bake.

Temp. 220–230°C (425–450°F).

Nougatines

180 g. (6 oz.) flaky or
  short crust
30 g. (2 oz.) butter
30 g. (2 oz.) sugar
1 egg
jam

chopped almonds (if liked)
30 g. (1 oz.) cake crumbs
30 g. (1 oz.) ground almonds
apricot marmalade
¼ teaspoon ratafia essence

Line moulds with pastry. Add jam. Beat butter and sugar and add egg, cake crumbs, ground almonds and essence. Put into cases covering the top with chopped almonds, if liked. Bake in a fairly hot oven but cover with greased paper to prevent burning. When cool brush over with apricot marmalade. *Temp. 220°C (425°F).*

Orange Pie

short pastry
1 cup sugar
1 tablespoon butter

pulp and juice of 7 oranges
1 cup breadcrumbs
3 eggs (yolks)

Line a pie dish with the pastry. Mix all together and pour into dish. Bake until set. Then beat the whites of the eggs stiffly with a teaspoon of sugar. Put on top of pie and bake until pale brown.

Temp. 210°C (400°F).

Patties

Patty casings are made by cutting rounds of puff pastry (a tumbler can be used). Then take a smaller glass and cut a circle out of half of the rounds. Just damp the edge of the circle and place one on the other. This cooks better and as the circle paste rises it leaves a good place for fruit or meat fillings.

Pumpkin Pie

3 eggs, well beaten
1 cup sugar
1 teaspoon salt
½ teaspoon cinnamon
2 cups milk, scalded

½ teaspoon nutmeg
½ teaspoon ginger
¼ teaspoon cloves
2 cups strained cooked pumpkin
or squash

Line a 25 cm. (9-in.) pie plate with pastry; combine eggs, sugar, salt and spices; gradually stir in milk, then pumpkin; turn into pastry-lined plate; bake in hot oven 230°C (450°F) for 10 minutes, then reduce heat to 175°C (350°F); bake 20–25 minutes longer or until knife comes out clean when inserted in custard.

Roly-Poly

1 cup flour
60 g. (2 oz.) butter
1 teaspoon baking powder
jam

water
30 g. (1 oz.) sugar
30 g. (1 oz.) butter
1 cup boiling water

Rub butter in flour, add baking powder and make paste. Roll out, spread jam, roll up and put in a Pyrex dish leaving plenty of room. Melt sugar and butter in boiling water, pour it over the Roly-Poly and cook for ¾ hour.

Treacle Tart

short pastry
juice of ½ a lemon (or 1 teaspoon
ground ginger if preferred)

treacle or golden syrup
½ cup breadcrumbs

Line a plate with the pastry. Fill with treacle or syrup, bread-crumbs and lemon juice mixed together. Bake in a hot oven.
Temp. 220°C (425°F).

Welsh Cheese Cakes

Pastry
125 g. (4 oz.) flour
pinch of salt
rind of ½ lemon
pinch of baking powder

Mixture
60 g. (2 oz.) butter or lard
water to mix jam
1 egg and its weight in
butter, sugar and flour

Make short pastry and roll out thinly. Cut into rounds. Line patty tins with pastry and put a little jam in each. Beat butter and sugar to a cream, add egg, flour, etc. Put one teaspoon of the mixture on top of jam. Bake in hot oven.
Temp. 220°C (425°F).

BREAD AND SCONES

Use of Dried Yeast

When a tin of yeast is opened it should be stored in the cool section of the refrigerator. For use, the dried yeast must always be allowed to stand in warm water, undisturbed, for about 10 minutes, or until soft, before being mixed into the flour for a dough.

Dried yeast is more active than fresh yeast. This is because when 30 g. (1 oz.) of dry yeast is reconstituted with water it is equivalent to about 40 g. (1⅜ oz.) of fresh yeast, and recipes should be adjusted accordingly.

In breadmaking remember that all utensils and ingredients must be kept just warm. Great heat spoils yeast and it will not work if cold.

Never put warm bread in a confined space such as a bread tin. Such bread is likely to go bad within a day or so.

See page 5 for hints on **Baking at high altitudes**.

To have scones nice and light, mix quickly, handle as little as possible and bake as soon as possible in a hot oven. Cakes, biscuits, etc., made with baking powder should not be mixed with sour milk or acid of any kind. Those mixed with bicarbonate of soda must always have acid added, such as sour milk or cream of tartar, and they should be baked quickly after being mixed, whilst the powders used for raising are still effervescing. When baked, stand on table for a minute before removing from the tin. Put on wire tray and cover with a clean cloth till cold or roll in a clean cloth.

Sour milk is much to be preferred to fresh in mixing scones, pancakes, soda bread, soda cakes and steamed puddings. Bicarbonate and cream of tartar (not baking powder) ought to be used as raising along with sour milk. The more acid that has developed in the milk, the less cream of tartar is required.

Home made Bread-Overnight Method

Process: Overnight cold water sponge.

INGREDIENTS FOR SPONGE

4 level teaspoons dried yeast   875 g. (1 lb. 12 oz.) plain flour
600 ml. (1 pint) cold water

Disperse the dried yeast in the cold water and then mix in the flour. A soft dough will be obtained which is allowed to rise in a cool place overnight or from 12—24 hours. During this time the sponge will more than treble volume and then collapse. Only after the sponge has collapsed will it be ready for the doughmaking part of the process.

This sponge will require a 4 litre (6 pt.) size saucepan or a 25 cm. (10 inch) diameter sufuria and during its fermentation should be covered by saucepan lid or damp cloth.

INGREDIENTS FOR DOUGHMAKING

750 g. (1 lb. 8 oz.) plain flour
4 level teaspoons salt
2 level teaspoons sugar
1 level teaspoon butter, lard or oil (if required)
300 ml. (½ pint) water

METHOD

Dissolve the sugar and salt in the water and pour this liquid into the sponge. If fat is being used this should be rubbed into the flour. The flour placed on a table and a bay formed into which is poured the sponge and liquids. Gradually mix the flour into the watery part of the mixture until no free liquid shows. Then with both hands and fingers wide apart shake the mixture together until a dough starts to form. When this stage is reached stretch and knead the dough until it is quite smooth. Return the dough to the container in which the sponge fermented and allow the dough to ferment in a cool place until double in size. Divide the dough into 620 g. (1 lb. 3 oz.) pieces for 500 g. (1 lb.) loaves.

Roll out each piece of dough to 6 mm. (¼ inch) thickness and as wide as the length of the tin to be used. Each piece of dough is then rolled up in the form of a swiss roll and placed closing downwards into the prepared baking tin. To prepare the baking tin clean it thoroughly with a dry cloth then smear a very little butter or fat on the baking surface. Rub this smear of fat thoroughly into the surface of the baking tin.

Prove the loaves in a warm place until nearly three times original volume. Keep the dough surface covered with a damp cloth to prevent a skin forming.

Bake the loaves in a hot oven 230°C. (450°F.) for about 45 minutes. Cool loaves thoroughly before placing in a bread storage tin.

White Bread-Quick Method
Stage 1.

INGREDIENTS FOR SPONGE

875 g. (1 lb. 12 oz.) plain flour
15 g. (½ oz.) dried yeast
   (two heaped teaspoons)

480 ml. (¾ pint) water at blood
   heat 36.9°C (98.4°F).
10 g. (¼ oz.) sugar (one level
   teaspoon)

METHOD OF MAKING SPONGE

(1) Place the water into a mixing bowl, add the yeast and sugar and allow the yeast to melt down for five minutes.

(2) Add the flour and mix until a smooth dough has been formed.

(3) Cover the bowl with a damp cloth and leave in a warm place for one and a half hours.

Stage 2.

INGREDIENTS FOR DOUGH—to be added to the sponge previously prepared.

435 g. (14 oz.) plain flour
220 g. (7 oz.) water
15g. (½ oz.) sugar (one level
   tablespoon)

25 g. (¾ oz.) margarine (one level
   tablespoon)
15 g. (½ oz.) salt (four level
   teaspoons)

METHOD OF MAKING DOUGH

(1)   Firstly rub the fat into the flour and dissolve the sugar and salt in the water.

(2)   Add the water to the sponge and mix in.

(3)   Now add the flour and mix all to a smooth dough.

(4)   Again cover the bowl and dough, with a damp cloth and allow to stand for 45 minutes in a warm place.

Stage 3.

MAKING THE BREAD

Divide the dough into four equal parts, each approximately 500 g. (one pound) in weight. Roll the rough pieces into a ball shape and allow to rest on the table covered with a damp cloth for ten minutes. Finally shape the dough pieces to fit the baking tins. Place the baking tins containing the dough into a warm cupboard or on top of the oven, until the dough has approximately doubled in size, this will take about 50 minutes. Wash lightly over the tops of the bread with a mixture of egg and milk and bake in a hot oven 230°C (450°F) for 30 minutes.

Brown Bread (with yeast)

250 g. (8 oz.) plain flour
25 g. (¾ oz.) dried yeast
   (3 heaped teaspoons)
300 ml. (½ pint) water at
   blood heat 36.9°C. (98.4°F.)
1 dessertspoon black treacle or
   syrup

15 g. (½ oz.) margarine (one level
   tablespoon)
15 g. (½ oz.) salt (four level
   teaspoons)
150 ml. (¼ pint) water at
   blood heat 36.9°C (98.4°F)
500 g. (1 lb.) wholemeal flour

METHOD

(1)   Place 300 ml. (½ pint) water into a mixing bowl, add the yeast and syrup and allow the yeast to melt down for about five minutes. Add the plain flour and beat with a wooden spoon to form a soft sponge.

(2)   Weigh the wholemeal and put this down one side of the mixing bowl. Place the margarine and salt on top of the wholemeal and set the bowl in a warm place such as an airing cupboard for 20 minutes.

(3)   Rub the margarine into the wholemeal. Add a further 150 ml. (¼ pint) warm water and mix all until a smooth dough is formed.

(4) Rest the dough for a further 15 minutes, then cut into three equal parts at about 440 g. (14 oz.) each. Mould the dough into the required shapes and place either on baking trays or into bread tins. Brush the surface with egg.

(5) Allow the shaped pieces to stand until about double their original size, this will take about 30 minutes.

(6) Place the dough pieces into a hot oven 225°C. (440.°F) and bake approximately for 30 minutes.

Brown Bread (without yeast)

1 teacup flour	3 teacups wheaten flour
1 teaspoon salt	¾ teaspoon bicarbonate soda
1 teaspoon cream of tartar	1 tablespoon syrup
sweet milk	

Mix dry ingredients, add syrup and sufficent sweet milk to make dough not too stiff. Grease tin and put in mixture. Cover with second tin, not flat in order to allow bread to rise, and bake in hot oven, ½ to ¾ hour.

Bread Boston

(a)

1 cup whole wheat flour	3 teaspoons baking powder
1 cup corn meal	1 teaspoon salt
1 cup rye meal or ground	¾ cup dark molasses
rolled oats	1 cup milk

Mix dry ingredients thoroughly. Add molasses to milk and add this to the dry ingredients. Beat thoroughly and put into greased moulds ⅔ full. Cover tightly and steam 3½ hours. Remove covers and bake in moderate oven until top is dry. This makes one large or three small loaves.

(b).

2½ cups flour	1½ cups mixed fruits (raisins
1½ cups milk	nuts, etc.)
¾ cup golden syrup	
heaped teaspoon bicarbonate of soda	

Clean the fruit and chop the nuts. Mix all the ingredients together and fill two 500 g. (1 lb.) round tins ¾ full. Steam for 3 hours.

Bread Cake

375 g. (¾ lb.) dough	185 g. (6 oz.) sugar
2 or 3 eggs	185 g. (6 oz.) lard or butter
dried fruits	vanilla essence and cinnamon

Take the dough from the bread bowl, after the bread has been kneaded ready for bread tins. Add the eggs, sugar, lard or butter, fruit, flavouring and cinnamon. Beat well and leave for ½ hour to rise. Put into two tins and bake for 45 minutes.

Bread Cottage (without yeast)

500 g. (1 lb.) sifted flour 1 teaspoon soda bicarbonate
1 teaspoon salt sour milk
(If no sour milk put two teaspoons cream of tartar.)

Sift the flour into a mixing bowl, mix in thoroughly the soda and salt, add sufficient sour milk to make a stiff dough, knead well, shape into breadcakes and bake for 1 hour.

This recipe for quickly made bread without yeast is particularly suitable for housewives in isolated places where fresh bread may be a little difficult to secure. Others will find it a pleasant change from the orthodox baker's loaf.

Bread Vienna

500 g. (1 lb.) flour 2 tablespoons yeast
300 ml. (½ pint) milk 30 g. (1 oz.) butter
30 g. (1 oz.) salt 1 teaspoon sugar
1 egg (if liked)

Melt the butter in the milk and make it lukewarm. Add sugar and salt to the milk, then the yeast and all the liquid to the flour; add beaten egg. Knead well and leave to rise till double its size (about 8 hours), knead lightly and make up into fancy shapes, cottage loaves, etc. Leave to rise for 20 minutes, then bake in a very hot oven for 15 minutes. Brush over with a little of the butter and milk to glaze them or they can be brushed with egg before baking.

Breakfast Rolls

(a)

500 g. (1 lb.) flour 1 teaspoon sugar
60 g. (2 oz.) butter 300 ml. (½ pint) tepid water
15 g. (½ oz.) dried yeast

Sieve the flour into a basin and rub in the butter lightly. While doing this, lift the flour well from the basin to allow the air to mix with it and to prevent the butter becoming soft. Make a well in the centre. In a smaller basin work together with a wooden spoon until creamy the dried yeast and sugar. When smooth pour on them the tepid water and strain the mixture into the centre of the flour. Mix the dough quickly, turn on to a well-floured board and knead until free from flouriness. Form into small rolls; this quantity will make 12. Put them on to a greased and floured tin to rise in a warm place for about 1 hour. Bake for 20 to 25 minutes until brown and crisp.

(b)

500 g. (1 lb.) flour 1 tablespoon butter
salt to taste 1 tablespoon baking powder
300 ml. (½ pint) milk

Rub butter into flour and mix into a stiff dough with milk. Make into rolls and allow to rise for 20 minutes in a warm place. Bake in a quick oven.

Bath Buns

250 g. (½ lb.) flour
60 g. (2 oz.) butter
15 g. (½ oz.) yeast
75 ml. (½ gill) milk

30 g. (1 oz.) lemon peel
1 large (1) egg
30 g. (1 oz.) sugar

Mix yeast with teaspoonful sugar and milk to warm and prove. Put to rise with the flour for ½ an hour. Melt the butter and add the egg, sugar and prepared fruit. Roll and place on well-greased flat tin. Allow to rise. Make into small buns. Bake in a moderate oven.

Hot Cross Buns
Stage 1. Ferment.

150 ml. (¼ pint) boiling milk
150 ml. (¼ pint) cold water
3 rounded tablespoons home baking flour
2 level tablespoons sugar
2 level dessertspoons dried yeast

Place the boiling milk and cold water into a 2.5 litre (4 pint) basin, add the yeast and allow it to soften. Finally stir in the flour and sugar. When the ferment is working vigorously it is ready to use. This will take approx. 10 minutes.

Stage 2.

To the ferment add the following:—
625 g. (1 lb. 4 oz.) flour
4 level tablespoons butter
2 rounded tablespoons sugar
2 medium eggs
1 level teaspoon salt
6 rounded tablespoons currants
1 rounded tablespoon mixed cut peel
½ teaspoon mixed spice
1 teaspoon cinnamon
lemon juice

Sieve the spices with the flour then rub in the butter. Make a bay and add the eggs, sugar and salt. Mix until a smooth dough is formed. Allow to rise to double volume then fold in the washed fruit, rest for ten minutes and divide into required size pieces. Make each piece round by rolling the dough on the table between cupped hands. Place onto a warm fat-smeared tray, allowing sufficient space between the buns to allow them to double in size without touching.

Cover the trays with a dry cloth and then allow the buns to prove until they are nearly touching.

Whilst the buns are rising prepare a piece of wood or stout card 5 cm. (2 in.) square, 3 mm. (⅛ in.) thick, making one edge smooth and slightly tapered.

To make the crosses, press down this smooth edge into and across the centre of the bun as far as the baking tray. Repeat at right angles to form the across marking. Glaze the buns with egg. Allow the buns to rise for a further 30 minutes in a warm humid place. Bake in a hot oven for approximately 15 minutes, or until they are a rich golden brown.

Depending on the size of the buns this recipe will produce between 20 and 30 Hot Cross Buns.

Bun Loaf

875 g. (1¾ lb.) flour
250 g. (½ lb.) currants
250 g. (½ lb.) raisins
185 g. (6 oz.) butter
185 g. (6 oz.) candied peel

480 ml. (¾ pint) water at
  blood heat 36.9°C (98.4°F).
185 g. (6 oz.) brown sugar
2 heaped teaspoons yeast
½ teaspoon mixed spice
  nutmeg

Rub butter into flour and add dry ingredients. Then mix as for white bread-quick method: Stage 2 (*see* page 171).

Milk Rolls

1.2 kg. (2 lb. 6 oz.) plain flour
15 g. (½ oz.) dried yeast
15 g. (½ oz.) salt
80 g. (2½ oz.) white fat

10 g. (¼ oz.) sugar
60 g. (2 oz.) milk powder
600 ml. (1 pint) water
  (warm to about blood heat)

METHOD OF MAKING DOUGH

(1) Place the yeast and water into the mixing bowl and allow to stand for 10 minutes.

(2) Add the salt, sugar and milk powder and whisk into the water.

(3) Add flour and then fat and mix until a close dough has been formed.

(4) Allow the dough to stand in the mixing bowl for two hours, cover with a damp tea-cloth.

MAKING THE ROLLS

(1) Weigh off 45 g. (1½ oz.) pieces and mould each piece into a ball shape and place them on a floured board.

(2) Cover with a warm cloth for ten minutes.

(3) Roll these round pieces out 20 to 25 cm. (eight to ten inches) long and twist into shapes as desired, and place on a lightly greased tray.

(4) Wash the rolls with an equal mixture of egg and milk.

(5) Leave the rolls until they have partly risen to about double their original size. This will take about 40–45 minutes.

(6) Now place the rolls in a hot oven 230°–260°C (450°–470°F) and leave approximately 15 minutes until they are a nice light golden colour.

This recipe will yield about 42 bread rolls.

Milk Loaf

6 tablespoons flour
1 tablespoon butter
pinch of salt
a few sultanas (if liked)

1 tablespoon sugar
2 eggs
2 teaspoons baking powder

Rub butter into flour and add eggs beaten. Handle lightly and cut into scones or make into loaf.

Muffins (American)

2 large cups flour
3 level teaspoons baking
  powder
1 egg
3 tablespoons sugar
2 tablespoons melted butter
1 cup milk

Mix dry ingredients and add milk, eggs, butter. Grease three 250 g. (½ lb.) baking·tins and half fill them with the mixture. Cover with lids and bake in a fairly hot oven for 25 minutes. When cold, cut in slices and butter.

Date Loaf

375 g. (12 oz.) chopped dates
1 cup sugar
3 teaspoons bicarbonate of soda
1 tablespoon butter
3 cups flour
2 cups boiling water

Pour 2 cups of boiling water on to the butter, dates, sugar and bicarbonate of soda. Add 3 cups of sieved flour and put into a greased loaf tin (1 kg. [2 lb.] size) or into two (500 g. [1 lb.] size) and bake in a moderate oven for an hour.

Rusks

12 cups flour
½ lb. butter
a little salt
3 cups sugar
2 cups yeast

Dissolve sugar and butter in about two cups warm water; add yeast, then pour over flour. Mix well. Make into small buns and keep in warm place to rise. Bake in fairly hot oven about 35 minutes. When cool break into halves and dry out in a warm oven.

Sally Lunns or Cookies

750 g. (¾ lb.) flour
15 g. (½ oz.) dried yeast
60 g. (2 oz.) butter
1 egg
300 ml. (½ pint) milk
a pinch of salt
1 teaspoon sugar for creaming the yeast

Have the flour very dry, sift it into a warm basin, add the salt and make a well in the centre. With a wooden spoon work the yeast and sugar together until smooth. Put the butter and milk into a saucepan and when lukewarm pour over the yeast. The milk must not be hot or it will kill the power of the yeast. When well mixed, strain this liquid into the centre of the flour, then add the well-beaten egg and with the hand mix all the ingredients together. Cover the basin with a cloth and let the dough rise in a warm place for about ¾ hour. Now turn the dough on to a well-floured board and knead lightly until it is free from cracks and flouriness. Grease and flour two or more shallow cake tins, put the dough in and set the tins on the rack to allow the cakes to rise again, for 15 minutes. Bake in a hot oven about 20 minutes until brown and firm to the touch. If it is desired to give the cakes a gloss, they should be brushed over with milk and sugar a few minutes before being removed from the oven.

Scones Aberdeen

500 g. (½ lb.) flour
pinch of salt
60 g. (2 oz.) butter
buttermilk or sour milk

½ teaspoon bicarbonate of soda
½ teaspoon cream of tartar
1 egg

Sieve the flour into a warm basin with the salt, soda and cream of tartar. Rub in the butter with the tips of the fingers and when free from lumps make a well in the centre of the flour. Into this put the beaten egg and enough buttermilk or sour milk to form a dough. Let the mixing be done quickly and then turn the dough out on a floured board. After kneading it lightly, form it, without the help of the rolling pin, into a round cake. Mark this into 4 with the back of a knife and bake for 20 minutes in a hot oven. These quarters should be split open, buttered and served very hot.

Scones Brown

250 g. (8 oz.) meal or bran
60 g. (2 oz.) flour
125 g. (4 oz.) butter
1 egg
nearly a cup of milk

1 tablespoon castor sugar
2 teaspoons cream of tartar
1 teaspoon bicarbonate of soda

Rub together all dry ingredients; add the egg and milk. Do not make too thick. Cut and bake in a hot oven.

Scones Cream

250 g. (½ lb.) flour
1 teaspoon baking powder
150 ml. (1 gill) fresh cream

30 g. (1 oz.) butter
1 egg

Rub dry ingredients together. Beat egg and add the amount of cream required, which largely depends on the dryness of the flour. Mix to a stiff dough; handle lightly. Bake in a quick oven.

Scones Drop

8 tablespoons flour
2 small teaspoons baking powder
1 teacup milk

1 or 2 eggs
¼ flat teaspoon salt
1 dessertspoon golden syrup
1 dessertspoon sugar (if desired)

Sieve the flour and salt into a basin. Make well in centre and add egg. Mix to smooth batter, adding syrup and milk as required. Beat very well. Add sugar and lastly baking powder. Drop mixture in small rounds on hot greased girdle. When surface rises in bubbles turn with knife and cook the other side. Cool in a clean cloth.

Scones Farmhouse or Girdle

1½ breakfast cups flour
½ teaspoon bicarbonate of soda
sour milk, cream, or buttermilk

salt
a little sugar (if liked)

Mix into a stiff dough. Roll out, cut, and bake in quick oven.

Scones Kenyan

1½ breakfast cups flour
1 tablespoon butter
milk

1 heaped teaspoon baking
powder
1 egg

Rub pinch of salt, sugar, baking powder and butter into the flour. Beat the egg and add milk to make a cupful. Mix to a light dough, cut into rounds and bake in quick oven.

Scones Potato

2 tablespoons flour
small cube of butter
1 pinch bicarbonate of soda
salt

1 pinch cream of tartar
3 freshly boiled potatoes
(average size)
milk

Rub butter into flour and add soda, salt and cream of tartar. Mix to a soft dough with milk (sour milk is preferable to fresh). Mash potatoes well and add to the dough. Dredge a board well with flour, as potato dough is apt to stick. Lift about a tablespoon of the dough on to the board and roll as thinly as possible; cut in four pieces, prick, and bake very quickly on a very hot girdle. When one side is baked turn and brown the other side. Have a clean cloth ready on a wire sieve, and as the scones are removed from the girdle place in the cloth, one on top of the other, and wrap up well for a short time to keep in the steam, otherwise the scones will be tough. Then open out and allow scones to dry. Potatoes left over from a meal can be used up in this way, but should be slightly warmed and made up in the proportion of 2 tablespoons potatoes to 1 of dough.

For maize meal scones *see* page 120

Scotch Pancakes

8 heaped tablespoons flour
2 eggs
1 level teaspoon bicarbonate
of soda

3 level tablespoons sugar
1 teacup milk
2 level teaspoons cream of
tartar

Beat eggs and sugar to a cream and add ½ of the milk. Put dry ingredients in a bowl. Make a hole in the centre of these and pour in the eggs, etc. Stir carefully and if necessary add the rest of the milk. Drop spoonfuls on smoking hot greased girdle. Turn and brown other side. Cool on a clean cloth.

Care must be taken not to over-grease the girdle; a lump of butter in a muslin bag is the best way to grease.

Sour Milk Girdle Cakes

2 cups flour
2 cups sour milk
1 egg

½ teaspoon salt
1 heaped teaspoon soda

Mix and sift all dry ingredients. Add sour milk and egg well beaten. Drop by spoonfuls on a greased hot girdle (or a frying pan), cook on one side. When puffed and full of bubbles, turn and cook on the other side. Serve with butter and, if liked, some syrup.

Syrup Scones

250 g. (8 oz.) flour
1 level teaspoon
  cream of tartar
30 g. (1 oz.) lard
2 level tablespoons syrup

1 level teaspoon bicarbonate
  of soda
pinch of salt
60 g. (2 oz.) seeded raisins
a little milk

Sieve the dry ingredients, rub in the lard, add the raisins and stir in the warmed syrup with just enough milk to make a soft dough. Roll out lightly to 1 cm. (½ inch) thickness, cut into rounds and place on a floured tray and bake in a hot oven 260°C (500°F), for 10 minutes or until well risen and brown. Wrap in a clean towel.

Yeast made with Potatoes

3 large potatoes
1 handful hops
1 tablespoon sugar

2 bottles cold water
1 tablespoon flour
½ tablespoon salt

Wash and cut up the potatoes with skins on. Boil in cold water with the hops. When potatoes are done, mash and leave to cool. Then strain and pour liquid on to flour, sugar, salt. Put into 2 bottles, ¾ full, and tie corks down. Leave for 3 days in a warm kitchen, when the yeast will be ready. This keeps good for 3 weeks, and when making a second brew, put into the yeasty bottles and it will rise in a few hours.

Baking Powder (Home-made)

60 g. (2 oz.) cream of tartar   30 g. (1 oz.) bicarbonate of soda
30 g. (1 oz.) rice flour

Mix all ingredients, rub three times through a hair sieve. Store in airtight tin.

CAKES

Secrets of Good Cake Making

(a) Before commencing to make a fruit cake, all fruit should be well washed and dried and then picked over. Damp fruit makes a cake heavy, so prepare fruit a few hours before mixing a cake. Remove sugar from candied peel before chopping it up.

(b) When mixing a fruit cake, care must be taken not to make it too wet, otherwise the fruit will sink.

(c) When creaming butter and sugar the butter may first be slightly warmed, but not oiled. Sugar and butter should always be very well beaten together until the texture and colour is that of thick cream.

(d) Always add eggs before flour.

(e) When beating eggs and sugar together, beat until white and free from streaks. The white speck in eggs should always be removed before commencing to beat.

(f) It is always advisable to break eggs separately before adding to others, as one bad egg will spoil the rest. Remember, too, that the object of beating is to introduce air into the mixture to cause lightness. Remember cake mixtures should never be beaten after baking powder has been introduced.

(g) Small cakes and buns require a quick oven all the time. Divide period of baking large cakes into three.

(1) Oven should only be moderately hot and place cake in lower part of oven so that the underheat will help it to rise to its fullest height before it starts to brown.

(2) When cake is risen, increase heat to form a crust and brown top.

(3) During third period reduce heat until cake is thoroughly cooked in the centre. Avoid opening the oven door too often, and for the first $\frac{1}{2}$ hour not at all. Never slam an oven door when food is being cooked in the oven, as at once the temperature is changed. Before removing a cake from the oven, test it by inserting a clean skewer, or a knife, into the centre. If the cake is sufficiently cooked the skewer or knife will come out dry.

(h) Sponge cakes and Swiss rolls require a very quick oven. Never turn out a sponge roll or layer cakes on to a plain cloth or paper. Sprinkle cloth or paper with castor sugar before turning out cakes.

(i) A dish of hot water in the oven when a cake is baking prevents the cake becoming too dry.

(j) Should there be any difficulty in removing a cake from the tin in which it has been cooked, place the tin on a damp cloth for a few minutes. The cake will then turn out easily.

(k) When making a gingerbread do not make the syrup or treacle very hot or the cake will be tough. Keep the oven at a steady heat, but not too fierce, as syrup and treacle burn easily.

(l) In addition to greasing cake tins, sprinkle them with mixed cornflour and castor sugar, and the cake, when cooked, will have a nice glaze.

(m) Should you want to use fewer eggs in any cake recipe, allow $\frac{1}{2}$ teaspoonful more baking powder and two tablespoonfuls more liquid for each egg left out; or a small quantity of vinegar can be used as a substitute.

Alma Cakes

2 tablespoons flour
1 tablespoon sugar
2 tablespoons butter or
   margarine
a pinch of salt

1 egg
½ teaspoon baking powder
apricot jam

Cream the butter and sugar and stir in the beaten egg and salt. Gradually add 2 tablespoons of flour with baking powder. Beat thoroughly and put into buttered patty pans. Bake in a hot oven till pale brown. Turn out, and when cool spread with apricot jam and castor sugar. Return to the oven until the jam is set.
Temp. 205°C (400°F)—10–15 minutes.

Almond Fingers

250 g. (½ lb.) flour
155 g. (5 oz.) butter
125 g. (4 oz.) castor sugar

60 g. (2 oz.) ground almonds
¼ teaspoon cinnamon
1 egg yolk

Rub butter into flour. Mix spice, ground almonds and sugar together and add to the flour. Beat yolk of egg with a little cold water and with it form the mixture into a stiff dough. Roll out into a long narrow strip, about 12 cm. (4½ inches) wide. Cut off a narrow strip, about 1 cm. (½ inch) wide, from each side of the strip and lay on top of the large strip along the edges. Put on baking sheet and bake in a good oven till nearly done.   *Temp. 205°C (400°F)—15–20 minutes.*
Before it is quite done fill with the following mixture.
Filling:

250 g. (½ lb.) sugar
3 whites of egg

90 g. (3 oz.) almonds (whole)
2 heaped teaspoons
   cinnamon

Cut almonds in 3 and put them into a small lined pan with the sugar and unbeaten whites of eggs. Stir continually till boiling, then add the cinnamon and mix well. Pour down the centre of the strip of pastry, leaving the raised edges clear, and finish off in the oven. When cracked and firm on the top take out and cut in fingers while hot and cool on a wire tray.

Angel Cake

60 g. (2 oz.) flour
1 teaspoon cream of tartar
pinch of salt

½ teaspoon almond essence
5 whites of egg
90 g. (3 oz.) sugar

Dry and sieve flour and cream of tartar several times. Add pinch of salt to white of eggs and beat to a stiff froth. Sieve sugar and fold it lightly in. Then the flour the same way and lastly the flavouring.

Do not stop beating and keep mixture light. Bake in a floured but ungreased tin in a moderate oven. When ready, turn the cake upside down on a sheet of paper and leave in tin until it can easily be slipped out.   *Temp. 175°C (350°F)—30 minutes.*

Applesauce Cake

3 cups sifted flour
2 teaspoons baking powder
¼ teaspoon salt
2 teaspoons cinnamon
1½ teaspoons cloves
2 cups chopped nuts

2 cups chopped raisins
1 cup chopped dates
½ cup butter or margarine
¾ cup packed brown sugar
2 eggs well beaten
2 cups thick applesauce

Mix and sift flour, baking powder, salt and spices. Mix about ½ a cup with nuts and fruit. Cream shortening, gradually add sugar creaming on till fluffy, then beat in eggs. Add flour mixture alternately with applesauce, beating well after each addition. Beat in fruit and nut mixture, turn into greased tins and bake in a moderately slow oven.

Temp. 165°C (325°F)—1 hour.

Apricot Baskets

90 g. (3 oz.) butter or margarine
90 g. (3 oz.) castor sugar
90 g. (3 oz.) flour
¼ teaspoon (a pinch) of baking
  powder
pistachio nuts or browned
  coconut

2 eggs
vanilla
apricot jam
lemon juice (or grated
  lemon rind)
angelica
cream

Cream the butter and sugar. Add the eggs. Beat the mixture thoroughly. Add flour, vanilla essence, and lemon. Half fill small deep tins with the mixture and bake in a hot oven. When cool cut out centres and coat with warm jam. Roll in chopped pistachio nuts or browned coconut. Put apricot jam or half an apricot in hollow in centre. Fill with whipped cream. Make handles of angelica.

Temp. 205°C (400°F)—15 minutes.

Birthday Cake Rich

750 g. (¾ lb.) flour
250 g. (½ lb.) castor sugar
250 g. (½ lb.) butter
250 g. (½ lb.) sultanas
250 g. (½ lb.) stoned raisins
250 g. (½ lb.) cherries
80 ml. (½ gill) milk

125 g. (¼ lb.) blanched almonds
125 g. (¼ lb.) mixed peel
rind of two lemons
10 g. (¼ oz.) allspice
1¼ (1) teaspoon baking powder
½ teaspoon salt
8 eggs

Line the cake tin with three thicknesses of white buttered paper. Clean and stone fruit; blanch and chop almonds; chop peel; grate lemon rind; and mix all together. Cream butter and sugar; well whisk the eggs; and add to butter and sugar. Sift flour, baking powder and salt, and add a little at a time. Lastly stir in remainder of dry ingredients and moisten with milk. Put mixture in a tin, cover with greased paper, and bake in a moderate oven from 2 to 2½ hours. Ice next day.
Temp. 175°C (350°F).

Butter Sponge

weight of 3 eggs in
  butter, sugar, and flour

1 teaspoon baking powder
2 tablespoons milk

Cream butter and sugar together, add eggs separately, and then flour, putting in baking powder with last quantity of flour. Bake in two tins in moderate oven. When cold put filling or jam in between and ice top if desired. *Temp. 205°C (400°F)—20–30 minutes.*

Buttons

90 g. (3 oz.) sugar
90 g. (3 oz.) butter or margarine
180 g. (6 oz.) flour
1 egg
½ teaspoon baking powder

Beat butter and sugar to a cream. Add the egg. Then add flour and baking powder. Beat well. Drop small spoonfuls on a hot greased tin, leaving space between the balls for rising. Sprinkle sugar on top before baking and bake in a moderate oven.

Temp. 205°C (400°F)—10–15 minutes.

Cherry Cake

1 teacup butter or margarine
1½ teacups sugar
4 eggs
1 cup crystallised cherries cut in halves
3 cups flour
1 teaspoon baking powder
1 cup milk

Cream the sugar and butter. Beat and add the yolks of the eggs. Add the flour, baking powder and milk. Add the cherries and lastly the whites of the eggs, beaten stiffly. Bake. Ice with white icing and decorate with cherries. *Temp. 190°C (375°F)—¾ hour.*

Chocolate Cake

250 g. (½ lb.) butter or margarine
1 level breakfast cup white
  sugar
¾ cup hot water
1 teaspoon soda
½ teaspoon vanilla essence
4 eggs
2 level cups flour
2 teaspoons cream of tartar
4 level tablespoons cocoa

Beat butter and sugar to a cream and add eggs well beaten. Mix flour, soda and cream of tartar, and add cocoa. Now add hot water to mixture of butter, sugar, and eggs; add vanilla essence; sift in flour, etc., very gently. When well mixed put in a greased tin and bake in bottom shelf of hot oven.

Temp. 175°C (350°F)—40 minutes.

Chocolate Cream Buns

30 g. (1 oz.) butter or margarine
castor sugar
80 ml. (½ gill) water
40 g. (1¼ oz.) flour
1 egg
vanilla essence
whipped cream (for filling)
chocolate icing

Put the butter and water into a pan. When the butter has melted and the mixture is boiling well, add the flour and stir quickly. Let it cook steadily for about 8 to 10 minutes, stirring all the time. Remove to the side of the stove and let it cool slightly, then beat in the egg and add the flavouring. Put this mixture in small round portions on to a greased baking sheet, using about a dessertspoonful for each. Bake in a moderately hot oven for about 20 minutes until biscuit coloured. When cooked put on a wire tray and leave till cool. Whisk some cream until it stiffens, sweeten with castor sugar and flavour with vanilla. Make a small opening in each bun and put in some of the cream. Stand the buns on a cake rack over a dish and coat with chocolate icing. *Temp. 205°C (400°F).*

Chocolate Coconut Cakes

60 g. (2 oz.) cocoa
250 g. (½ lb.) flour
1¼ (1) teaspoon baking powder
1 egg
milk

185 g. (6 oz.) castor sugar
125 g. (¼ lb.) butter or margarine
30 g. (1 oz.) desiccated coconut
vanilla essence

Sieve the flour, cocoa and baking powder. Add the coconut and mix together. Beat the sugar and butter to a cream. Add the egg, stir it in quickly and beat for a few minutes. Stir in the dry ingredients with some milk as required and mix all together. Add a few drops of vanilla. Put in small greased cake tins, or baking cups, and bake in a hot oven about 15 to 20 minutes. *Temp. 205°C (400°F).*

Chocolate Gâteau

90 g. (3 oz.) butter or margarine
155 g. (5 oz.) flour
½ to ¾ teaspoon baking powder

155 g. (5 oz.) castor sugar
45 g. (1½ oz.) cocoa
3 eggs

Sieve cocoa, flour and baking powder together. Cream butter and sugar. Add each egg separately, stir it in quickly and beat well before adding the next. When all are added stir in the flour, cocoa and baking powder and mix together lightly. Put in a greased cake tin and bake in a moderately hot oven for about 40 minutes. Put on a rack until cold. *Temp. 205°C (400°F).*

Butter filling:
250 g. (8 oz.) icing sugar
125 g. (4 oz.) butter

vanilla

Roll the lumps out of the sugar then rub it through a fine sieve. Add the butter and beat both to a cream. Add vanilla to taste. Split the cake into halves, spread the butter icing, then replace together.

Chocolate icing:
125 g. (¼ lb.) icing sugar
30 g. (1 oz.) cocoa

1 tablespoon boiling water
vanilla

If the cake has risen in the centre it is better to cut off a slice and turn it upside down before icing it. Sieve the cocoa and icing sugar and add the boiling water carefully until the icing is of the right consistency. Add vanilla to flavour.

Chocolate Maids of Honour

375 g. (¾ lb.) flaky pastry (use as required)
2 teaspoons cocoa or chocolate
75 g. (2½ oz.) castor sugar
1 egg
jam

weight of egg in ground rice and butter
almond or vanilla flavouring
chocolate icing (*see* Icings)
3 or 4 pistachio nuts for decoration

Roll out the pastry rather thinly, cut into rounds and line about 12 patty pans. Put a very small quantity of jam in the bottom of each.

Mix the ground rice and cocoa together. Beat the sugar and butter to a cream. Separate the yolk from the white of egg. Whisk the white to a very stiff froth. Stir the yolk into the creamed butter and sugar and beat well for a few minutes. Add the ground rice, cocoa, and flavouring to taste, and mix together. Add the whisked white and fold in lightly. Put a small quantity of mixture into each patty pan. Stand them on a baking sheet and bake in a very hot oven for about 15 minutes. When cold, make some chocolate icing and ice the tops. Decorate the centres with a slice of blanched pistachio nuts.

Temp. 230°C (450°F).

Chocolate Nut Fingers

200/250 g. (6 or 8 oz.) flaky pastry
125 g. (¼ lb.) castor sugar
30 g. (1 oz.) ground rice
white of 1 egg
30 g. (1 oz.) almonds

1 dessertspoon cocoa or chocolate
60 g. (2 oz.) ground almonds
vanilla or almond flavouring
apricot jam

Roll out the pastry thinly and line the bottom of a small baking tin. Blanch, skin and chop up the almonds. Mix the cocoa, ground rice, sugar and almonds together. Whisk the white of egg to a stiff froth and add with a few drops of flavouring. Mix all to a soft paste; if necessary a little water may be added. Spread just a very thin layer of jam over the pastry, then cover with the prepared mixture and spread evenly. Brush the surface over with water and sprinkle the chopped almonds on top. Bake in a hot oven for about 15 to 20 minutes. When almost cooked, froth up a little white of egg extra to that given in the recipe and brush the mixture over with it. Then dredge freely with castor sugar. Return to the oven for a few minutes until lightly browned, then place on a sieve to cool. Put on to a flat surface and cut into fingers with a sharp knife.
Temp. 230°C (450°F).

Chocolate Petits Fours

30 g. (1 oz.) cocoa or chocolate
95 g. (3 oz.) ground almonds
125 g. (4 oz.) icing sugar
vanilla flavouring

about ¾ to 1 white of egg
a few glacé cherries
30 g. (1 oz.) shelled walnuts

Chop the walnuts very finely. Rub the lumps out of the sugar and put it through a sieve. Add the cocoa, walnuts and ground almonds and mix together. Whisk the white of egg slightly and add to the dry ingredients as required. Mix all to a stiff paste, together with a few drops of vanilla. When well mixed work it until smooth, then divide into about 16 portions. Roll each piece in the palm of your hand and make into a smooth round shape. Then press your little finger in the centre, not through the bottom, and make a small hole. Put on a plate and brush the sides over with yolk of egg to glacé them. Stick ½ a cherry in the centre. Put on top of the browning shelf in a cool oven to dry for about 15 minutes.

Chocolate Roll

90 g. (3 oz.) flour	1½ dessertspoons cocoa
90 g. (3 oz.) castor sugar	½ teaspoon baking powder
2 eggs	1 tablespoon hot water

Grease a small baking tin and line with greased paper to stand just above the sides. Whisk eggs and sugar together until thick and creamy. Sieve flour, cocoa and baking powder together and stir in lightly. Add the water and mix all together. Put into prepared tin and spread evenly with hot knife. Bake in a hot oven from 7 to 10 minutes, till it feels spongy. Turn on to sugared paper, cut off hard outside edge from each side. Roll up and leave on sieve till cold, then unroll and spread with following filling: *Temp. 205°C (400°F).*

Cream filling: 180 g. (6 oz) icing sugar, 2 tablespoons cream, vanilla essence. Roll the lumps out of sugar and rub it through a fine sieve. Whisk cream until thick, stir in sieved sugar and a few drops of vanilla, mix, and spread on with hot knife.

Chocolate Sandwich

90 g. (3 oz.) castor sugar	125 g. (¼ lb.) flour
1 egg (or 2 small)	½ teaspoon cream of tartar
vanilla flavouring	⅛ flat teaspoon bicarbonate of
30 g. (1 oz.) cocoa or	soda
a little melted chocolate	30 g. (1 oz.) butter or margarine
milk	

Sieve the flour, cocoa, cream of tartar and bicarbonate of soda together. Whisk the egg and sugar until thick and creamy and free from dark streaks of egg. Put the butter into a saucepan and warm it sufficiently to melt it. Stir the flour into the egg and sugar and mix all lightly, together with the melted butter and a few drops of vanilla. Stir in about a spoonful of milk if required. Put into a greased sandwich tin and spread over evenly. Bake in a hot oven 230°C (450°F) for about 10 minutes. When cooked, put on to a sieve and leave until cold.

Filling:

125 g. (¼ lb.) icing   60 g. (2 oz.) butter   vanilla flavouring
sugar

To make the filling: roll the lumps out of the sugar, then rub it through a fine sieve. Add the butter and beat both to a cream. Flavour with vanilla. Split open the sandwich, spread the prepared filling over it, then put together again and dust with sieved icing sugar.

Cinnamon Sponge

1 tablespoon butter or margarine	2 level breakfast cups flour
½ breakfast cup sugar	2 teaspoons baking powder
3 eggs	¼ teaspoon soda
2 tablespoons treacle	1 teaspoon cinnamon
milk	

Beat butter and sugar to a cream; add eggs well beaten. Mix soda in treacle and slightly warm it. Add cinnamon, sifted flour, baking powder, and milk if needed. Put in 2 sandwich tins and bake in a quick oven. When cool, put jam between.

Temp. 205°C (400°F)—20–30 minutes.

Coconut Buns

2 tablespoons butter or margarine	1 tablespoon grated coconut
4 tablespoons fine sugar	6 tablespoons flour
1 egg	2 teaspoons baking powder
	a little milk if necessary

Beat the butter and sugar to a cream. Add the yolk of the egg. Then add the coconut, the flour to which the baking powder has been added, and a little milk if necessary. Lastly add the white of the egg well beaten to a froth. Bake in a very quick oven for 10 minutes.

Temp. 230°C. (450°F).

Coffee Buns

250 g. (8 oz.) flour	125 g. (4 oz.) butter or margarine
125 g. (4 oz.) Demarara sugar	90 g. (3 oz.) currants or sultanas
1 egg	½ teaspoon bicarbonate of soda
½ teaspoon cream of tartar	1 teaspoon coffee essence

Cream butter and sugar, add other ingredients and put into little mounds on a greased tin. Bake 7 to 10 minutes in a hot oven.

Temp. 230°C (450°F).

Cookies

4 cups of flour	250 g. (½ lb.) butter or margarine
1½ cups of sugar	¼ teaspoon salt
½ cup milk	½ teaspoon bicarbonate of soda

Put butter, sugar, milk and soda in a saucepan together, bring to the boil, when cool mix with flour. Knead well, roll out and cut into rounds or squares. Prick some with a fork, leave others plain.

Delicious with icing sugar fillings between two. They will keep for months in airtight tin.   *Temp. 230°C (450°F)—15 minutes.*

Cornflour Cake

125 g. (4 oz.) cornflour	3 eggs
185 g. (6 oz.) butter or margarine	125 g. (4 oz.) plain flour
185 g. (6 oz.) sugar	1 teaspoon baking powder
a little vanilla essence	

Prepare and bake as for Madeira Cake (*see* page 194).

Cream Lilies

4 eggs
4 tablespoons sugar
1 cup flour
¼ teaspoon bicarbonate of soda
½ teaspoon cream of tartar
a pinch of salt
1 dessertspoon boiling water

Have ready a good hot oven and a sheet of baking paper. Beat eggs and sugar until light and creamy (10 minutes). Add boiling water and again beat. Mix soda, cream of tartar and salt with the flour and fold into beaten eggs very gradually till all is absorbed. On a hot oven shelf place the sheet of baking paper and drop the mixture on in dessertspoonfuls, allowing room to spread. Place in the hot oven without loss of time. Have a clean cloth ready on a wire cooler. In about 5 minutes, or when the mixture is a golden-brown, take out. Slip a large clean knife under each cake and take them off the paper without breaking. While hot turn each cake on the finger in the shape of an arum lily and place on the cloth. Lay them against each other to keep them from opening. When cool fill each lily with whipped cream, flavoured if desired.

This amount should make 15 cakes. If the oven shelf is too small to take all the mixture at once, it does not harm by standing till the first lot are cooked. *Temp. 205°C (400°F)—7–10 minutes.*

Date Cake

2 cups flour
2 eggs
1 cup milk
1 cup sugar
1 teaspoons baking powder
2 tablespoons butter or margarine
1 teaspoon cinnamon
a little nutmeg
250 g. (½ lb.) finely chopped dates

Cream the butter and sugar. Add the eggs well beaten, then the milk. Add one teaspoon baking powder to the flour, then the spices and dates, and bake 1½ hours in a cake tin lined with buttered paper. *Temp. 190°C (375°F)*

Date Dainties

500 g. (1 lb.) stoned and chopped dates
1 cup chopped nuts
5 tablespoons flour
¾ cup sugar
2 level teaspoons baking powder
⅛ teaspoon salt
1 teaspoon vanilla essence
3 eggs

Sieve the flour with the baking powder. Mix all the other ingredients, the eggs unbeaten. Add the flour. Bake in a shallow greased pan in a moderate oven for about 45 minutes. Cut in squares and sprinkle powdered sugar. *Temp. 190°C (375°F).*

Date and Nut Sandwich Cake

2 eggs
their weight in flour,
 butter and sugar
1 teaspoon baking powder
1 teaspoon vanilla essence
a little milk
a pinch of salt

Sieve the flour, baking powder and salt together. Cream the butter and sugar. Add the yolks of eggs and beat well. Stir in the sieved flour, adding the milk as required. Lastly fold in the stiffly beaten whites of eggs and the vanilla essence. Pour the mixture into a shallow sandwich tin, approximately 15 cm. (6 ins.) in diameter, which should previously be well greased, and bake in a moderately hot oven for about 30 to 35 minutes. Cool on a wire tray or sieve.

Temp. 203°C (400°F).

Filling:

Soak 90 g. (6 oz.) dates in a little warm water. Remove the stones and chop. Mix with a little whipped cream. Split the cake in two and spread the top of one piece with the dates and cream. Sprinkle with chopped almonds, place the other half on top and coat with caramel icing made with brown sugar.

Delicate Cakes

1 cup flour	1 teaspoon vanilla essence
½ cup cornflour	125 g. (¼ lb.) butter
3 eggs	½ cup water
2 teaspoons baking powder	¾ cup sugar

Cream butter and sugar together and add well-beaten eggs. Sift flour, cornflour and baking powder together and add alternately with water to the first mixture. Lastly add vanilla. Put in small greased tins. Sprinkle with desiccated coconut and bake in moderate oven.

Temp. 205°C (400°F)—15–20 minutes.

Doughnuts with Yeast

250 g. (½ lb.) flour	15 g. (½ oz.) yeast
¼ teaspoon salt	75 g. (½ gill) milk (warmed)
10 g. (¼ oz.) sugar	30 g. (1 oz.) butter or margarine
1 egg	a little jam
cinnamon	

Mix the flour and salt. Warm milk and melt the butter in it and add yeast and beaten egg. Beat very well and put to rise for an hour or more. Roll out and cut into rounds. Put a little jam on half the number of rounds and place the rest on top. Put to rise again for 10 minutes. Fry in smoking-hot deep fat and toss in sifted sugar and cinnamon.

Doughnuts with Baking Powder

250 g. (½ lb.) flour	60 g. (2 oz.) castor sugar
1 teaspoon baking powder	milk
60 g. (2 oz.) butter	1 egg
¼ teaspoon spice	lemon essence
cinnamon	

Rub butter into flour. Add spice, sugar and baking powder. Mix the egg, milk and essence to form a stiff dough. Roll out and cut into rings and rounds. Fry in smoking-hot fat and toss in sugar and cinnamon.

By adding more milk to make a softer dough the mixture may be cooked by dropping from a tablespoon into smoking-hot fat.

Dundee Cake

180 g. (6 oz.) butter or
  margarine
180 g. (6 oz.) sugar
180 g. (6 oz.) sultanas
300 g. (10 oz.) flour

60 g. (2 oz.) peel
3 large eggs
30 g. (1 oz.) almonds
salt

Cream the butter and the sugar. Beat in eggs one by one. Add the flour gradually, and then the fruit. Put in a tin lined with greased paper. Bake for about 2½ to 3 hours. Place strips of almonds on top after the first hour. *Temp. 175°C (350°F).*

Fairy Cakes

4 eggs
¾ cup fine sugar (castor)
90 g. (3 oz.) butter
1 cup cornflour
lemon juice
cochineal

a pinch of salt
1 small teaspoon baking
  powder
vanilla essence
cocoa or chocolate

Beat eggs thoroughly, then add sugar and beat again. Cream the butter and beat all well together. Add the lemon juice and stir in gently the cornflour and a little ordinary flour to which has been added the baking powder. Stir all lightly and divide into two portions: into one put a few drops of cochineal, into the other 2 heaped teaspoons cocoa and a few drops of vanilla. Grease some flat tins and drop the mixture, a half teaspoon at a time, on to the tins, leaving room between each drop for spreading. Bake very lightly for a few minutes. Turn out on to a wire tray. When cool put a small portion of the following mixture on each pink cake and place a chocolate one on top. *Temp. 230°C (450°F)—10 minutes.*

Mixture:
Beat together equal quantities of butter and icing sugar, one small egg or a little cream, and a few drops of vanilla essence.

Fruit Cake Family

250 g. (8 oz.) flour
180 g. (6 oz.) butter
180 g. (6 oz.) currants, raisins,
  and sultanas

180 g. (6 oz.) sugar
3 eggs
vanilla essence (if liked)
1 teaspoon baking powder

Rub butter into flour and mix all dry ingredients. Add the eggs and sufficient milk to make the mixture rather moist. Bake in a hot oven for about 1¾ hours. *Temp. 205°C (400°F).*

Genoese Cake

4 eggs
125 g. (4 oz.) castor sugar

90 g. (3 oz.) flour
90 g. (3 oz.) butter

Melt the butter and sift the flour. Whisk the eggs and sugar over hot water till light and thick, then whisk till slightly cooled. Add the flour and cooled butter lightly to the mixture. Turn into a greased and papered baking tin and bake in a very steady oven till firm and brown.   *Temp. 230°C (450°F)—30 minutes.*

The above mixture forms the foundation of many small cakes and can be iced with butter or glacé icing and decorated to taste. Sweet fillings may be spread between the layers and almond paste may be used to cover the small cakes entirely, or to decorate the top, the sides being coated with apricot marmalade and ratafia crumbs.

German Cake

180 g. (6 oz.) sugar	250 g. (½ lb.) flour
90 g. (3 oz.) butter	1 teaspoon cream of tartar
2 eggs	½ teaspoon bicarbonate of soda
nuts	300 ml. (½ pint) milk

Cream the sugar and butter and add the eggs well beaten, then the flour, cream of tartar and soda. Moisten with the milk. Butter a flat cake tin, pour in the mixture, and sprinkle nuts, mixed with sugar and a little ground cinnamon, on top. Bake in a moderate oven, as the nuts are apt to burn.   *Temp. 190°C (375°F)—45 minutes.*

Gingerbread

a)

4 cups flour	1 cup milk
1 cup sugar	1 teaspoon of soda dissolved in
1 cup butter	the milk
1 cup golden syrup	1 tablespoon ginger
1 dessertspoon cinnamon or mixed spice.	

Warm together in basin, syrup, butter and milk. Mix together other ingredients in another basin. Pour syrup, etc., into the dry ingredients. Mix well and pour into a greased tin, allowing room to rise. Bake in a moderate oven for about 1 hour. If desired, fruit may be added to this mixture (sultanas, currants, peel, etc.).
                                    Temp. 175°C (350°F).

(b)

1 cup sifted flour	¼ teaspoon nutmeg
½ teaspoon baking soda	1 egg slightly beaten
¼ teaspoon salt	5 tablespoons brown or white
2 teaspoons cinnamon	sugar
1 teaspoon ginger	¼ cup syrup
¼ cup melted butter	¼ cup milk

Mix and sift flour, soda, salt and spices. Combine egg, sugar, syrup, milk and butter; heat slightly. Add to flour mixture and beat vigorously until smooth. Turn into greased pan and bake in moderate oven.   *Temp. 175°C (350°F)—30 minutes.*

Honey Drop Cakes

$\frac{1}{3}$ cup butter
$\frac{1}{4}$ cup sugar
$\frac{1}{2}$ cup honey
$1\frac{1}{2}$ teaspoons baking powder

1 egg
$\frac{1}{2}$ tablespoon lemon juice
$1\frac{1}{2}$ cups flour

Cream the butter and add sugar slowly. Add honey, beaten egg yolk and lemon juice. Mix well and add flour and baking powder which has been sifted together. Fold in beaten egg white. Put into greased individual tins, or drop far apart on greased baking sheet, and bake in hot oven 10 to 15 minutes. *Temp. 230°C (450°F).*

Jam Sandwich

6 heaped tablespoons flour
1 cup milk
2 or 3 eggs (according to size)
30 g. (1 oz.) butter

3 heaped tablespoons sugar
1 teaspoon baking powder
jam

Cream butter and sugar together, add beaten eggs, flour and milk alternately, and lastly the baking powder. Pour quickly into two large greased sandwich tins. Bake for about 20 minutes in a hot oven. When cold put jam in between and sugar or icing on top.
Temp. 205°C (400°F).

Kabete Sandwich Cake

1 cup sugar
$1\frac{1}{2}$ cups flour
2 teaspoons baking powder
$\frac{1}{4}$ teaspoon salt
$\frac{1}{4}$ cup cocoa

2 medium-sized eggs
$\frac{1}{3}$ cup melted butter
$\frac{2}{3}$ cup milk
$\frac{1}{2}$ teaspoon vanilla

Mix the dry ingredients. Beat eggs and add to melted butter, milk and vanilla in one basin. Pour all the wet ingredients into the dry ones and when mixed together beat well for about 2 minutes. Place in two greased tins and bake in fairly hot oven for about 25 minutes. When cold put cream or butter filling between. This cake is very quickly made because little beating is required.
Temp. 205°C (400°F)—25 minutes.

Kisses

1 egg
1 cup sugar
$\frac{1}{2}$ cup butter
$\frac{1}{2}$ cup milk
cinnamon

$\frac{1}{2}$ teaspoon bicarbonate of soda
1 teaspoon cream of tartar
enough flour to make a stiff
dough

Beat butter and sugar. Add egg well beaten. Then add milk and gradually stir in flour and baking powder. Drop from a teaspoon into a greased pan. Sprinkle with coarse sugar and cinnamon and bake in a quick oven. They can be stuck together with cake fillings or jam. *Temp. 230°C (450°F)—10-15 minutes.*

Ladies' Fingers

(a)

300 g. (10 oz.) flour	¼ cup milk
1 cup sugar	1 teaspoon cream of tartar
½ cup butter or margarine	½ teaspoon soda
1 egg	1 teaspoon vanilla
a little salt	

Beat the butter and sugar to a cream. Add the egg yolk and the white beaten stiff. Mix the dry ingredients. Now mix all together. Roll out about 1 cm. (½ in.) thick. Cut into strips and roll round with the hand on the board. Roll in sugar and bake on a greased tin in a quick oven. If liked, add pounded cinnamon to the sugar in which you roll them. *Temp. 230°C (450°F).*

(b)

60 g. (2 oz.) butter	grated rind and juice of ½
60 g. (2 oz.) sugar	lemon
1 egg	¼ teaspoon cream of tartar
125 g. (4 oz.) finely sifted flour	a pinch of bicarbonate of soda

Cream the butter and sugar and add the beaten egg. Then gradually mix in the flour to which the cream of tartar and soda have been added, beating all the time. Put into a shallow pan lined with buttered paper and bake in a moderately hot oven for about 10 minutes. Turn on to a sheet of white paper sprinkled with castor sugar. Cut into fingers and serve either hot or cold. *Temp. 205°C (400°F).*

Lemon Cake

125 g. (4 oz.) flour	½ teaspoon baking powder
75 g. (2½ oz.) butter	grated lemon rind
75 g. (2½ oz.) castor sugar	sliced citron peel
2 eggs	

Cream butter and sugar, beat in egg one at a time, add lemon rind, mix in flour gradually, then baking powder. Put in prepared and greased tin, bake in moderate oven, decorate with peel.
Temp. 175°C (350°F)—45 minutes.

Lemon Queens

125 g. (¼ lb.) butter or margarine	¾ tablespoon lemon juice
125 g. (¼ lb.) sugar	4 eggs
grated rind of one lemon	5 oz. flour
¼ teaspoon bicarbonate of soda	¼ teaspoon salt

Cream the butter and sugar and beat well. Then add the grated rind, the lemon juice and the well-beaten yolks of eggs. Mix and sieve the flour, soda and salt together and stir into the first mixture. Beat hard and then add the well-beaten whites. Put in greased pans and bake for 20 minutes. *Temp. 230°C (450°F).*

Madeira Cake

250 g. (8 oz.) flour	1 teaspoon baking powder
155 g. (5 oz.) butter	grated lemon rind
155 g. (5 oz.) castor sugar	sliced citron peel
4 eggs	

Line cake tin with buttered paper. Sift flour. Cream butter and sugar. Beat in eggs one by one. Add lemon rind. Stir in flour gradually and lightly mix in baking powder. Put mixture in prepared tin and bake in a moderate oven 1½ hours. Decorate top with citron peel.

Temp. 205°C (400°F).

By adding cherries, sultanas, carraway seeds or grated coconut, this mixture gives a variety of cakes.

Many Cakes from One Recipe

1 large tablespoon butter or margarine	1 heaped teaspoon baking powder
1 teacup sugar	½ cup milk
1½ teacups flour	2 eggs
pinch of salt	

From the above ingredients the following are made:—

VANILLA LOAF. Cream butter and sugar together thoroughly, stir in whipped eggs, add flour sieved twice with baking powder, salt, and lastly milk. Flavour with vanilla and beat the whole vigorously; then bake in loaf form in good steady oven for about 1 hour. Ice with boiled icing. *Temp. 190°C (375°F).*

SMALL LEMON CAKES are made by adding to the above mixture extract of lemon and a grating of nutmeg. Bake in patty tins, sprinkling the cakes with sugar before putting in oven.

CHOCOLATE CAKE is made by adding two squares of unsweetened chocolate (melted over steam) to the above mixture, baked in two layers, which are put together with icing flavoured with lemon.

ORANGE CAKE. Add to above recipe the grated peel of ½ orange. Bake in a shallow tin. Ice thickly with orange icing. Cut cake in squares when serving.

GRATED LEMON PEEL makes another change, and with this use a little grated nutmeg or powdered ginger. Care should be taken that no lemon juice falls into the batter, as the acid neutralises the effect of baking powder.

FRUIT CAKE is made by adding a cup of seeded and chopped sultanas and raisins.

LOAF CAKE is made by adding figs or dates to mixture, just before putting into tin.

NUT CAKE. Add a cup of chopped nuts to the same ingredients.

GINGERBREAD can be made by substituting syrup for milk, and bicarbonate of soda for baking powder. Flavour with ginger and spices.

Marble Cake

½ cup butter or margarine
1½ cups sugar
grated rind of ½ orange
1 egg and 1 yolk
45 g. (1½ oz.) unsweetened chocolate or cocoa

2½ cups flour
¼ teaspoon salt
2 teaspoons baking powder
1 cup milk

Cream the butter. Add sugar and orange rind. Add beaten egg yolks. Sift together flour, baking powder and salt, and add alternately with the milk. Lastly fold in one beaten egg white. Divide the batter into two parts. To one part add the chocolate. Put in by tablespoons, alternating dark and light batter, into three greased layer-cake pans. Bake in a moderate oven for 20 minutes. Put butter icing between.
Temp. 205°C (400°F).

Meringues *See* Cold Puddings.

Mocha Tier Cake

2 cups sifted flour
2 teaspoons baking powder
½ teaspoon salt
1 cup butter
2 cups sugar

¼ teaspoon almond essence
½ teaspoon vanilla essence
4 eggs, separated
85 g. (3 oz.) melted chocolate
1 cup strong coffee

Mix and sift flour, baking powder and salt, cream butter, gradually add sugar until very fluffy. Add flavouring and beat in egg yolks, then chocolate. Add flour alternately with coffee, beating until smooth after each addition. Fold in thoroughly the stiffly beaten egg whites, turn into sandwich tins and bake in moderate oven, 175°C (350°F), about 15 minutes. Put layers together with butter filling. Spread coffee-flavoured water icing on sides and top.

Nut Cake

250 g. (½ lb.) peanuts or ground almonds

125 g. (¼ lb.) castor sugar
5 eggs

Warm and skin the nuts and put through the mincing machine. Beat well with yolks of eggs. Whip whites of eggs stiff, then add alternately with sugar into the nuts and yolks. Beat very well, then bake for 40 minutes, during which time do not open the oven door. No flour is required for this cake. *Temp. 150°C (300°F).*

Orange Cake

125 g. (4 oz.) butter or margarine
125 g. (4 oz.) sugar
3 eggs

180 g. (6 oz.) flour
1 orange
1 teaspoon baking powder

Beat butter with sugar till creamy and add to sugar and butter the yolks of eggs, beating the whole with a wooden spoon. Grate off rind of orange; squeeze out juice, strain and add to mixture. Mix flour and baking powder together and stir in. Beat whites of egg to a stiff froth and add. Line a tin with buttered paper and pour in the mixture. Bake in a moderate oven from 45 to 50 minutes.
Temp. 205°C (400°F).

Orange Cakes

(*a*)

2 tablespoons butter	grated rind of 1 orange
4 tablespoons sugar	6 tablespoons flour
1 egg	½ teaspoon baking powder
a little milk	

Cream the butter and sugar and the grated rind of orange. Mix the flour and baking powder and add gradually. Add enough milk to make the mixture rather moist, stirring slowly. Grease patty pans and fill with the mixture. Bake in a quick oven and when cool cover with orange icing (*see* Icings).

Temp. 230°C (450°F)—15-20 minutes.

(*b*)

180 g. (6 oz.) flour	120 g. (4 oz.) castor sugar
60 g. (2 oz.) butter	1 orange
2 eggs	1 teaspoon baking powder

Sift the flour and baking powder together; cream butter and sugar. Beat eggs in, one at a time. Stir in lightly flour and baking powder and grated rind and juice of orange. Put in tin lined with buttered paper and bake in a moderate oven for 45 minutes.

Temp. 205°C (400°F).

Petits Fours

2 eggs (yolks and whites separate)	60 g. (2 oz.) castor sugar
	jam (any kind)
60 g. (2 oz.) flour	crystallised violets
glacé icing (any flavour)	chopped nuts or almonds

Sieve the flour on to a sheet of paper. Put the egg yolks and castor sugar into a basin and beat till white and creamy. Whisk egg whites to a very stiff froth, add flour and stir very lightly into the creamed yolks and sugar. Brush the insides of small fancy patty tins with melted butter. Half fill them with the mixture and bake in a moderate oven for 10 minutes. When cold place two together with jam between and pour over them the glacé icing. Decorate with violets, pistachio nuts, or almonds.

Temp. 205°C (400°F)

Plum Cake

250 g. (½ lb.) flour	500 g. (1 lb.) currants
4 eggs	125 g. (¼ lb.) candied peel
180 g. (6 oz.) butter	60 g. (2 oz.) almonds
180 g. (6 oz.) brown sugar	60 g. (2 oz.) treacle
150 ml. (1 gill) milk	¼ teaspoon bicarbonate of soda

Beat the sugar and butter with a wooden spoon until they are smoothly mixed and light. Add the treacle and mix it in. Beat up the eggs in a small basin and stir them little by little, beating all the time. Then add the milk and mix it in. Wash, dry and clean the currants thoroughly and cut the peel into thin strips. Stir in and mix. Mix the soda with the flour and stir it in gently, not beating but only mixing. Pour the mixture into a prepared cake tin and bake in a slow oven for at least 2 hours. It is best not to cut this cake for a month at least.   *Temp. 150°C (300°F).*

Queen Cakes

120 g. (4 oz.) flour
60 g. (2 oz.) butter
60 g. (2 oz.) sugar
60 g. (2 oz.) currants, cherries or peel

rind of lemon grated
½ teaspoon baking powder
1 egg

Cream the butter and sugar. Add the flour and egg gradually, beating well between times. Add raisins, peel and lemon rind. Beat again and lastly add baking powder and mix well. Fill small greased tins three parts full and bake in oven, very hot at first, then cooler. Cook till pale brown and firm to touch.

Temp. 230–175°C (450–350°F)—15–20 minutes.

Raspberry Buns

250 g. (½ lb.) flour
a pinch of salt
1 teaspoon baking powder
90 g. (3 oz.) butter

60 g. (2 oz.) sugar
1 egg
a little milk
jam

Mix flour, salt and baking powder. Rub in butter, add sugar, mix egg and milk and make a light dough. Divide in 12 and shape into buns. Make a hole on top, put in a little jam, close up, brush with water and sprinkle with sugar. Bake on greased tin 15 to 20 minutes.

Temp. 205°C (400°F).

Refrigerator Cake

1 pkt. plain biscuits
1 egg
125 g. (¼ lb.) butter or margarine

250 g. (½ lb.) icing sugar
1 small bar milk or
plain chocolate

Melt butter, sugar and chocolate. Add beaten egg and then crushed biscuits. Place in lightly greased ice holders or baking tin in refrigerator until needed. Will keep indefinitely.

This can be varied by adding chopped nuts, almond essence, coffee, sultanas, raisins, etc.

Rock Cakes

250 g. (½ lb.) flour
1 teaspoon baking powder
90 g. (3 oz.) butter
60 g. (2 oz.) sugar

1 egg
60 g. (2 oz.) currants
vanilla essence
a little milk

Cream the butter, sugar and egg. Then add the flour, baking powder, currants and essence and milk sufficient to make a very stiff dough. Lift with a fork and drop on a hot greased baking tin and bake in a hot oven for 10 minutes, then reduce heat.

Temp. 230°C. (450°F)

Sandwich cake, two coloured

3 eggs
2 tablespoons sugar
1 teablespoon milk

3 tablespoons flour
½ teaspoon baking powder
2 tablespoons butter

Beat yolks and whites of eggs separately, using two bowls, and to each add half the above ingredients in the following order: butter and sugar beaten together till creamy, flour and baking powder mixed together, and lastly milk. Beat the mixtures well and bake in two cake tins for about 20 minutes. On removing cakes from oven one will be found to be yellow and the other white. Spread one side with jam and place the other half on top, which may be iced if desired.

Temp. 205°C (400°F).

Scotch Bun

Crust:
1½ breakfast cups flour
120 g. (4 oz.) butter

½ teaspoon baking powder
beaten egg, and water

Mixture:
500 g. (1 lb.) flour
1 kg. (2 lb.) raisins
1.5 kg. (3 lb.) currants
250 g. (½ lb.) brown sugar
1 teaspoon (small) white pepper
½ teaspoon black pepper
3 eggs (or more)
milk to mix
1 tablespoon brandy (optional)

185 g. (6 oz.) sweet almonds
60 g. (2 oz.) citron
60 g. (2 oz.) lemon peel
125 g. (4 oz.) orange peel
15 g. (½ oz.) cinnamon
15 g. (½ oz.) ground ginger
1 large teaspoon bicarbonate of soda
1 large teaspoon cream of tartar
a large pinch of salt

Make pastry and line a greased cake tin with it, reserving a piece the size of the tin for the top. Mix together all the dry ingredients after preparing fruit, etc. Add eggs and liquid and make fairly stiff. Beat well. Put mixture into lined tin, flatten the top, damp edges round and seal remainder of pastry on. Make four holes right down to bottom of cake with a skewer. Prick with fork all over top. Brush with beaten egg. Bake till ready (probably about 3 hours). Keep for about a week before cutting. *Temp. 150°C. (300°F).*

Simnel Cake

185 g. (6 oz.) butter
125 g. (¼ lb.) candied peel
125 g. (¼ lb.) sultanas
5–6 eggs
½ teaspoon mixed spice

185 g. (6 oz.) castor sugar
500 g. (1 lb.) currants
280 g. (9 oz.) flour
1 tablespoon caramel
375 g. (¾ lb.) almond icing

Cream the butter and sugar together until they are white, then beat in the eggs one at a time. Stir in lightly the flour, currants, candied peel (cut up small), sultanas, spice and caramel. Put this mixture into a cake tin lined with buttered paper and bake in a moderate oven for 2 hours. Next day split the cake in two. Divide the almond paste and roll it into two rounds the size of the cake. Put one round between the two layers of cake and press them well together. Put the second round on the top, smooth it over and mark a pattern on it with a small knife. Brush the top over with a little beaten egg and bake in a quick oven for 20 minutes until the top is slightly brown. Decorate with small Easter eggs in almond paste, according to taste.

Temp. 190°C (375°F).

Slab Cake

125 g. (¼ lb.) flour
125 g. (4 oz.) butter
90 g. (3 oz.) sugar
60 g. (2 oz.) raisins
60 g. (2 oz.) currants
75 ml. (½ gill) milk

60 g. (2 oz.) peel
2 eggs
1 level teaspoon spice
1 heaped teaspoon baking powder

Line a meat tin with very slightly greased paper. Beat butter and sugar to a cream. Beat and add eggs. Sieve flour, spice and baking powder and add to the mixture. Add gradually fruit and milk. Put into tin. Smooth over and bake in a moderately hot oven for 40 minutes or a little longer if necessary. *Temp. 205°C (400°F).*

Sponge Cake Simple

3 eggs
3 tablespoons sugar
½ teaspoon baking powder

jam or fruit
3 tablespoons flour

Beat eggs and sugar till very light, about 10 minutes. Mix flour and baking powder well together and add them to eggs and sugar very gradually, mixing very gently. Add any flavouring desired. Place in well-greased tin and bake without loss of time in a quick oven. Turn out on to a clean cloth and, when cool, split and spread with jam or fruit. *Temp. 230°C (450°F)—10–15 minutes.*

Sultana Cake

375 g. (12 oz.) flour
250 g. (8 oz.) butter or margarine
250 g. (8 oz.) castor sugar
4 eggs

375 g. (12 oz.) sultanas
3 tablespoons milk
1 teaspoon baking powder

Cream butter and sugar, add eggs well beaten with flour. Add fruit. Put milk and baking powder in bowl and mix, then fold into cake mixture. Bake at temperature 190°C (375°F) for 1½ hours in the middle of oven.

Swiss Roll

3 eggs
85 g. (3 oz.) castor sugar
85 g. (3 oz.) flour

1 tablespoon milk or warm water
1 small teaspoon baking powder

Whisk eggs, add sugar, then whisk till thick and spongy (10–15 minutes). Fold in flour, baking powder and water lastly very lightly. Bake near the top of the oven, 8–9 minutes. Place a sugar paper on a damp cloth. Turn out the sponge and quickly trim off the edges. Spread on warm jam. Roll up tightly with join underneath. Trim edges again if necessary when cool. Dredge with sugar.

Temp. 230°C (450°F).

Swiss Tarts

185 g. (6 oz.) flour
125 g. (4 oz.) butter
60 g. (2 oz.) sugar

½ egg or 1 tablespoon water
or milk
jam

Sieve the flour into a basin. Rub in the butter and sugar and mix together. Pour in the egg, water or milk and mix thoroughly into a lump with your hand. Divide into 6 equal portions. Round each into a smooth ball, grease 6 small cake tins and put one ball into each. Press your little finger into the centre of each ball and make a hole almost to the bottom. At the same time press the ball to the shape of the tin. Drop jam into the hole and decorate the top with a knife, making sharp cuts from the centre all round the cake. Bake in a moderate oven about 20 minutes until very light brown in colour. Cool on sieve and sprinkle a little sieved icing sugar on the top of each.

Temp. 205°C (400°F).

Walnut Cake

2 cups sifted flour
2½ teaspoons baking powder
½ teaspoon salt
⅔ cup butter or margarine
6 tablespoons milk

1 cup sugar
1 teaspoon vanilla
3 eggs
1 cup chopped walnut

Mix and sift flour, baking powder and salt, cream butter, gradually add sugar, creaming until fluffy. Add vanilla and beat in thoroughly one egg at a time. Add nuts and beat well. Add flour, alternately with milk, beating until smooth after each addition. Turn into greased pans and bake in moderate oven, temperature 350°, about 1 hour.

Wedding Cake

1 kg. (2 lb.) butter
1 kg. (2 lb.) flour
2 kg. (4 lb.) currants
250 g. (½ lb.) citron peel
20 (18) eggs
500 g. (1 lb.) cherries
160 ml. (1 gill) brandy
1 kg. (2 lb.) moist brown sugar

500 g. (1 lb.) raisins
250 g. (½ lb.) sweet almonds
250 g. (½ lb.) mixed peel
1 tablespoon mixed spice
1 kg. (2 lb.) sultanas
a little caramel
a pinch of salt

Sift the flour. Cream the butter and sugar in a basin with the hand until it is quite white. Beat up the eggs with butter and sugar, adding them one at a time; if the mixture shows any sign of curdling add a little flour, but this is not usually necessary. Stone the raisins; chop the citron; cut up the peel; blanch the almonds and cut them into three parts. Stir in lightly the flour, raisins, citron, peel, almonds, currants, cherries, sultanas, spice and brandy. Colour the mixture a pale brown with caramel and put it into a tin, greased and lined with paper. Tie a thick layer of brown paper round the outside of the tin and bake in an oven fairly warm at first, then cooler afterwards, from 6 to 7 hours. When baking a cake of this size in an oven with bottom heat, put a tin of sand underneath the baking tin to prevent its burning.

Temp. 175°C (300°F).

With half the above quantities a Christmas cake can be made.

Christmas Cake

250 g. (½ lb.) flour
250 g. (½ lb.) butter
250 g. (½ lb.) brown sugar
250 g. (½ lb.) raisins
 (stoned and cut up)
250 g. (½ lb.) sultanas and
 currants
½ teaspoon bicarbonate of soda
a pinch of salt

125 g. (4 oz.) mixed peel
125 g. (4 oz.) almonds (blanched
 and chopped)
6 eggs
1 tablespoon brandy (if liked)
1 teaspoon caramel
a little milk
a little mixed spice

Cream the butter and sugar. Add the eggs one at a time and beat in thoroughly. Stir in flour and salt. Add fruit, spice, spirits, etc., the soda last of all. Put into a cake tin, lined with brown and white paper. Bake in a moderate oven for 3 or 4 hours. Ice with almond paste and Royal Icing. (see Icings).   *Temp. 175°C (350°F).*

FILLINGS AND ICINGS FOR CAKES OR PASTRY

Almond Paste or Marzipan

500 g. (1 lb.) ground almonds
250 g. (½ lb.) icing sugar
250 g. (½ lb.) castor sugar
1 teaspoon vanilla essence
2 whole eggs, or 3 or 4 whites
1 teaspoon brandy or rum

¼ teaspoon ratafia essence
juice of 1 lemon
½ teaspoon orange flower
 water (if available)

Mix the ground almonds and sugar. Add flavouring and eggs and mix to a stiff paste. Put all in a basin or mortar and knead or pound thoroughly. Roll out to size of cake. Brush cake with white of egg before putting on almond paste.

Banana Filling

As for date filling but ½ cupful banana pulp instead of dates.

Boiled Icing

1 cup sugar
⅛ teaspoon cream of
 tartar

½ cup water
white of one egg
1 teaspoon vanilla

Bring water and sugar slowly to boiling point. Add cream of tartar when it has boiled and continue boiling until it threads. Then pour on to the beaten egg. Beat until stiff and cold. Add vanilla and pour over the cake. Never stir the syrup after it has come to the boiling point as stirring makes it sugary.

Butter Filling (for Coffee Cake, Chocolate Cake, etc.)

120 g. (4 oz.) icing sugar. Beat to a cream with 60 g. (2 oz.) butter, flavour with coffee essence, or vanilla, or teaspoonful cocoa dissolved in a very little water, or coconut. Colour pink or green, if liked.

Caramel Icing
250 g. (8 oz.) brown sugar
100 ml. (⅔ gill) milk   25 g. (¾ oz.) butter
½ teaspoon vanilla essence   pinch of bicarbonate of soda

Heat the sugar with the milk until a soft ball forms when dropped into cold water. Remove from the fire, add the butter, vanilla essence and soda bicarbonate. Beat with a whisk till the mixture becomes thick and creamy, then pour over the cake. Decorate with small pieces of sliced dates and almonds.

Chocolate Icing
(a)
¼ cup milk   1½ tablespoons cocoa
1 yolk of egg   1 teaspoon melted butter
a few grains salt   some icing sugar

Mix the cocoa and milk. Put in the saucepan to heat with the salt and butter, then add the yolk of egg. Take care not to let it boil. Remove from the fire and stir in icing sugar until it is of a consistency to spread.

(b) Melt 50 g. (2 oz.) plain chocolate, or a teaspoon of cocoa, in a tablespoon of boiling water and stir in icing sugar until it is of the right consistency. Vanilla may be added to flavour, and if cocoa is used the addition of a little butter is an improvement.

Chocolate Icing (Creamy)
50 or 60 g. (2 oz.) chocolate   2 egg yolks well beaten
½ cup milk   1 tablespoon butter
1½ cups sugar   1 teaspoon vanilla

Heat chocolate and milk until chocolate is melted, beat until smooth. Gradually stir sugar into egg yolks, then chocolate-milk mixture. Cook 8–10 minutes or until fixed, stirring frequently. Add butter and vanilla and cool. When lukewarm beat until thick enough to spread.

Coconut Filling
Take a heaped cupful of grated coconut, add to it ½ cupful sugar and if desired a well-beaten egg. Mix together and use as filling for pastry. It is as well partially to cook the pastry before adding the filling, as it only requires enough cooking to melt the sugar into the coconut.

Confectioner's Custard
250 ml. (½ pint) milk   25 g. (1 oz.) castor sugar
2 yolks of eggs   20 g. (¾ oz.) cornflour
¼–½ teaspoon vanilla essence

Mix cornflour and milk to a smooth paste. Stir until it boils, then let it simmer for 10 minutes. Add yolks of eggs, sugar and vanilla, stir and heat until the custard thickens: it should not be allowed to boil. When cool the custard is ready for use and may be used instead of whipped cream for filling eclairs, etc.

Cream Filling

$\frac{3}{4}$ cup sugar
$\frac{1}{3}$ cup flour
$\frac{1}{4}$ teaspoon salt

4 egg yolks or 2 eggs
2 cups milk, scalded
1 teaspoonful vanilla

Combine dry ingredients and mix with slightly beaten egg. Stir in enough hot milk to make a thin paste. Add paste to remaining hot milk and cook over boiling water 5 minutes, stirring constantly. Cook 10 minutes longer or until mixture is thick enough, stirring occasionally. Cool and add vanilla. For a richer filling, add 2 tablespoons butter and cooked custard.

Custard Filling

A little custard powder, made into a rather thick paste with milk, well sweetened and flavoured and boiled 3 minutes.

Date Filling

2 spoons sugar
1 cup milk
vanilla
1 cup chopped dates

1 tablespoon butter
2 eggs
2 tablespoons flour

Mix the flour with a little of the cold milk. Boil the rest of the milk and add sugar to it. Cook until the mixture leaves the sides of the pot. Take off the stove and add butter and beaten eggs and stir well. Add dates, recook for a minute and cool before using.

Gentlemen's Favourite Filling

2 apples
$1\frac{1}{2}$ teaspoons grated lemon rind

3 tablespoons lemon juice
1 cup sugar

Peel and grate apples, add lemon rind, juice and sugar. Cook for 5 minutes, stirring constantly. Cool.

Ginger Filling

To be made the same as Pineapple Filling, using ginger syrup in place of pineapple juice. Add a little chopped ginger when cooked.

Grenadilla Filling

(a) 1 dessertspoon butter. 6 dessertspoons icing sugar. Mix well and add grenadilla juice which has been strained to remove pips.

(b) Take some grenadillas, cut open and scoop out the contents. Put these in a small saucepan with a little water or the juice of a lemon or orange. Bring to boil and then pass through a sieve. Add a little butter and sugar and thicken with a little cornflour. When cool add the white of an egg, well beaten.

Lemon Filling

2 eggs
1 lemon

1 cup sugar
1 teaspoon butter

Grate the rind of the lemon and put in saucepan with sugar, butter, juice of lemon and egg, well beaten. Put on fire, cook till it thickens and remove immediately. Allow to cool.

Lemon Icing

1 egg white   1 teaspoon lemon juice
about 1 small teacup icing sugar

Beat egg white until frothy, then sprinkle with lemon juice and gradually beat in sugar until stiff enough to spread.

Mock Cream Filling (for Sponge Cake)

55 g. (2 oz.) butter   1 tablespoon milk
55 g. (2 oz.) castor sugar   1 tablespoon hot water
flavouring

Beat the butter and sugar to a cream. Mix in the milk. Beat well. Add hot water gradually and beat very well. Add flavouring.

Orange Filling

(a)
The juice of two or three oranges and a little grated rind. Add sugar to taste, small piece of butter and thicken with 1 heaped teaspoon of cornflour. Spread when cold.

(b)

2 yolks of eggs   250 g. ($\frac{1}{2}$ lb.) castor sugar
30 g. (1 oz.) butter   1 orange (juice and rind)
15 g. ($\frac{1}{2}$ oz.) cake crumbs   1 teaspoon lemon juice

Melt butter in a saucepan, add sugar, yolks of eggs and juice and grated rind of orange. Stir until the mixture thickens, but do not boil or it will curdle. Add cake crumbs and lemon juice. When cold the mixture is ready for use.

Orange Icing

When the cake is baked and still warm put the following icing on top: Squeeze out the juice of one orange into sufficient icing sugar to make a stiff icing. Put this on the cake and decorate with angelica, crystallised oranges and cherries. To dry the icing quickly, add to it a teaspoon of cornflour.

Pineapple Filling

Mince 3 slices of pineapple after removing the core and eyes. Be careful to catch all the juice and place in a small saucepan with sugar to taste. Boil for 15 minutes and then thicken with a heaped teaspoon of custard powder mixed in a little cold water. When cold add whipped cream.

Royal Icing

500 g. (1 lb.) icing sugar   1 tablespoon lemon juice
2 whites of eggs, beaten a   a little water if necessary
   little   a squeeze of blue from blue bag

Beat all ingredients together with a wooden spoon for 5 or 10 minutes; make it a good colour. Pour on cake and smooth with a knife dipped in boiling water.

This is used to cover almond paste on Christmas and birthday cakes. It can also be used in an icing syringe or bag to decorate cake.

Seven-Minute Frosting

1 egg white, beaten   1 cup sugar
4 tablespoons cold water

Put in double boiler and set in boiling water. Beat continuously for 7 minutes. Remove boiler from water, add flavouring. Stir now and again until it cools. If too thick, thin out with cream; if too thin, cook longer.

Transparent Icing

500 g. (1 lb.) sugar   juice of ¼ lemon   300 ml. (½ pint) water

Dissolve the sugar and water together in a saucepan and boil until the mixture threads. While boiling the sugar must be well skimmed and the sides of the pan brushed down with a little clean water. Pour it into a clean basin, add lemon juice and beat with a wooden spoon until it is thick and white. It is then ready to pour over the cake.

If liked this can be used to form a last coat on a cake which has been iced with Royal icing. It gives a smooth finish.

Walnut or Almond Filling

85 g. (3 oz.) ground almonds   1 tablespoon walnuts or almonds
3 tablespoons apricot jam   (chopped)
1 teaspoon vanilla essence

Rub the jam through a hair sieve. Mix all together and use as required.

The addition of whipped cream is an improvement, but the filling must then be used at once.

Water Icing

250 g. (½ lb.) icing sugar, sieved and crushed. Add warm water carefully and flavour with the juice of orange or lemon, cocoa dissolved in a little water, coffee, vanilla, or other essence. Colour as desired.

Zabbaglione Filling

2 yolks of eggs   1 tablespoon sugar
2 tablespoons sherry or marsala

Beat all together and cook in a double cooker until it thickens.

Decorations for the Tops of Cakes

1. COCONUT browned in oven, or coloured pink or green by mixing on a plate with a drop of colouring and a little water. Dry in cool oven.

2. ALMONDS and GROUNDNUTS blanched, dried in oven until light brown and roughly chopped.

3. CRYSTALLISED FRUITS AND FLOWERS (cherries, angelica, violets, rose leaves, etc.).

4. GRATED CHOCOLATE.

5. WALNUTS, PISTACHIO, HAZEL NUTS.

6. COARSE COLOURED SUGAR.

BISCUITS

A good general rule for biscuits, and one that can be safely followed, is that if the recipe allows less than half the quantity of butter to flour, the butter should be rubbed in to the flour as in short pastry. If, however, a richer biscuit is desired and the recipe allows more than half the quantity of butter to flour, the butter should be beaten to a cream with the sugar.

Paste for biscuits improves if left overnight in the refrigerator.

Abernethy Biscuits

(a)

90 g. (3 oz.) butter or margarine   15 g. (½ oz.) carraway seeds
500 g. (1 lb.) flour   milk
60 g. (2 oz.) castor sugar

Rub the butter in to the flour, then add the sugar and carraway seeds. Moisten with a little milk. Roll out till paste is 1 cm. (½ inch) thick. Cut with a small cutter, prick with a fork and bake in a quick oven until golden-brown.

(b)

500 g. (1 lb.) self-raising flour   ½ teacup sugar
125 g. (4 oz.) margarine   ½ teacup milk
125 g. (4 oz.) lard

Rub in fat until like fine breadcrumbs. Heat milk and sugar until melted. Let cool and add to flour. Cut with round cutter and prick with fork. Bake in oven, temperature 150°–175°C (300°–350°F), until golden-brown.

Almond Biscuits

1½ cups flour   ½ teaspoon essence of almonds
125 g. (¼ lb.) butter   ½ teaspoon baking powder
125 g. (¼ lb.) sugar   1 egg

Cream the butter and sugar. Add the eggs and essence and stir in the baking powder and flour. Roll into small balls, put on a tin and bake slowly in a moderate oven. A split almond or cherry should be placed on each biscuit.   *Temp. 175°C (350°F)*

Brandy Snaps

60 g. (2 oz.) syrup   ½ teaspoon ground ginger
50 g. (1¾ oz.) flour   60 g. (2 oz.) butter or margarine
50 g. (1¾ oz.) sugar   ½ teaspoon grated lemon rind
½ teaspoon brandy or lemon juice

Melt the syrup, sugar and butter in a saucepan. Stir in the flour, ginger and lemon rind and juice. Mix the ingredients well together. Drop the mixture in small teaspoons on a greased baking sheet, about 7.5 cm. (3 in.) apart. Bake in a cool oven from 7 to 10 minutes. When brown and slightly set, roll up at once.   *Temp. 150°C (300°F)*.

Chocolate Biscuits

225 g. (9 oz.) sifted flour
a pinch of salt
150 g. (6 oz.) butter

100 g. (4 oz.) castor sugar
50 g. (2 oz.) plain chocolate
vanilla essence

Cream the butter and sugar. Dissolve the chocolate in 1 tablespoon of water (this to be done at low heat). When melted add to the mixture. Stir in the flour very lightly. Add a little vanilla essence. Turn on to a floured board. Roll out and cut into fancy shapes. Bake in a moderate oven for about 12 minutes. *Temp. 175°C (350°F).*

Chocolate Squares ("Brownies")

2 eggs
1 cup sugar
⅓ cup butter or margarine
vanilla essence

½ teacup flour
2½ squares unsweetened
chocolate

Beat the 2 eggs till frothy. Beat in the sugar slowly. Melt together over hot water the chocolate and butter and add to the egg mixture with vanilla essence. Mix thoroughly, adding flour. Bake in a hot oven, in a flat baking tin. Before removing from the tin and while hot, cut into squares. *Temp. 205°C (400°F).*

Coconut Biscuits

250 g. (8 oz.) flour
250 g. (8 oz.) desiccated
coconut

185 g. (6 oz.) castor sugar
125 g. (4 oz.) butter
1 egg

Mix the ingredients together with the hand, working in the butter last of all. If it is too stiff, a few drops of milk may be added. Roll out to 6 mm. (¼ in.) thickness and cut into rounds. Put on a floured baking sheet and bake in a fairly slow oven until they are a light brown colour. These biscuits keep for a long time if they are put into tightly closed tins. *Temp. 175°C (350°F).*

Coconut Cones

180 g. (6 oz.) coconut
120 g. (4 oz.) castor sugar

30 g. (1 oz.) flour
2 whites of egg

Mix the sugar, coconut and flour together. Add the whites of eggs which have been well beaten. Put the mixture in little heaps, or fill wetted egg cups with mixture and turn out on to greased baking tin. Bake for about 15 minutes in moderately hot oven. Half the mixture may be coloured with a few drops of cochineal.
Temp. 175°C (350°F).

Cream Crackers

4 heaped tablespoons butter
or margarine
250 g. (8 oz.) flour

pinch salt
½ cup milk

Rub the butter into the flour and salt, mix to a fairly stiff dough with the milk. Roll out very thinly, the thinner the better. Cut into squares, prick with fork, place on lightly floured baking tin. Bake in a quick oven about 10 minutes. *Temp. 205°C (400°F).*

These are just like the bought variety.

Crunches

(a)

95 g. (3 oz.) flour
155 g. (5 oz.) brown or
   white sugar

250 g. (8 oz.) rolled oats
185 g. (6 oz.) butter
pinch of salt

Melt butter and sugar, add other ingredients. Press flat into well-greased tin. Bake 20–25 minutes in moderate oven, temperature 175°C (350°F). Cut into fingers while hot.

(b)

1 large cup flour
1 large cup coconut
1 large cup porridge oats
375 g. (12 oz.) sugar

1 teaspoon bicarbonate of soda
125 g. (4 oz.) butter
1 large tablespoon syrup
2 tablespoons boiling water

Mix all dry ingredients. Melt the syrup and butter. Add the soda bicarb. to boiling water and then the syrup and butter. Mix well and add to the dry ingredients. Pat into a greased baking tin and bake in a slow oven, temperature 150°C (300°F), for 30–40 minutes. While still hot cut the mixture into oblong cakes and leave to cool.

German Biscuits

95 g. (3 oz.) butter or margarine
250 g. ($\frac{1}{2}$ lb.) flour
60 g. (2 oz.) sugar
a pinch of salt

jam
$\frac{1}{2}$ teaspoon baking powder
$\frac{1}{2}$ egg
pink or white icing

Sift flour, baking powder and salt together. Add the sugar, rub in the butter, and add the $\frac{1}{2}$ egg. Work till quite smooth. Roll out thinly and cut in small rounds. Bake in a rather cool oven for about 10 minutes. When cool put two biscuits together with jam between and ice on top either with pink or white icing.

Temp. 150°C (300°F).

Ginger Snaps

1 cup sugar
1 cup golden syrup
$\frac{1}{2}$ cup butter or margarine
$3\frac{1}{2}$ cups flour

$\frac{1}{2}$ teaspoon bicarbonate of
   soda
1 tablespoon ground ginger
a pinch of salt

Heat the treacle to boiling point and pour over the butter. Add the dry ingredients. Cool thoroughly; then turn out on a floured board and roll as thin as possible. Cut with a round cutter; put on a buttered baking tin and bake in a moderate oven. *Temp. 150°C (300°F).*

Jubilee Biscuits

185 g. (6 oz.) sugar
185 g. (6 oz.) butter or margarine
375 g. (12 oz.) flour
3 eggs

$\frac{3}{4}$ teaspoon baking powder
1 tablespoon cornflour
$\frac{1}{2}$ teaspoon vanilla

Cream the butter and sugar. Add the eggs and beat well. Add the flour, baking powder and cornflour, sifted together. Roll out and cut into shapes. Dust with castor sugar and bake in a moderate oven. *Temp. 150°C (300°F).*

Jumbles (old English recipe)

155 g. (5 oz.) flour
45 g. (2½ oz.) butter
1 teaspoon grated lemon rind

30 g. (1 oz.) ground almonds
45 g. (2½ oz.) castor sugar
1 yolk egg

Cream the butter and sugar and add the yolk of egg. Mix in the flour, lemon rind and almonds. Roll out fairly thinly and shape into a variety of fancy shapes. (For children, if possible have cutters shaped as animals or letters of the alphabet.) Put on a greased baking sheet and bake in a moderate oven for about 10 minutes.

Temp. 205°C (400°F).

Macaroons

(*a*)

125 g. (4 oz.) ground almonds
125 g. (4 oz.) castor sugar

whites of 2 eggs

Mix together the almonds and castor sugar, then stir in the whites of egg beaten to a stiff froth. Drop the mixture in little piles on wafer paper and bake to a pale brown. When nearly cooked, put half an almond on each.

(*b*)

Same as above but add 30 g. (1 oz.) grated chocolate.

Melting Moments

250 g. (½ lb.) butter
185 g. (6 oz.) flour

60 g. (2 oz.) cornflour
80 g. (2½ oz.) sugar

Melt butter in saucepan and when cool stir in sugar. Sieve flour and cornflour and add to butter and sugar. Bake as small rock cakes.

Temp. 205°C (400°F).

Oat Biscuits

125 g. (4 oz.) oats
60 g. (2 oz.) flour
125 g. (4 oz.) butter or margarine
1 egg

95 g. (3 oz.) sugar
60 g. (2 oz.) coconut
1¼ (1) teaspoon baking powder

Put the oats, flour, sugar, coconut and baking powder together. Rub in the butter and add the egg, well beaten. Put in small heaps on greased baking sheet and cook in a moderate oven.

Temp. 175°C (350°F).

Oat Fingers

125 g. (4 oz.) oats
95 g. (3 oz.) butter or margarine
1 teaspoon treacle or syrup

95 g. (3 oz.) brown sugar
1 teaspoon ginger or mixed
 spice (if desired)

Melt butter, sugar and treacle in saucepan. Lightly stir in oats. Turn into a greased square tin and bake from 15 to 20 minutes. When cooling turn out and cut into fingers.

Temp. 175°C (350°F).

Oatcakes

(a)

375 g. (¾ lb.) medium oatmeal   1 tablespoon flour
1 tablespoon lard or butter   1 teaspoon salt
a pinch bicarbonate of soda

Put all the ingredients in a basin and pour on enough boiling water to make a stiff dough. Mix well and leave to cool. Then roll out and cut into desired shapes, using dry oatmeal to dust. Place on a dry baking tin and bake in the oven.   *Temp. 175°C (350°F)—20–30 minutes.*

(b)

2 breakfast cups fine   1 tablespoon bacon fat or
   oatmeal   lard
salt

Mix with boiling water and allow to stand. Roll out on floured board, cut into triangles and bake in a hot oven.

Oatmeal Biscuits

155 g. (5 oz.) flour   ½ teaspoonful baking powder
220 g. (7 oz.) medium oatmeal   1 teaspoon castor sugar
125 g. (4 oz.) butter or margarine   ½ teaspoon salt

Sieve the flour, baking powder and salt. Rub the butter into the flour and add oatmeal and sugar. Mix the egg with a little water and add enough to the flour to make a stiff dough. Roll out thinly. Cut into squares and oblong pieces and mark neatly with knife. Bake in a moderate oven for 15 or 20 minutes.   *Temp. 175°C (350°F).*

Oatmeal Macaroons

1 cup sugar   ½ teaspoon salt
1 tablespoon melted butter   2½ cups rolled oats
vanilla   2 level teaspoons baking
2 eggs   powder

Mix the sugar with the butter. Add the egg yolks, salt and rolled oats. Then add the baking powder, beaten egg whites and vanilla. Mix thoroughly. Drop on greased tins, about ½ teaspoon to each macaroon, allowing space for spreading. Bake for about 10 minutes in a moderate oven.   *Temp. 175°C (350°F).*

Perkins

250 g. (8 oz.) flour   16 blanched almonds
125 g. (4 oz.) sugar   4 dessertspoons syrup
1 teaspoon bicarbonate of   250 g. (8 oz.) oatmeal
   soda   125 g. (4 oz.) butter or margarine
1 teaspoon ginger   1 teaspoon allspice

Grease a baking sheet. Blanch the almonds and split them. Mix the flour, sugar, baking powder, spices and oatmeal together in a basin. Melt the butter, add the syrup and make it hot. Add to the dry ingredients and mix to a paste. Turn on to a floured board, knead slightly. Roll out to about 1 cm. (½ in.) thick. Cut into rounds with a plain cutter and place half an almond on each. Bake in a very moderate oven for 20 minutes. Allow to become firm before removing from the tin.　　　　　　　　　　*Temp. 175°C (350°F)—20–30 minutes.*

Shortbread

(*a*)

185 g. (6 oz.) flour　　　　　　　125 g. (4 oz.) salt butter
60 g. (2 oz.) rice flour　　　　　　60 g. (2 oz.) sugar (castor)

　　Put all the ingredients into a baking bowl and knead with the hands until the butter absorbs all the rest of the ingredients. Place on a floured baking board and, with the hands, knead and pat into a round (or if desired 2 or 3 rounds or ovals) about 1 cm. (½ in.) thick. Pinch a border with the finger and thumb and prick the remainder of the cake with a fork. Cook in a moderate oven until a golden-brown for about ½ hour, but time depends on thickness of cake.
　　　　　　　　　　　　　　　　　Temp. 175°C (350°F).

(*b*) (*Pitcaithley Bannocks*)

　　These are made in the same way as above with the addition of some carraways mixed into the paste and strips of candied peel and hundreds and thousands sprinkled on the top.　　　　*Temp. 175°C (350°F).*

(*c*)

250 g. (8 oz.) flour　　　125 g. (4 oz.) butter　　60 g. (2 oz.) sugar
　　Cream the butter and sugar thoroughly and work in the flour gradually. Roll out and cut in squares or rounds as desired. Bake in a moderate oven till golden-brown.　　　*Temp. 175°C (350°F).*
　　The cooler the time of making shortbread the better. Early morning or evening is the best time.

Shortbread Biscuits

250 g. (½ lb.) flour　　　　　　　125 g. (¼ lb.) butter
95 g. (3 oz.) sugar (castor)　　　　1 egg yolk
a pinch of salt　　　　　　　　　1 tablespoon cream or milk

　　Sift the flour and salt into a basin. Add the castor sugar and rub in the butter. Mix this with the yolk of egg and cream. Turn the mixture on to a pastry board and work it with the hand till smooth. Roll out 6 mm. (¼ in.) thick and cut into fancy shapes. Put them on to a greased baking sheet and bake in a moderate oven 15 to 20 minutes.
　　　　　　　　　　　　　　　　　Temp. 175°C (350°F).
　　If liked, these biscuits may be decorated with pistachio nuts, almonds, cherries, citron or violets, before they are baked. For Easter Cakes add 30 g. (1 oz.) currants and a little spice or grated nutmeg. Cut in large rounds.

Sweet Biscuits

6 cups flour
2½ cups sugar
3 eggs
¾ cup butter
½ cup milk

¾ cup lard or dripping
15 g. (½ oz.) mixed spice
15 g. (½ oz.) bicarbonate of soda
½ tablespoon ground cloves
or ginger

Rub the butter into the flour and mix well. Beat the eggs and add. Add the soda to sufficient milk to form a dough stiff enough to roll out. Leave for 3 hours, then roll, cut out and bake on greased pans in a moderate oven. *Temp. 175°C (350°F).*

Water Biscuits

280 g. (9 oz.) sifted flour
60 g. (2 oz.) butter

a pinch of salt
water

Rub the butter and salt into the flour and add enough water to make a very stiff dough. Roll out very thinly, cut and prick with a fork. Bake in a very slow oven. *Temp. 150°C (300°F).*

Wexford Biscuits

125 g. (4 oz.) butter
250 g. (8 oz.) flour
185 g. (6 oz.) sugar

yolks of 2 eggs
white of 1 egg
tablespoon brandy

Rub butter well into flour. Add the sugar, yolks of eggs, the beaten white and the brandy. Mix well. Turn out on a baking board and roll the paste thin. Cut with a wineglass or tin cutter. Brush over the tops of each with white of egg and sift on a little sugar. Bake in a warm oven. *Temp. 175°C (350°F).*

SAVOURY SANDWICHES

General Hints

Use bread which is not more than one day old. For either sandwiches or rolled bread it is a good plan to cut the crusts off a new loaf the day before (or several hours before the bread is to be used), wrap the bread in a damp cloth and keep in a cool place till required.

The bread may be cut in thin slices lengthwise, if desired. See that the butter is soft and creamy. Fillings should be chopped finely, minced or sieved.

It is considered an improvement to moisten the filling with creamed butter, salad cream, mayonnaise or fresh cream.

If using mustard or curry powder, cream it with the butter.

Lettuce or watercress, salted, may be put on one side of the bread and butter and used with fillings.

Press sandwiches well together and cut into fancy shapes. If several kinds of sandwiches are made, cut each kind into a different shape and label each plateful with a small flag.

After making sandwiches, keep them covered with a damp cloth, lettuce leaves or a piece of banana leaf, till the moment they are to be eaten.

Asparagus Rolls

asparagus tips

a little mayonnaise (if liked)

salt and pepper

brown or white bread

Cut off crusts and roll loaf in damp cloth as described in general hints or butter thin slices of new bread, after removing crust. Place on each slice 1 large asparagus tip or 2 small ones, pointing outwards. Add seasoning. Roll up.

Asparagus Sandwiches

Mash asparagus tips, add seasoning.

Avocado Pear

avocado pear, mashed up

with a fork

salt and pepper

Worcester sauce or

mayonnaise to taste

Banana and Cream

3 bananas cut in rings or

mashed

a little lemon juice

75 ml. ($\frac{1}{2}$ gill) whipped cream

2 tablespoons raspberry jam

Beef and Tomato Sauce

Very thin slices of beef spread with the sauce and salt and pepper sprinkled over.

Instead of the tomato sauce the following could be used with cold beef: horseradish sauce, curry powder (creamed with butter) or grated radishes.

Cheese Sandwiches

60 g. (2 oz.) grated cheese

a little mustard

$\frac{1}{2}$ teaspoon vinegar

15 g. ($\frac{1}{2}$ oz.) butter

salt and pepper

Cheese and Anchovy Sauce

grated cheese and anchovy essence or sauce.

Cheese and Chutney

grated cheese and chutney (or pickles).

Cheese and Date Sandwiches

125 g. ($\frac{1}{4}$ lb.) dates cut up

125 g. ($\frac{1}{4}$ lb.) grated cheese

1 tablespoon cream

lettuce leaves for decoration

213

Checker Board Sandwiches

2.5 cm. (1 in.) slices   2.5 cm. (1 in.) slices
  brown bread   white bread
butter (creamed)   any sandwich paste

    Butter thickly 1 slice of brown and 1 slice of white bread and press buttered sides together. Cut this thick sandwich into 2.5 cm. (1 in.) slices, crosswise. Spread each of these slices again thickly with butter and any desired sandwich paste on outside, showing the brown and white layers. Press the slices together in pairs to form long blocks 5 cm. (2 in.) square, the brown and white alternating as in a checker board. Put in a cool place under a light weight. Cut each block in thin slices. Arrange on plate to show checks.

Cheese and Egg

    Same as Cheese Sandwiches above with 1 hard-boiled egg (chopped) added to the mixture.

Chicken Sandwiches

60 g. (2 oz.) cooked chicken   1 tablespoon white sauce
30 g. (1 oz.) butter   pepper and salt
1 dessertspoon chutney if desired

Chocolate Sandwiches

grated chocolate   whipped cream
vanilla essence

    Make the chocolate into a stiff paste with cream and add vanilla.

Cream Cheese and Celery

cream cheese seasoned and finely chopped celery or celery salt.

Cream Cheese and Nuts

cream cheese, salt and pepper, and chopped walnuts.

Cucumber Sandwiches

  (1) cucumber plain and sliced thinly with salt and pepper.
  (2) cucumber sliced thinly and put into vinegar to which a very small slice of onion has been added for flavouring. Drain cucumber, use for sandwiches sprinkled with salt and pepper.
  (3) cucumber chopped   a little onion juice
      finely   mayonnaise
     chopped parsley

Date and Nut Savoury

125 g. (¼ lb.) dates cut finely   60 g. (2 oz.) chopped nuts
2 tablespoons cream or ½   1 apple, grated, if liked
  butter and cream

Egg Sandwiches

hard-boiled egg (chopped
  finely)

salt and pepper
cream or butter

Egg Sandwiches for Children

1 egg scrambled
chopped parsley, if desired

salt

Egg and Anchovy

2 eggs hard-boiled (chopped
  finely or sieved)
pepper

15 g. (½ oz.) creamed butter
2 teaspoons anchovy essence
  or 2 chopped anchovies

Egg and Cold Beef

3 hard-boiled eggs
1 teaspoon Worcester
  sauce
salt

60 g. (2 oz.) cold minced beef
15 g. (½ oz.) butter
chopped parsley

Pound the yolks and mix with the other ingredients. Spread on buttered bread and sprinkle over this the finely chopped egg whites.

Egg and Olive

1 hard-boiled egg (sieved)
cream or butter

2 or 3 olives (chopped)
salt and pepper

Egg and Tomato Sandwiches

1 hard-boiled egg chopped
  finely
salt and pepper

1 tomato skinned and
  sieved or chopped

Foie Gras Sandwiches (imitation)

125 g. (4 oz.) calf's liver
60 g. (2 oz.) bacon
½ small carrot
½ small onion

minced
  or
chopped

salt and pepper
parsley, thyme, bay leaf
nutmeg
butter or cream

Fry bacon slightly: then add all the other ingredients, except the cream. Cook gently for about 10 minutes. Pound till smooth or rub through a sieve. Add cream or butter gradually till a soft paste is obtained.

Ham Potted for Sandwiches

cooked ham
nutmeg and mace

cayenne pepper
butter

Mince cold ham and mix with it a dash of cayenne, grated nutmeg and a little mace. Press into a buttered dish. Put greased paper on top and bake in the oven for 25 minutes. Pack into jars and put a layer of clarified butter on top. Any meat or fish paste may be made in the same way, *e.g.* chicken and tongue.

Ham Sandwiches

ham, minced   mustard creamed with butter

Harlequin Sandwiches

Filling (1) :—

90 g. (3 oz.) cooked ham, tongue, lobster or salmon	30 g. (1 oz.) butter salt and pepper

Filling (2):—

shredded lettuce seasoning	60 g. (2 oz.) butter

Remove crust, cut bread into 6 mm. (¼ in.) thick slices. Put alternate fillings between slices of bread, making 4 layers. Press well. Slice from top to bottom into sandwiches 6 mm. (¼ in.) thick.

Lentil and Anchovy Paste

cooked lentils sieved seasoning	butter anchovy essence

Marmite Sandwiches

Mix a little Marmite with 3 times as much butter and use this paste for sandwiches.

Marmite paste, combined with either cheese, cucumber, celery, egg or tomato, makes a good filling.

Nasturtium and Egg Sandwiches

young nasturtium leaves a little cream or butter	hard-boiled egg, chopped salt and pepper

Nut Sandwiches

Any kind of salted nuts peeled and chopped and sprinkled over buttered bread; or nuts chopped with mayonnaise and cayenne added.

Ribbon Sandwiches

Proceed as for Harlequin Sandwiches but use 4 different fillings, e.g. lettuce, tomato, chopped hard-boiled egg and grated cheese.

Salmon Sandwiches

remains of cold salmon butter	salt and pepper grated nutmeg

Mash salmon thoroughly and pound to a smooth paste with other ingredients. If put into a glass jar and covered with melted butter, this paste will keep a day or two, not longer. It may be cooked in the oven.

Sardine Sandwiches

sardines mashed or sieved
a little lemon juice or
  vinegar'

salt and pepper
creamed butter

Sardine and Egg

Add hard-boiled egg, chopped finely, to the sardine mixture as above.

Sardine and Tomato

Add tomato sauce or sieved tomato to mashed sardines and season well.

St. James' Sandwiches (for picnics)

puff pastry
finely chopped chicken,
  ham or tongue
cream

butter
lemon juice
1 egg
salt and pepper

Roll the paste 2 cm. ($\frac{3}{4}$ in.) thick and cut 6 or 7 cm. ($2\frac{1}{2}$ in.) long by 2.5 cm. (1 in.) wide. Brush over well with yolk of egg and bake in the oven. Prepare the chicken, ham or tongue, moisten with butter and cream and a few drops of lemon juice, then add seasoning. When the pastry is ready remove the top from each section with a knife and fill with the preparation. Brush the edges with white of egg and replace tops. Return to oven for a few minutes to set fillings and serve either hot or cold.

Tomato and Egg (cooked filling)

See under **Toasties**. This mixture is excellent for sandwiches.

Tongue (or Meat) Sandwiches

cold tongue minced

mustard creamed with butter
  or a little white sauce
  (well seasoned)

JAMS, JELLIES AND PRESERVES

GENERAL HINTS FOR JAM-MAKING

1. If jam is properly made it will keep for years, so give your personal attention to it.

2. Fruit used for jam should be under-ripe or just ripe.

3. When water is used the fruit should simmer in it very slowly before adding the sugar as this releases the pectin and acid in the fruit and helps it to set. Warm the sugar before adding to the fruit, stir in gradually with a wooden spoon, cook very gently until the sugar is completely dissolved, then turn on full heat and boil hard (the jam must boil so hard that it spits). Skim if necessary at the end of the boiling but frequent skimming is wasteful. Test the jam by putting a little on a cold plate and leave a minute; if the jam wrinkles when the plate is tilted it has reached the setting point.

One teaspoonful of pure glycerine added when the jam is almost ready will prevent the jam going sugary in storage.

4. When making marmalade or jam, butter the bottom of the preserving pan before putting in the fruit. This will prevent the contents from burning and lessen the danger of boiling over.

5. To sterilise bottles, jars and rubbers, put in the oven until thoroughly hot and dry. Only remove from oven when the jam is ready to bottle.

6. To prevent jam turning mouldy on top, cover with a piece of paper dipped in brandy, white of egg or clear mutton fat, before screwing on the lid.

Apple Jelly

apples   water
sugar   cloves (if liked)
lemon rind

Take any quantity of apples; wash well, cut in pieces. Put in preserving pan and cover with water. Boil to a pulp and strain through a jelly bag. To 600 ml. (1 pint) of liquid add 500 g. (1 lb.) of sugar. Boil for about 20 minutes or until a drop will jell on a cold plate. Lift from fire, skim carefully, bottle in hot jelly jars and cover when set.

Apricot Jam (Dried Fruit)

500 g. (1 lb.) dried apricots   2.5 l. (4 pints) water
1.75 kg. (3½ lb.) sugar   30 g. (1 oz.) almonds

Wash the fruit and soak from 24 to 48 hours in the water. Add sugar and let it dissolve. Boil for 1 hour. Add the almonds, blanched and cut in halves. Boil a few minutes longer and put in heated jars and cover.

Blackberry Jelly

Take any quantity of fruit; cover with water and boil to a pulp; strain and measure, allowing 600 ml. (1 pint) fruit juice to 500 g. (1 lb.) sugar. Return to preserving pan; boil until it jells and bottle in hot glass jars. Cover when set.

Cape Gooseberry Jam

Wash and prick the fruit with a fork. Add just a little water and a ½ cup lemon juice and boil till tender. Allow to stand overnight. Next morning weigh and strain off juice; add 500 g. (1 lb.) sugar to 600 ml. (1 pint) of pulp and juice. Put juice and sugar on the boil and when sugar is melted strain and allow to cool. Add fruit and boil till syrup jellies.

Green Fig Preserve

Scrape figs and slit on top. (If a little butter or fat is rubbed on the fingers and the figs are soaked in cold water, the fingers will not become sore during the scraping process.) Lay in cold water mixed with lime (2 tablespoons to 100 figs). About 12 hours later take out and wash clean. Have ready a saucepan of boiling water in which place a pinch of soda and a little salt and let the figs boil in this, leaving the lid off the pot. Take out when soft enough to be easily pierced with a straw. Drain through a colander or on a cloth. Take 1 kg. (2 lb.) of sugar more than the weight of fruit; make a clear syrup (1 cupful water to 1 cupful sugar) and when it is strained and cool, lay the figs in it for a night. The next day cook on a low heat till the fruit is quite clear.

Grenadilla Jam

Take any quantity of grenadillas, not over-ripe. Cut in halves, remove the juice and seeds and boil them with a little water. Strain through a hair sieve. Now boil skins until tender, in plenty of water. Strain away the water and scoop out the inner skin. Add juice from the seeds to this, measure and add 375 g. (1 lb.) sugar to 500 g. (1 lb.) pulp. A little lemon juice may be added. Boil until clear.

Guava or Loquat Jelly

Wash and cut up any quantity of fruit available; if loquats, remove the pips which are poisonous if cooked. Put fruit into a saucepan and just cover with water. Boil to a pulp. Pour all into a thick muslin bag and hang up to drip overnight, with a basin underneath. With loquats, a little lemon rind improves the flavour. Add 500 g. (1 lb.) sugar to 600 ml. (1 pint) of juice, bring to boiling point and then remove to the side of the stove. Simmer until a drop will jell on a cold plate. Bottle when hot and cover when set.

Kei Apple Jelly

Choose good ripe fruit; cut up and put into a preserving pan. Cover with water and cook to a pulp. Strain through a sieve. Weigh and add 625 g. (1¼ lb.) sugar to 600 ml. (1 pint) of liquid. A few guavas added to this counteract the acidity.

Kijabe Fig Jam (ripe fruit)

4 cups figs

4 cups sugar

juice of 1 lemon

grated rind of lemon and orange

Peel figs thinly and cut into small pieces. Add sugar and boil till amber-coloured. Bottle in heated jars.

Lemon Curd

500 g. (1 lb.) sugar

4 eggs

juice of 3 lemons

grated rind of 1 lemon

125 g. (¼ lb.) butter

Put the sugar, butter, juice and rind of lemon into a double saucepan; stir well and bring to the boil. Add well-beaten eggs, stirring continuously till the mixture thickens. Then bottle.

Lemon Curd (for immediate use)

juice of 2 lemons

1 teaspoon custard
   powder

1 egg

sugar to taste

Heat juice and sugar. Stir in custard powder mixed with a little cold water. When thick beat in yolk of egg and when cool add white of egg well beaten.

Peach Jam

Skin all peaches and cut into quarters. Crack half the stones and add kernels to the fruit. Cover fruit with water and boil until quite white and soft. Then add 500 g. (1 lb.) sugar to every 500 g. (1 lb.) fruit. To every 1 kg. (2 lb.) fruit add the juice and strained boiled pulp of 1 large lemon. Boil till it jellies and the pulp gets clear and the juice brownish.

Pineapple, Crystallised

pineapple

water

sugar

Cut pineapple into cubes. Just cover with water and boil 20 minutes. Strain off liquid. Allow 2 cups sugar to 1 cup liquid. When sugar is dissolved allow to cool. Add fruit and allow to stand for 1 day. Next day boil till transparent. Leave in syrup a further 2 days, then roll the cubes of fruit in sugar.

Pineapple Jam

pineapples   lemon   sugar

Peel and remove brown eyes of pineapples. Cut away hard core. Mince, being careful to catch all juice; add 1 cup of water to 5 cups of pulp and boil up for 15 minutes, counting from the time it starts to boil. Take care not to burn it. Weigh and add 375 g. (¾ lb.) sugar to 500 g. (1 lb.) pulp. Boil rapidly. Add strained juice of 1 lemon to each

5 cups. If lemon juice is not added it will not jell. A couple of apples peeled and cored may be used instead of each lemon. Boil again till it is clear and will not flow when cooled on a plate. Bottle and cover.

Pineapple and Vegetable Marrow Jam

1 fresh pineapple   sugar
1.5 kg. (3 lb.) vegetable marrow   salt

Cut and peel the marrows; weigh them and put into salt water, allowing 2 tablespoons of salt to 5 litres (1 gallon) of water. Set in a cold place overnight. Drain the marrow dry and cut into pieces about 5 cm. (2 in.) square. Place these in a large earthenware dish and to each pound of marrow allow 375 g. ($\frac{3}{4}$ lb.) sugar. Add the pineapple cut into squares, and the pineapple juice, and leave for 24 hours. Boil till clear (about 2 hours) and seal in jars.

Plum Jam

3 kg. (6 lb.) plums   3 kg. (6 lb.) preserving sugar
320 ml. ($\frac{1}{2}$ pint) water

Wipe the plums, removing all blemished fruit. Stone the plums; remove kernels from half the stones; blanch and skin the kernels. Tie the rest of the stones in muslin. Put the water and sugar in a preserving pan and let it dissolve slowly. Add the plums and the stones tied in muslin. Stir over a moderate heat till it boils. Boil rather quickly for about 30 minutes, skimming frequently and stirring to prevent burning. Test the jam on a cold plate; if it sets throw in the kernels and boil up well. Remove the stones and pour into hot, dry jars and cover at once.

Rhubarb Jam

2.5 kg. (5 lb.) rhubarb   2.5 kg. (5 lb.) sugar
80 g. ($2\frac{1}{2}$ oz.) whole ginger

Wipe rhubarb with clean, damp cloth and cut into small pieces. Put into jar or basin with sugar, cover, and leave for 2 days stirring now and again. Pour off syrup into preserving pan, add ginger and boil 30 minutes. Then pour over rhubarb and leave 24 hours. Put all into pan and boil till proper consistency (an hour or more).

Strawberry Jam

Remove the stalks and clean strawberries, weigh and add 500 g. (1 pound) of sugar for 500 g. (1 pound) of fruit. Put some of the strawberries in a deep basin, sprinkle with sugar and repeat until all strawberries and sugar are used. Allow to stand for 24 hours. Pour off the liquid in the basin into the preserving pan and bring to boil, stirring frequently. Add strawberries and boil for about 20 minutes. Skim, and when set, pour into hot jam-jars.

Some varieties of strawberries may be cooked immediately with the sugar. If this is done, add a cupful of water or fruit juice to moisten the sugar. This prevents the fruit getting broken whilst the sugar is melting.

Tomato Preserve

(a)

4 kg. (8 lb.) tomatoes
juice of 4 lemons
3.5 kg. (7 lb.) sugar

30 g. (1 oz.) sliced ginger and
mace mixed

Take small, sound, green fruit. Prick each several times. Add sugar
and the lemon juice, ginger and mace. Bring all slowly to the boil
together and let it cook till the fruit has a transparent appearance. Lift
out each fruit on a skimmer and arrange in a single layer on dishes.
Boil the syrup till it thickens, pack the fruit into jars and fill with syrup.
Cover when cold.

(b)

3.5 kg. (7 lb.) tomatoes
juice of 3 lemons

3.5 kg. (7 lb.) sugar

Weigh out firm, ripe tomatoes, blanch and peel and let stand
overnight with sugar and lemon juice. Drain off all the resultant
syrup and boil it, skimming carefully. Then add the tomatoes, being
careful not to break them, and boil together for 20 minutes. Take each
fruit out with a skewer and arrange in a single layer on dishes. Boil
the syrup down rapidly till it thickens. Pack the fruit into jars, pour
the hot syrup over and let it get cold before covering tightly. If the
flavour is preferred not too sharp, add the lemon juice to the syrup just
before the latter thickens.

A good hint is to let tomatoes stand overnight in a weak solution
of salt and water, allowing 2 tablespoons of salt to 5 bottles of water.
Rinse well before adding to syrup, allowing 3 kg. (6 lb.) sugar to 500 g.
(5 lb.) fruit. The salt water keeps the tomatoes firm.

Tree Tomato Jam

Choose large ripe fruit. Cut it up and put all into a pot. Just cover
with water and boil until it is reduced to a pulp, then pass through
a sieve. Weigh and add 500 g. (1 lb.) of sugar to 500 g. (1 lb.) of pulp.
Boil quickly until a nice colour.

Vegetable Marrow Jam

1 or 2 marrows to weigh 3 kg. (6
lb.) when peeled and cored
375 g. (¾ lb.) sugar to each pound
of marrow

750 g. (1½ lb.) preserved ginger
juice and rind of 2 lemons
60 g. (2 oz.) root ginger

Weigh marrow and cut into small cubes. Place in a bowl and cover
with sugar. Leave until next day, then strain off syrup and boil with
juice and rind of lemons and root ginger (tied in muslin bag). Cut
preserved ginger into small pieces and add with marrow to boiling
syrup. Boil for another hour, or less if transparent sooner. Remove
bag of ginger and pour into hot jam jars.

Whole Preserves. Oranges and Tangerines

Scrape the rind on a grater, or peel very thinly, just cutting through pores. Cut 1 cm. (½ in.) cross at the flower end of the fruit and put into cold water for 2 days, changing the water at least once during that time. Then put the fruit into a saucepan of boiling water and boil until fruit is soft enough to be pierced by a straw. Remove from the water and drain well.

Make a syrup, allowing 1 kg. (2 lb.) more sugar than the original weight of the fruit; a cup of water for every cup of sugar makes a good syrup. Boil up the syrup, strain and when lukewarm pour it over the boiled fruit and leave overnight. Next day, put the pan containing the fruit and syrup on the stove and preserve very slowly by keeping the syrup at simmering, not boiling, point. When the fruit is clear, put into widemouthed bottles; fill up with syrup and when cold cover carefully.

MARMALADES

Marmalade—Orange Jelly

As many Seville or bitter oranges as are required

1.25 litres (2 pints) water to 500 g. (1 lb.) oranges
1 kg. (2 lb.) sugar to 500 g. (1 lb.) oranges

Stalk and wipe oranges and weigh them. Put into jelly pan and pour over them cold water in above proportions. Bring to boil and let them boil gently till oranges are tender, covering them with plate to keep them under water. Boil 1½ hours, allow to cool, then lift the oranges out on to a colander and drain. Do not throw away water.

Cut oranges into quarters and scrape out soft pulp and pith into a clean bowl, tying pips up in a small muslin bag. Next cut the best of the peel with a sharp knife or a pair of scissors into very fine shreds, rub pulp through a sieve, scraping the sieve underneath from time to time. Return shredded peel, sieved pulp and pips (in bag) to the water in which oranges were boiled. Mix together, bring nearly to the boil, then add sugar. Dissolve sugar slowly, then boil up and continue to boil till it jells when dropped on a cold plate. Stir frequently and skim the top. When ready pour marmalade into dry, heated glass jars and when cool tie or screw down and make airtight. If orange jelly only is wanted, a very few of the shreds, or none at all, should be put in.

Marmalade—Orange

9 Seville or bitter oranges
2 extra sweet oranges
2 lemons

sugar in proportion of
500 g. (1 lb.) to 600 ml.
(1 pint) pulp
water in proportion of
1.25 l. (2 pints) to 500 g. (1 lb.)
oranges

Wipe oranges and lemons carefully with a damp cloth. With a sharp knife cut fruit into very thin slices and put into a large basin. (The pips should be put into a muslin bag and soaked in water sufficient to cover them. They are important in helping marmalade to jell.) Cover the cut up fruit with the water and allow to soak for 24 hours. Then boil, along with the pips and water in which they were soaked, until peel can be pulped between the fingers, probably after an hour or 1½ hours. Return fruit to basin and allow to stand overnight. Next day add the sugar. Bring again to the boil, skim well and test occasionally till the juice thickens at once when put on a cold plate. Dish into sterilised, hot jam jars, cover when cold.

Marmalade—Lemon or Grapefruit

As above.   (Orange Marmalade.)
Put 625 g. (1¼ lb.) sugar to 500 g. (1 lb.) pulp if for long keeping, or if bitter fruit.

BOTTLING FRUIT

Method I

A simple way if special jars are not available, suitable for stone fruit and gooseberries.

Choose dry fruits without blemish. Wipe and remove leaves and stalks. Pack the fruit tightly into glass jam jars. Place the jars on a pad of paper on a tin in a very moderate oven and leave until some of the fruit just begins to crack and change colour. Draw out the jars singly, fill up with boiling water to within 1 in. of the top, pour on some melted clarified mutton fat to come to top of the jars. Leave undisturbed till set. Cover with jam pot covers, or layers of waxed brown paper. Store, taking care not to shake or disturb.

Method II

This is suitable for any fruit except strawberries when screw-topped jars, with lid and rubber ring, are available.

Choose fruit which is just ripe. Wash or wipe and pack into wet jars. Cover with cold water till overflowing. Put on a perfect rubber ring top and screw. Release screw slightly to allow for expansion.

If a proper steriliser is not available, put into a fish kettle, or saucepan, but place on a false bottom made of pieces of wood crisscross, cardboard, paper or straw. Never stand jars direct on the bottom. Fill with cold water up to the necks of the bottles, put on lid of boiler and bring very slowly to about 75°C, well below boiling point. This should take 1½ hours at least. Allow to remain at this heat 5 to 10 minutes, depending on age and size of fruit. (Older and larger fruit takes longer). Remove from water, dry and screw down tightly. If no thermometer is available, heat very slowly till water in pan just begins to simmer, then remove bottles at once. Next day test screw and see if top is perfectly sealed; if not, fruit must be re-sterilised.

When fruit is to be used, pour off the liquid, add sugar to it and bring to the boil. Put fruit in for a few minutes and serve. For pies, etc., use straight from the bottle with sugar added.

For tomatoes add 1 teaspoon of salt to each jar and fill the jars to overflowing.

CHUTNEYS AND PICKLES

Chutney turns dark if overcooked. Therefore, if when cooked it appears to be too thin, it is better to add a little starch or cornflour than to cook it longer. The starch should be blended with a little vinegar and added to the boiling chutney.

Chutney may be covered, while hot, with melted mutton fat, which will come off easily when cold. This helps to prevent the lids from rusting.

Apple Chutney

750 g. (1½ lb.) cooking apples   ¾ teaspoon cayenne pepper
375 g. (¾ lb.) raisins or sultanas   1 teaspoon salt
250 g. (½ lb.) sugar   6 cloves
250 g. (½ lb.) small onions   4 chillies
600 ml. (1 pint) vinegar

Mince apples and onions. Stone the raisins and chop them. Sultanas may be left whole. Put all the ingredients except the vinegar into an enamel saucepan and cook for ½ hour. Add the vinegar and simmer for 3 hours. Pour into warm, dry jars and cover while hot.

This recipe is very good made with half apples and half mangoes.

Banana Chutney

(a)
12 bananas   2 carrots minced
250 g. (½ lb.) minced dates   2 tomatoes
2 teaspoons curry powder   1 tablespoon salt
1 kg. (2 lb.) minced onions   1 litre (1½ pints) vinegar
250 g. (½ lb.) brown sugar   1 tablespoon ground ginger
cayenne pepper to taste   a sprig of mace

Slice bananas, put into saucepan with other ingredients, cook to a pulp. Sieve, bring to the boil and bottle hot.

(b)

500 g. (1 lb.) onions	250 g. (½ lb.) seedless raisins
8 firm bananas	1 rounded teaspoon salt
15 g. (½ oz.) mixed pickling spice	125 g. (¼ lb.) crystallised ginger
480 ml. (¾ pint) of malt vinegar	185 g. (6 oz.) brown sugar
150 ml. (1 gill) syrup from a tin of pineapple	

Peel and coarsely mince the onions with the raisins and peeled bananas. Put into a pan with the salt, spices (tied in a muslin bag) and vinegar and cook for 15 minutes. Remove the bag of spices. Mince or chop the crystallised ginger and add with the sugar and pineapple juice. Cook, stirring, until the chutney is thick and beginning to turn brown and there is no free vinegar to be seen: fill at once into hot, sterilised jam jars. When cool, cover with cellophane paper or a screw-top lid.

Fruit Chutney

4 guavas	a little cayenne pepper
4 apples	500 g. (1 lb.) sugar
6 bananas or other fruit	1 teaspoon salt
500 g. (1 lb.) stoned raisins	2 large onions
250 g. (½ lb.) apricots	2 bulbs garlic
1·25 l. (2 pints) vinegar	

Soak apricots overnight. Chop the fruit and onions into small pieces. Boil with the vinegar and other ingredients until thick, stirring continuously.

Mango Chutney

To every 2 kg. (4 lb.) mangoes, weighed whole, measure out the following spices:

3 tablespoons mustard seed	a few chopped chillies
1 tablespoon coriander seed	2·5 l. (2 quarts) vinegar
1 level tablespoon pounded garlic	125 g. (4 oz.) raisins
	salt
3 heaped tablespoons minced onion	

Peel and slice the mangoes. Simmer the raisins till soft in half the vinegar. Boil the rest of the vinegar, add 3 heaped tablespoons salt, the mustard, coriander, garlic and chillies, tied in a muslin bag. Simmer for a few minutes, then add the onion, pour all on to the mangoes and simmer till tender, stirring well. The ingredients may all be minced to save time. Time required for cooking, about 1 hour.

Military Pickle

1 fair-sized marrow	1 cucumber
500 g. (1 lb.) cauliflower	500 g. (1 lb.) onions
500 g. (1 lb.) French beans	500 g. (1 lb.) sugar
7 chillies	2·5 l. (2 quarts) vinegar
30 g. (1 oz.) ginger	30 g. (1 oz.) turmeric powder
1 breakfast cup flour	

226

Cut vegetables small, cover with salt, leave for 12 hours, then drain. Put into saucepan, add the vinegar and boil for 6 minutes. Mix the powder ingredients to a smooth paste and add while boiling. Boil all for at least ½ hour, stirring well to prevent burning. Bottle and tie down.

Mushroom Ketchup

Peel and wash 3 kg. (6 lb.) of mushrooms and break them into earthenware jars, sprinkling them with 125 g. (¼ lb.) salt. Put them in a cool place for 12 hours, then strain and measure the juice and boil ¼ hour. Add for each 1·25 l. (one quart) of juice 10 g. (¼ oz.) allspice, 15 g. (½ oz.) ground ginger, 2 blades of mace and 30 g. (1 oz.) pepper. Let boil gently for ½ hour, then strain and allow to cool. Bottle, cork and seal.

Pawpaw Chutney

3 medium-sized pawpaws	750 g. (1½ lb.) seedless raisins,
6 large onions minced	chopped
3 tablespoons salt	6 small red chillies chopped
about 2 l. (3 pints) vinegar	2 teaspoons ginger
12 green tomatoes, skinned	1 teaspoon mustard
1 tablespoon mixed spice	750 g. (1½ lb.) sugar

Take pawpaws which are almost ripe, peel, and cut into neat strips about 2·5 cm. (1 in.) long. Place in a large bowl. Add the onions, mix the two ingredients well and cover with salt. Leave uncovered for 24 hours. Put the vinegar in a preserving pan, add the pawpaw and onion, bring to the boil and simmer for ½ hour. Add tomatoes, raisins, chillies, ginger, mustard, spice and lastly sugar. Keep well stirred and boil for about 1 hour, till every ingredient is cooked through and the chutney is of the right consistency.

Pickled Beetroot

beetroot	sugar
vinegar	a few peppercorns
salt	a little allspice (if liked)

Boil the beetroot (*see* page 108), slice it and put into a jar. Boil some vinegar with a little salt, sugar and a few peppercorns. When cold pour over the beetroot. This is ready for use in a day or two.

Pickled Cabbage

1 red cabbage	1 dessertspoon pickling spice
salt	12 peppercorns
1 litre (2 pints) vinegar	

Wash a large red cabbage and drain very dry. Shred it finely with a sharp knife, put into a basin and sprinkle well with salt. Leave this to stand for 48 hours and then drain off the salt.

Boil the vinegar with the pickling spice for 10 minutes. Put the cabbage into jars and press it well down. As soon as the vinegar is quite cold pour it over the cabbage. Cover the jars and stand them in a dark place. It is important that the vinegar is cold or the cabbage will go soft and flabby.

Pickled Cucumbers

small cucumbers
vinegar
salt
garlic

whole ginger
peppercorns
cloves

Using cucumbers of similar size, make a strong brine of salt and water and when boiling pour over cucumbers. Cover closely and let stand overnight. Place cucumbers on a sieve to drain and dry with a cloth. Make a pickle of sufficient vinegar to which add the spices and boil. When boiling add the cucumbers. Cover saucepan and boil fast for a few minutes. Put the pickles in wide-mouthed bottles, cork and tie down.

Pickled Egg Fruit (Brinjal)

6 small brinjals
onion
green chilli
vinegar

cloves
peppercorns
bay leaf
salt

Boil brinjals in salt water for 10 minutes. Cool, press all water out, add a few pieces of onion and green chilli. Pack in bottle with a few cloves, peppercorns and bay leaf. Cover with vinegar. If too sour a little sugar can be added to the vinegar. Ready for use in a few days.

Pickled Onions

2·5 kg. (5 lb.) small
  white onions
1·25 l. (1 quart) vinegar

30 g. (1 oz.) whole black
  peppercorns
15 g. (½ oz.) whole ginger, bruised.
1 saltspoon of cayenne pepper

Boil the vinegar with the spices and strain. Skin the onions and pack in bottles. Pour the vinegar over when cold and cover the jars. If liked very hot, alternate layers of chillies (which have been punctured with a fork) may be used with the onions. Ready for use in 7 to 10 days.

Tomato Chutney

1·5 kg. (3 lb.) tomatoes
750 g. (1½ lb.) apples
1 teaspoon allspice
60 g. (2 oz.) salt
2 large onions

1 litre (1½ pints) vinegar
125 g. (4 oz.) brown sugar
60 g. (2 oz.) ground ginger
250 g. (½ lb.) sultanas
125 g. (¼ lb.) blanched ground
  nuts

Scald tomatoes; remove skins; peel, core and chop apples and onions. Put into an enamel saucepan with other ingredients and boil gently for ½ hour. Just before removing from heat add ground nuts. Bottle when cold.

Tomato Chutney (Sweet)

2 kg. (4 lb.) ripe tomatoes
250 g. (½ lb.) onions, sliced
2 chillies, sliced

500 g. (1 lb.) sugar
2 breakfast cups vinegar
1 tablespoon salt

Peel and slice tomatoes. Boil all ingredients except vinegar for 1½ hours, then add vinegar and boil again till thick. Bottle while hot and cover to exclude the air.

Tomato Ketchup

6 kg. (12 lb.) red tomatoes	1 onion or 2 or 3 garlics
500 g. (1 lb.) sugar	¼ teaspoon cinnamon
45 g. (1½ oz.) salt	75 ml. (about ⅛ pint) tarragon
10 g. (¼ oz.) paprika or pinch	vinegar
cayenne pepper	600 ml. (1 pint) good vinegar
36 cloves	

Wash and cut up tomatoes. Place in pan over low heat and cook till they become pulped, stirring all the time to prevent sticking. Rub through a fine sieve. Return to pan and add all the other ingredients. Bring to boil, continue stirring and boiling till of a creamy consistency. Bottle in sterilised bottles, warmed. Cork and seal with paraffin wax.

Tomato Relish (Green Tomatoes)

1·5 kg. (3 lb.) green tomatoes	6 small onions
600 ml. (1 pint) malt vinegar	250 g. (½ lb.) brown sugar
2 teaspoons salt	2 teaspoons made mustard
1 teaspoon black pepper	

Wipe the tomatoes and slice them. Peel and shred the onions. Place all the ingredients in a preserving pan and cook gently for 2 hours, stirring occasionally. When all is soft, rub through a coarse sieve. Reboil the pulp. Pour into jars or bottles and cover immediately.

This is excellent for serving with cold meats and is a good method of using up tomatoes which do not ripen.

FRUIT DRINKS AND HOME MADE WINES

All cool drinks are greatly improved when iced.

Apple Water

3 apples	1 tablespoon sugar
½ lemon rind	3 breakfast cups water

Peel and cut the apples up in small pieces and put them into a jug, adding the lemon rind and sugar, then pour in the boiling water, cover and cool.

Barley Water

60 g. (2 oz.) barley	1·25 l. (1 quart) water
½ lemon rind	1 dessertspoon sugar

Wash the barley well and put it in a saucepan with the cold water. Add the rind of the lemon, very thinly pared off, and boil for ½ hour. Afterwards add the sugar and strain into a jug to cool.

Boston Cream

3·75 l. (3 quarts) cold boiled
water
750 g. (1½ lb.) white sugar
1½ teaspoons lemon essence

60 g. (2 oz.) tartaric acid
whites of 2 small eggs

Into the water stir all the other ingredients beating the 2 egg whites stiffly first and mix well. Put away in bottles for use.

When using it, put into a tumbler about ½ saltspoon of bicarbonate of soda, half fill the tumbler with water and mix. Pour in a glassful of the cream and a froth will rise to the top immediately, making a delicious drink, similar to lemonade.

Fruit Cocktail

Fill a shaker half full of broken ice.
Add juice of 1 orange
   juice of 1 lemon
   a little plain syrup (apricot or other fruit syrup)
   3 sprigs of mint
   a little white of egg
Shake well and strain.

Ginger Beer (Syrup)

2 litres (1½ quarts) boiling water
2 tablespoons tartaric acid
juice of 4 lemons

3 breakfast cups sugar
1½ teaspoons essence of
   ginger

Pour boiling water over the sugar and tartaric acid. Stir well till dissolved, then add the essence of ginger and lemon juice. When cold add the white of 1 egg and bottle for use. It will keep well. When using it, put ½ saltspoon of bicarbonate of soda in a tumbler and half fill with water; then add about 2 tablespoons, or more if preferred of the ginger syrup. A froth rises to the top when stirred.

Lemonade

1 lemon
1 tablespoon sugar

250 to 300 ml. (about ½ pint)
   boiling water

Cut a few pieces of the thin yellow rind from the lemon, then squeeze out the juice; put the rind and juice in a jug with the sugar and pour over boiling water. Cover closely and, when cold, strain.

Lemon Syrup

The juice of 50 lemons. To every 1·25 l. (one quart) of juice add 1·5 kg. (3 lb.) sugar.

Place in an earthenware bowl in a pot of hot water and steam until the juice becomes like thin honey.

Lime Drink

1 teaspoon lime juice
4 teaspoons rum
½ tumbler hot water

2 teaspoons sugar
a little nutmeg

Put the ingredients into a tumbler and drink while still hot. Very good for a cold!

Lime Juice

60 g. (2 oz.) citric acid	juice and rind of 12 lemons
30 g. (1 oz.) tartaric acid	2 kg. (4 lb.) sugar
30 g. (1 oz.) Epsom salts	2 litres (3 pints) boiling water

Pour boiling water over all other ingredients. Allow to stand overnight, so that the dry ingredients are dissolved. In the morning strain and bottle.

Orangeade

14 oranges	60 g. (2 oz.) tartaric acid
30 g. (1 oz.) Epsom salts	30 g. (1 oz.) citric acid
1·75 kg. (3½ lb.) sugar	1·25 l. (2 pints) boiling water
grated rind of 6 oranges	

Put juice, rind, sugar, salt and acid into pan. Add boiling water. Stir till ingredients have dissolved. Bottle while warm.

Orange Cup

1 large lump ice	500 ml. (1 pint) fresh orange
juice of 1 lemon	juice
75 ml. (½ gill) of syrup	1 litre (1 quart) iced water or
75 ml. (½ gill) of fruit syrup	soda water

Put all the ingredients into a jug, adding the water last. Stir well. Decorate with thinly cut slices of orange.

Pineapple Punch

1 large pineapple	juice of 1 large grapefruit
juice of 6 oranges	750 g. (1½ lb.) sugar
juice of 4 lemons	1·25 l. (2 pints) boiling water

Mix in a bowl the pineapple (grated), juice of grapefruit, oranges and lemons. Dissolve sugar in boiling water and when cold pour over fruit. Allow to stand for 1 or 2 hours, then strain, and it is ready for immediate use. Allow one-third of this mixture to two-thirds of water or soda.

Sufficient for 20 or 30 guests.

Pineapple Syrup

1 large pineapple   sugar

Remove core and rind and weigh remaining fruit. Take an equal weight of sugar. Mince fruit finely, put half of sugar in a basin and cover with fruit, placing remaining half of sugar on top. Place a large plate, weighted, on basin and allow to remain for 24 hours or longer. Then put in an enamel pan and boil for not less than 1 hour, stirring frequently. As some pineapples give out more juice than others it is sometimes necessary to boil several hours, to reduce to a thick liquid, which when cold should be of the consistency of condensed milk or cream. Use 2 teaspoons to a tumbler of water or soda, to which may be added some lemon, if desired.

Wineberry Syrup

1 kg. (2 lb.) wineberries   30 g. (1 oz.) citric acid
875 g. (1¾ lb.) sugar   1½ breakfast cups water

Mix the citric acid and the water together and pour both over the fruit. Let it stand for 24 hours and then strain it through a jelly bag. Now add the sugar and heat it until dissolved or merely allow it to stand for 1 day until quite dissolved. When cold, bottle for use.

Syrups may be made from different varieties of fruit in a similar manner and if well corked will keep for years.

SWEETS AND FONDANTS

Notes on Sugar Boiling

1. Sugar must first be dissolved over gentle heat and then brought to boiling point; never try to boil and dissolve sugar at the same time. When it boils, remove scum. -

2. Unless otherwise stated, do not skim or shake during the boiling process, as any disturbance is likely to cause the syrup to grain, or become sugary.

3. Toffee should be cooled at an even temperature and marked out when lukewarm. A buttered or oiled knife should be used and the top should be marked straight through. The knife should not be dragged across.

4. Certain toffees are pulled. To do this, allow the toffee to become cool enough to be handled.

Temperatures

The temperatures given below are those at sea level. It has been found that in Nairobi, altitude 1,675 m. (5,500 ft.), the temperatures should be reduced by about 5°C (10°F).

THE THREAD

Boil the sugar and water 2 or 3 minutes. Dip the finger and thumb in cold water, dip into the syrup and then again into cold water. Pinch the finger and thumb together, pull apart, when a fine thread should be seen.   *Temp. 110°C (230°F).*

THE BALL

The syrup is tested by dipping the finger and thumb into water and into the syrup and back into water. The syrup, when ready, can be rolled into a soft ball. The boiling, if continued a little longer, will bring the syrup to a hard ball.   *Temp. 115°C (238°F).*

THE CRACK

This is the temperature usually required for toffees. The syrup is tested as before and forms a piece of toffee which can be cracked. For "hard crack" it must be boiled 1 or 2 minutes longer.

Temp. 140–150°C (280–300°F).

CARAMEL

The syrup changes colour rapidly and becomes "caramel". Prolonged boiling darkens it, until eventually it browns.

Temp. 175°C (350°F).

Almond or Ground Nut Pralines

250 g. (½ lb.) sweet almonds   250 g. (½ lb.) granulated sugar
240 ml. (1½ gills) water

Blanch the almonds, dry and leave whole. Put the sugar into a strong saucepan, add the almonds and stir continuously over a very steady heat until the almonds are brown and brittle and the sugar sandy. Add the water. Stir until sugar is dissolved and beat until a hard ball will form when tested in water. Drop from a teaspoon in small heaps on to an oiled tin.

Boiled Fondant

500 g. (1 lb.) sugar   160 ml. (¼ pint) water
30 g. (1 oz.) glucose or a good pinch of cream of tartar

Put sugar and water into a pan and dissolve very slowly. Then bring to the boil and add cream of tartar. Boil quickly and test for "soft ball". Have ready a marble or enamel slab sprinkled with water, pour on the syrup and leave for a few minutes to cool. Then with a palette knife work the edges of the syrup towards the centre, until the fondant is cool enough to handle. Knead well with the hands till smooth and firm. Divide into portions, colour and flavour as desired. If a slab is not available, the fondant may be creamed in a bowl till thick and then kneaded on sugared greaseproof paper, but it is more difficult to obtain an even creaminess by this method.

Unboiled or Plain Fondant

1 kg. (2 lb.) best icing sugar   whites of eggs
a good pinch of cream of   1 dessertspoon lemon juice
  tartar

Roll and sieve icing sugar. Add cream of tartar, lemon juice and beaten egg whites, using enough to make a pliable paste. Knead thoroughly for 5 minutes, then leave for 1 hour before using.

Unboiled fondant does not keep.

Cherry Creams (Fondant)

Make small ball of fondant, coloured pale pink; put halves of preserved cherries on each side and add a stalk of angelica.

Coconut Ice

(a)

1 kg. (2 lb.) sugar	1 dessertspoon butter
250 g. (½ lb.) coconut	pinch of cream of tartar
300 ml. (½ pint) milk	colouring

Put milk and sugar on to boil slowly. Stir all the time. Boil until the mixture will spin a thread between the fingers (15 minutes), add pinch of cream of tartar and butter. Take off fire and stir in coconut until thick. Pour half amount into greased tin. When skin forms add other half coloured.

(b)

3 cups sugar	¾ breakfast cup milk

Boil for 10–15 minutes. Add 1 cup coconut and boil for a few minutes. Take off and beat until creamy, then pour into well-greased tin. Repeat for top layer but add a few drops of cochineal. Cut into squares while slightly soft.

Coffee Cream Fondant

Add coffee essence to plain fondant and knead well.

Cream Fondant

500 g. (1 lb.) icing sugar	¼ teaspoon cream of tartar
2 tablespoons cream	1 white of egg

For method *see* Unboiled Fondant.

Harlequin Creams or Rainbow Fondant

Divide 500 g. (1 lb.) of fondant into 4 portions. Colour 1 portion yellow and flavour with lemon; colour another portion pink and flavour with rose water; colour another pale green and flavour with orange flower water; colour the remainder pale mauve and flavour with sweet violet essence. Make into fancy shapes and place a pistachio nut on each.

Mocha Fondant

Into 250 g. (½ lb.) of warm fondant stir enough coffee essence to colour to a pale brown. Allow to cool, then form the fondant into large balls. Press half walnut on each side of the balls and leave them to dry.

Nut Creams (Fondant)

Take fondant coloured pink or green and flavoured with vanilla. Make into round sweets and place a ground nut or hazel nut on each. Ground nuts should be blanched previously and slightly browned in the oven.

Peppermint (Creams Fondant)

Add essence or oil of peppermint to plain fondant, mould and dry for some hours.

Rainbow Sweets (Fondant)

Roll out some violet fondant 6 mm. (¼ in.) thick, moisten with white of egg and place a layer of plain marzipan on top. Moisten again with white of egg and cover with a layer of rose fondant. Each layer should be very flat and 6 mm. (¼ in.) thick. Roll slightly and cut into small squares, rounds or diamonds. Leave to dry for 24 hours.

Rose Creams (Fondant)

Add rose essence and pink colouring to plain fondant.

Violet Creams (Fondant)

Take fondant, flavour with essence of violet and add a few drops of violet colouring. Make into flat sweets and put a walnut or crystallised violet on top.

Fudge

(*a*)

1 kg. (2 lb.) brown sugar	300 ml. (½ pint) fresh milk
60 g. (2 oz.) butter	1 tablespoon syrup
½ tin condensed milk	

Mix all together and boil slowly for 30 minutes. Test for soft ball. Remove from heat and beat well for 3 minutes until thick and creamy. Pour into greased tin and cut when cool but not cold.

(*b*)

1 kg. (2 lb.) sugar	1 tin condensed milk
1 teacupful milk	2 teaspoons vanilla
125 g. (4 oz.) butter	

Put all ingredients except vanilla into pan and stir well before putting on fire and boil for 25 to 30 minutes. Test for soft ball, take from heat to a cool place and add vanilla. Stir until the mixture begins to grain and pour into a buttered tin and cut into squares when set. 60 g. (2 oz.) of chopped nuts may be added if desired.

Jubilee Fudge

750 g. (1½ lb.) sugar	½ cup walnuts or almonds
½ cup syrup	¼ cup cherries
1 cup water	2 stiffly beaten egg whites
1 teaspoon vanilla essence	

Put sugar, syrup and water on to boil. Beat egg whites and when syrup, etc., forms a tough drop, pour half on the egg whites and mix. Return rest of syrup to stove until it forms a very crisp drop. Pour into egg mixture, whisking well. Add vanilla, nuts, cherries and any colouring desired. After it is well beaten pour on to a flat buttered dish. Cut as soon as it sets, while still warm.

Mayfair Fudge

2 cups castor sugar
⅔ cup milk
½ cup raisins

2 tablespoons butter
½ cup stoned dates
½ cup shelled walnuts

Pour sugar and milk into a saucepan and bring to boiling point, stirring occasionally. Boil until the soft ball degree is reached and then stir in butter, chopped dates, raisins and walnuts. Cool and when tepid beat till creamy. Pour into a buttered tin and cut into squares when cold.

JELLIED SWEETS

Creme de Menthe

30 g. (1 oz.) gelatine
500 g. (1 lb.) sugar
12 drops oil of peppermint

juice of 1 lemon
1 teacup water

Soak gelatine with water and lemon juice; add sugar and boil for 5 minutes. Add peppermint and colour to taste. Put in deep, damp dish to set. Cut in squares with sharp scissors and dip in equal quantities of sugar and cornflour.

Ginger Squares

30 g. (1 oz.) powdered gelatine
320 ml. (2 gills) cold water
440 g. (14 oz.) castor sugar
240 ml. (1½ gills) boiling water
cornflour

125 g. (4 oz.) chopped crystallised
  ginger
1 tablespoon lemon juice
icing sugar

Soak the gelatine in the cold water. Boil the sugar and boiling water together for 10 minutes. Add the gelatine and boil for 15 minutes. Add the lemon juice and ginger, cool and then pour into a damp tin. Stand for 24 hours. Cut into neat squares and allow to stand for a few hours. Toss in equal quantities of icing sugar and cornflour.

Marshmallows

30 g. (1 oz.) gelatine
320 ml. (2 gills) cold water

125 g. (4 oz.) icing sugar
white of 1 egg

2 tablespoons orange essence (or caramel essence, orange and vanilla mixed)

Put the gelatine, sugar and water into a basin, set over a saucepan of boiling water and stir till dissolved. Remove the basin and let the mixture cool slightly. Add the flavouring and the stiffly whipped white of egg. Whisk till the mixture is almost set and pour into a tin which has been dusted with cornflour. When firm, cut into squares or rounds and roll in equal quantities of cornflour and icing sugar. Half of the marshmallows may be dipped in melted chocolate.

Raspberry Delight

30 g. (1 oz.) gelatine
raspberry essence

500 g. (1 lb.) loaf sugar
carmine colouring
320 ml. (½ pint) cold water

Dissolve the gelatine and the sugar in the water and boil for 2 minutes. Then add the colouring and essence to taste. Have ready some tins dipped in cold water; pour the mixture into these, making it about 1 in. thick. When set, cut into blocks, using a knife constantly dipped in boiling water, and roll in icing sugar previously rubbed through a sieve.

Turkish Delight

May be made as Creme de Menthe but different flavourings and colourings should be used.

MARZIPANS, ETC.

Marzipan

250 g. (½ lb.) ground almonds
250 g. (½ lb.) icing sugar
white of egg

1 teaspoon vanilla essence
1 teaspoon orange flour
water

Mix the ingredients, add flavourings and enough white of egg to make a soft but dry paste. Colour as desired and use to make up into fancy shapes or fruits.

Marzipan Carrots

Use orange and red colouring to get the correct shade, form into small carrot shapes and mark a few lines around each with a skewer. Insert thin pieces of angelica in top.

Mock Marzipan

125 g. (4 oz.) cake crumbs
30 g. (1 oz.) semolina
95 g. (3 oz.) castor sugar

2 teaspoons almond essence
¼ teaspoon lemon essence
½ egg

Mix all dry ingredients with hand, add egg and essence and bind well. Divide into portions and colour.

Marzipan Potatoes

Mould the marzipan into small potatoes, making dents with a skewer to represent the eyes. Roll in cocoa or chocolate powder and dry.

Marzipan Walnuts

Colour marzipan pink and roll into small balls. Press half walnut on 2 sides with the marzipan as a centre. Almonds, dates, prunes, crystallised cherries and other fruits may be used with marzipan to make various sweets.

Nougat

125 g. (4 oz.) icing sugar
125 g. (4 oz.) honey
30 g. (1 oz.) glacé cherries

250 g. (8 oz.) almonds
2 whites of eggs
wafer paper

Blanch and dry the almonds thoroughly. Line a tin box carefully, first with white paper and then with wafer paper. Put the sugar, honey and whites of eggs into a strong pan and stir by the side of the heat till the mixture becomes thick and white. Drop a little into cold water: if it hardens at once, remove from the heat. Stir in the almonds. Dredge a slab with icing sugar, turn the nougat on to it, and press well to make compact. Press into the prepared tin, cover with wafer paper, put a weight on it and stand for 24 hours. When cold cut with a sharp, hot knife.

Stuffed Dates

Pour boiling water over the dates, strain immediately and dry on a clean cloth. Remove stones. Stuff with one of the following:

Piece of walnut, or almond, which should be blanched and slightly dried in oven.

Marzipan, coloured and flavoured.

Piece of fondant.

After stuffing, roll in sieved icing or castor sugar, or dip in Royal icing (*see* page 204) and drain or roll in desiccated coconut.

TOFFEES

Almond or Groundnut Toffee

500 g. (1 lb.) sugar
30 g. (1 oz.) butter
95 g. (3 oz.) chopped almonds
a little almond essence
2 tablespoons golden syrup

150 ml. (1 gill) water
¼ teaspoon cream of tartar
2 or 3 drops acetic acid or
1 teaspoon vinegar

Bring water and sugar to the boil. Add butter, cream of tartar, acid and golden syrup. Boil again for a few minutes to the crack degree. Pour on to a greased tin and sprinkle chopped nuts over it. When nearly set, cut into squares.

Butterscotch

1 tin unsweetened milk
4 tablespoons golden syrup
440 g. (14 oz.) sugar

95 g. (3 oz.) butter
240 ml. (1½ gills) water

Put all ingredients into a pan; heat gently and boil; cook until it forms a hard ball when tested. Pour into an oiled tin and mark out when nearly set.

Chocolate Toffee

60 g. (2 oz.) cocoa
500 g. (1 lb.) sugar
vanilla flavouring

1 tin sweetened condensed milk
125 g. (¼ lb.) butter

Melt the butter in a saucepan, add the sugar and dissolve slowly over a gentle heat. Stir in the milk mixed with the cocoa, bring to the boil for 15 to 20 minutes. Test for hard ball degree; stir well while boiling. When ready flavour with vanilla and pour into a buttered tin. When nearly set, cut into squares with a sharp knife.

Everton Toffee

1 kg. (2 lb.) sugar
80 ml. (⅓ gill) water

375 g. (¾ lb.) butter
1 tablespoon vinegar

Boil all ingredients over a gentle heat until the toffee thickens. Turn out on a buttered dish and cut in pieces.

Helensborough Toffee

(a)

500 g. (1 lb.) brown sugar
1 tin sweetened milk

1 teaspoon vanilla essence
250 g. (½ lb.) butter
1 tablespoon milk

Put sugar, milk and butter into a pan. Stir until it boils and continue stirring for 10 minutes. Beat slightly. Test for soft ball. Take off stove add vanilla and pour into greased tins. When nearly cool mark in squares.

(b)

½ cup water
125 g. (¼ lb.) butter
1 kg. (2 lb.) sugar

1 tin sweetened condensed milk
1 teaspoon vanilla or almond
essence

Put water in pan and add butter and sugar and bring to boil. Add the condensed milk, boil until sugary and test in cold water after 20–30 minutes. Remove from stove, add vanilla essence stirring rapidly. Pour into buttered trays.

Peanut Brittle

1 kg. (2 lb.) peanuts

500 g. (1 lb.) sugar

Put sugar and 1 dessertspoonful of water into a large pan. Stir until sugar is dissolved and becomes a light-brown colour. Mix in chopped nuts, turn on to buttered flat dish.

Russian Toffee

250 g. (½ lb.) sugar
125 g. (¼ lb.) butter
vanilla or other flavouring

150 ml. (¼ pint) cream
1 tablespoon red currant or
guava jelly

Place the sugar, butter and cream in a stewpan and stir till the mixture thickens and leaves the sides of the pan clean. Add jelly and flavouring. Pour on to a buttered tin and when cold cut into squares.

Toffee (simple)

2 teacups sugar
2 tablespoons butter
2 tablespoons water

2 tablespoons vinegar
2 tablespoons syrup

Put all ingredients in a pan and stir slowly. Bring to boil and boil for 15 minutes. Do not stir after it boils. Turn out into a buttered tin. Before quite cold and set, mark in squares. When cold break into pieces and wrap in cellophane or waxed paper.

Toffee Treacle

750 g. (1½ lb.) brown sugar   500 g. (1 lb.) treacle
250 g. (8 oz.) butter   240 ml. (1½ gills) water
a pinch of cream of tartar

Put all the ingredients, except the cream of tartar, into a pan; cover and bring to the boil rapidly. When the toffee boils, add the cream of tartar, dissolved in a little cold water. Replace the lid, continue boiling for a few minutes longer, remove the lid, wash down the sides of the pan with a brush dipped in cold water, then boil until a drop of the mixture forms a hard ball in cold water. Pour into oiled tins to cool, mark with a knife, break into squares when cold and wrap in waxed paper or cellophane. Store in airtight tin.

INVALID COOKERY

The following list of dishes suitable for invalids cannot fail to be useful to those who have the care of the sick. During the convalescence of a patient every effort should be made to see that meals are tempting and as varied as the nature of the illness allows. Food should be served in small quantities, as daintily as possible, and should be very nourishing and easily digestible.

Albumen Water

Take the white of a fresh egg and put it on a plate and with 2 knives cut all ways for a minute. Add a tablespoon of cold boiled water and mix well. Put into a cup and flavour with a pinch of salt or a little lemon.

Arrowroot Cup

1 teaspoon arrowroot   1 teaspoon castor sugar
280 ml. (½ pint) milk

Mix the arrowroot with a little cold milk. Boil the remainder of the milk and pour it over the arrowroot. Stir and boil for 5 minutes. Add the sugar and serve. If more of a pudding is desired use 2 teaspoons of arrowroot to 280 ml. (½ pint) of milk.

In case of acute stomach trouble arrowroot should be cooked with water only, till clear like starch. It is then a good medium for any stimulant such as rum or brandy.

Barley Water

60 g. (2 oz.) pearl barley   30 g. (1 oz.) sugar
1·25 l. (1 qt.) water   1 lemon (if desired)

Blanch the barley, then put it with the water in an enamel saucepan and simmer for 2 hours. Strain, add sugar and cool. Lemon juice may be added.

Barley water should be made fresh daily as it does not keep well.

Beef Tea

500 g. (½ lb.) gravy beef or rump steak   300 ml. (½ pint) water
a pinch of salt

Wipe the meat thoroughly, removing all the fat. Scrape and place the pulp in a jam jar with the water and salt. Stand covered for ½ hour to draw out the juices, pressing from time to time; then cover with greased paper, put the jar in a pan of cold water, bring to the boil and simmer slowly for from 2 to 3 hours. Strain and serve hot and free from grease.

Particles of grease can be removed by skimming the surface of the beef tea lightly with soft paper.

Cooked beef tea should only be subjected to very gentle heat as the albumen will then be in a light and digestible form. If a double saucepan is used, care must be taken to prevent overheating. When beef tea has to be provided quickly it can be made by omitting the standing and by placing the ingredients straight into a pan and then heating them slowly for 1½ hours, or for a shorter time if necessary. A fresh quantity of beef tea should be made every day. Provided it is cooked slowly, the covered jar containing the beef tea can be placed in a moderate oven from 2 to 3 hours.

Beef Tea Custard

2 egg yolks   300 ml. (½ pint) beef tea
pinch of salt

Beat the eggs, add the beef tea and salt, beating until well mixed. Strain into a buttered cup or small mould, cover with greased paper. The water should be boiling when the custard is put in the pan, which should then be covered and the heat reduced so that the custard sets lightly. Cook for 20 minutes, or until firm. Serve hot or cold with crisp toast or a plain biscuit.

Creamed Chicken

125 g. (¼ lb.) breast of chicken (partially cooked)   60 g. (2 oz.) breadcrumbs
salt
300 ml. (½ pint) chicken or veal broth   1 or 2 tablespoons cream

Soak the breadcrumbs in milk; mince the chicken, or chop very finely. Strain the breadcrumbs, put them into a pan with the meat, broth and salt, then stir. Bring to the boil, stir in the cream and serve.

Chicken Jelly

Cut up the chicken and put the pieces in a jar with just enough cold water barely to cover the meat. Cover the top of the jar and place in a pan of boiling water, adding more hot water from time to time. Simmer for 6 hours and then strain and add a pinch of salt. When cold skim off the fat. A nourishing jelly remains. When partially cooked the breast can be removed and used for Creamed Chicken.

Chicken Soup

Put the chicken into a little cold water with a bunch of herbs, 2 leeks and 1 carrot, salt and pepper, and simmer for 3 hours. Strain the soup before serving. If liked a little vermicelli or rice may be boiled in the soup after straining.

Chops Steamed

Trim the chops and remove all fat. Butter 2 plates and place the chops between them. Add 1 tablespoon water, to make steam. Set on pan of boiling water and cook till tender.

Egg, boiled for invalid

The best way to boil an egg for a child or an invalid is to place the egg in boiling water, draw the pan to the side of the stove and leave the egg to simmer for 5 minutes. The cooking is thus slower and as a result the white is not too hard and the yolk is more perfectly cooked.

Egg Flip

Beat a new laid egg with 1 teaspoon of sugar and put into a large tumbler. Add very gradually 300 ml. ($\frac{1}{2}$ pint) of hot milk. One teaspoon of brandy may also be added.

Egg Jelly

150 ml. (1 gill) lemon juice   15 g. ($\frac{1}{2}$ oz.) gelatine
300 ml. ($\frac{1}{2}$ pint) water   95 g. (3 oz.) loaf sugar
2 eggs

Put the sugar, water and gelatine into a pan, stir gently and simmer for 10 minutes. Cool a little, add the lemon juice and strain on to the beaten yolks of the eggs. Return to the pan and stir till the yolks thicken the liquid, but, on no account allow to boil. Cool and when nearly cold, fold in the beaten whites of eggs. Turn into small wet moulds. When set, dip the moulds in hot water and turn out.

Gruel

30 g. (1 oz.) medium oatmeal   300 ml. ($\frac{1}{2}$ pint) water or milk
pinch of salt   or 150 ml. ($\frac{1}{4}$ pint) water and
      150 ml. ($\frac{1}{4}$ pint) milk

Soak the oatmeal in the water for 1 hour, stirring occasionally. Strain the liquid into a pan, add the salt, bring to the boil, stirring constantly, and simmer for 15 minutes. This makes a thin gruel. If a thicker gruel is required, use more oatmeal.

Water gruel assists perspiration whereas milk retards.

Ice Cream (*see recipes on page* 154)

Liver

Ways of Cooking:
Fried.
Lightly grilled with tomato.
Mince made with fresh liver.
Baked liver (sliced and spread with forcemeat and onion stuffing and a rasher of bacon, baked 1½ hours, with a little stock in the dish).

Liver Jelly

125 g. (¼ lb.) minced liver
about 15 g. (¼ to ½ oz.) gelatine
300 ml. (½ pint) brown stock
1 hardboiled egg or a few neat pieces of cooked vegetable
   to decorate moulds

salt and pepper
1 teaspoon Bovril

Dissolve the gelatine in the stock with the Bovril; strain and season. Rinse out 4 small moulds with cold water and put a slice of egg or a few pieces of vegetable at the bottom of each. Set these with a little jelly mixture, then fill up with the rest of the jelly mixture to which the minced liver has been added. Turn out when set and arrange on watercress or lettuce.

Liver Soup

Method as for Kidney Soup (*see* Soups), allowing to simmer gently only ¾ hour. Rub through fine sieve, thicken and add a little gravy colouring if necessary.

Milk Jelly

600 ml. (1 pint) milk
15 g. (½ oz.) gelatine

45 g. (1½ oz.) castor sugar
strip of lemon rind

Heat the milk with the lemon rind and allow to stand for a few minutes to extract the flavour. Add the gelatine and sugar and stir gently till dissolved. Strain into a basin. Pour into wet moulds and turn out when cold.

Milkless Pudding (uncooked)

4 eggs
1 tablespoon castor sugar
   to taste

15 g. (½ oz.) powdered gelatine
1 teacup water or orange juice

Separate yolks and whites of eggs. Beat yolks with half sugar till light and creamy. Soak gelatine and slightly warm in water or orange juice till thoroughly melted; add beaten yolks and sugar. Whip up whites with remainder of sugar and stir in gently. Chill.

If water is used flavour with lemon or vanilla essence.

Rice Water

60 g. (2 oz.) rice   1·25 l. (1 quart) tepid water

Carefully wash the rice in cold water. Soak rice in tepid water on top of the stove for 3 hours, then boil slowly for 1 hour and strain. When cold give to the patient adding flavouring if this is allowed.

A useful drink in cases of diarrhoea or dysentery; made in a few hours.

Sour Milk Junket

When milk has "turned" but has not yet become thick, pour it into custard glasses. When it becomes solid, sprinkle with sugar and cinnamon or a little nutmeg and serve as junket. To hasten the process of souring, a little buttermilk may be added to fresh milk. This dish is much used on the Continent and is most excellent for children and invalids, as the lactic acid developed in the milk makes it more easily digested than fresh milk.

Buttermilk is the milk which remains after the butter has been separated from the cream by churning.

Other Invalid Dishes

Beef Extract made with milk.

Bovril or Marmite.

Chicken braised or boiled, chicken creams or shapes (*see* Chicken Dishes).

Jellies, milk puddings, junket, lemon sponge, baked apple (*see* Cold Puddings.)

Mutton and veal broths (strained), milk soup, clear soup.

Poached eggs and omelettes (*see* Breakfast Dishes).

Steamed fish, fish baked in milk, fish soufflé, fish custard (*see* Fish Section).

Stewed sweetbreads, tripe or brains (*see* Entrées).

Steamed mutton chops (*see* Entrées).

HOUSEHOLD HINTS

CLEANING HINTS

To Clean and Cure Poultry Feathers

When feathers are to be cured for home use it is best to take the feathers into a shed, to prevent them blowing about. In the event of the feathers having been kept in a damp place, they will be stuck together and must be separated.

When sorting, throw out any feathers which are dirty or have blood or bits of skin on them. Have a box to put these in to keep them out of the way. Do not throw the tail or wing feathers away, as they can be stripped and mixed with the good feathers. Any feathers with stiff quills should also be picked out and stripped. Put into a bag. Wash in disinfectant. Rinse in clean water. Dry and bake in a warm but not hot oven or in an outside boiler previously dried and warmed.

To Clean Carpets and Rugs

To revive the colours, wash over with a cloth wrung out in vinegar and water or salt and water after the carpet has been cleaned. If very dirty, wash with foam from detergent solution.

To Clean Tapestry

Rub well with warm bran.

To Clean a White Felt Hat

Place the hat on a clean table or paper. Throw a few handfuls of maize meal on the hat and dry clean in the usual way, rubbing it in with a cloth. This rubs up the felt. To restore the smooth appearance, rub gently with a clean soft cloth or brush.

To Clean Leather-covered Furniture

Rub transparent or neutral coloured boot polish well in and polish with a soft cloth.

To Clean Glassware

All tumblers, glass bowls, etc., should be washed in a lather of soapy water. When thoroughly clean rinse in cold water, then dry with a clean glasscloth and before using polish with a similar cloth.

To Clean Decanters

Chop up a few peeled potatoes and place in the decanter and shake to keep crystal-clear.

Decanters which have been stained with wine can be made quite clean if a teaspoonful of raw rice is added to a little water inside the decanter, or a little coarse salt and vinegar used. Shake the decanter well and rinse in cold water.

To Clean Windows

(a) Apply paraffin oil with a cloth. Leave for 10 minutes, then polish with a soft cloth. This will deter flies.

(b) A rag dipped in methylated spirits will remove dimness and dirt.

To Clean Mirrors

Never use water for mirrors as if water gets behind the mirror, it will cause discoloration; use methylated spirits and polish well.

To Clean Sponges

If a bath sponge becomes slimy try the following:—
(a) Immerse in vinegar and water, or,
(b) immerse in 30 g. (2 oz.) of washing soda and water for 2 hours.

To Clean a Porcelain Bath

Use paraffin or petrol on a soft rag and dry well. This keeps a bath clean and shiny and is better than powders which scratch the surface and in time make the bath difficult to clean.

Remove rust stains

(a) by covering the marks with a mixture of paraffin and bath brick and leaving for 2 hours.

(b) with spirits of salts diluted with water.

(c) with detergents.

To Clean a Water Filter

Take the filter to pieces and remove the candles. Place these in a basin of lukewarm water and scrub off the slimy dirt with a clean brush. Soak the candles for an hour in a solution of permanganate of potash and water, then rinse in clean boiled water and replace in filter. This should be done at least every 10 days.

To Clean Shoes

When too liberal an amount of polish has been used, rub with a sliced half lemon, allow to dry, then polish in the usual way with shoe cream. Boots and shoes are apt to harden after getting wet, so to make them recover their original softness wipe off all dirt with a cloth, then rub dubbin well into them. After a little while the leather will become more pliable. Polish in the usual way.

To Clean Ivory

Prepare a paste of french chalk, sal volatile and olive oil, rub on the ivory and leave to dry. Then brush off.

To Wash Hair Brushes

Use lukewarm soapy water to which 1 teaspoon of paraffin or ammonia has been added. Rinse in lukewarm water in which a pinch of soda bicarbonate has been dissolved. This will keep the bristles white. In the last rinsing water put 1 teaspoon of alum or salt, previously dissolved in hot water, to stiffen the bristles. Plunging in really cold water immediately after washing also stiffens the bristles.

To Clean Silver

(a) (Suitable for table silver.) Wash the articles in warm water to which a little ammonia has been added, rinse and allow to drain, dry well and polish with a soft cloth.

(b) Clean with powdered whitening or plate powder moistened with water or methylated spirits. When dry, brush off and polish.

(c) Wash silver in soap suds, dry well, then polish with a chamois leather and a little plate powder.

(d) **For Indian Silver,** make a paste with a tablespoon of olive oil and camphorated chalk. Rub this over the article with a toothbrush then wash in warm soapy water and dry with a soft cloth, finally polishing with a soft pad and a small amount of camphorated chalk.

Indian silver, no matter how badly discoloured, will become brilliant by this method.

To Clean Brass and Copper

Kitchen utensils of brass and copper should not be cleaned with metal polish but with salt and lemon juice or vinegar. Wash in hot water and polish with a clean cloth.

Brass and copper ornaments or chests should be cleaned with metal polish thinned down with a little paraffin. Rub with a rag and finally polish with a newspaper. This does away with cloths which are always difficult to wash.

Floor Polish

(a) A mixture of beeswax and turpentine makes an excellent polish for linoleum and all types of polished floors. The wax should be shredded or grated finely and turpentine added in the proportion of 300 ml. ($\frac{1}{2}$ pint) to 60 gm. (2 oz.) wax. The mixture should be placed in a jam jar or other vessel with a wide mouth and stood in a basin of boiling water until the wax has melted. It should be stirred occasionally but on no account should the polish be allowed to stand on or in the vicinity of a fire, on account of the inflammable nature of the turpentine.

(b) Another good floor polish is made as follows: melt a tin of ordinary floor polish and add $\frac{1}{2}$ bottle of paraffin and stir well. When cold this will be found to be of a creamy consistency and easy to apply evenly and is very economical.

(c) A good non-slip floor polish is made by mixing together equal parts of linseed oil, turpentine and vinegar. Always mix thoroughly before using and just rub in gently.

(d) WOODWORK. Here is a good preparation for oiling all woodwork, floors, doors, etc. Mix well together in the proportion of $\frac{1}{2}$ bottle raw linseed oil, $\frac{1}{2}$ bottle turpentine, $\frac{1}{4}$ bottle vinegar and $\frac{1}{4}$ bottle fresh lime or lemon juice. Always shake this mixture well before applying.

To Remove Hot Water Marks from a Polished Surface.

Make a paste of linseed oil and salt and apply to the mark. Leave to soak in, for some hours, then polish with a soft cloth. Camphorated oil rubbed on a small discoloration darkens the spot and makes it almost imperceptible.

Staining Wood. Sandpaper the wood to make it smooth. Dissolve permanganate crystals in hot (not boiling) water and apply with a pad of rag tied at the end of a stick. Leave for 24 hours. Rub linseed oil well in and leave for another 24 hours. Then apply turpentine on a cloth and polish well.

Glossy Paintwork should never be treated with soap, which leaves a smeary surface, but a teaspoonful of turpentine in warm water will make the cleaning simple. This method also does away with the danger of scratching the paint.

GENERAL HOUSEHOLD HINTS

Butter. If it is tainted, knead it in cold water to which a pinch of soda bicarbonate has been added and leave it soaking for about 2 hours, when the butter should be absolutely fresh.

Wool that has been unravelled can be made to look fresh and new if it is wound round a thin piece of cardboard and held over the steam of a kettle.

New Uses for Old Brushes

(*a*) Old shaving brushes may be used for extracting dust from ledges which cannot be reached with a duster.

(*b*) Old tooth brushes can be used to clean embossed silver or brass, for applying paint on small articles or polish on shoes.

(*c*) To sweep walls, tie a duster or piece of cloth on an old broomhead and rub gently over wall to collect the dust.

Bread Saving. Save all your outside crusts not wanted for any other purpose, dry them in a slow oven and when cool pound or roll them until finely crumbed. A bottle, pint size, makes a good crusher.

Soap Saving. Collect the old pieces of soap then chop them or shred thinly and put in an empty tin with cold water. Place the tin on to the stove and leave till the soap is dissolved. When cold this sets into a jelly and can be used in the kitchen. Scraps of white soap should be kept separate from the blue soap as the white soap jelly is useful for washing woollens and fine articles. Scented and coloured soaps should not be used for this purpose.

Silk or Nylon Stockings that are laddered beyond repair make an excellent medium for knitting floor rugs. Start cutting from the top of the leg round and round the stocking till the heel is reached. Wind into balls after sewing pieces together.

Vinegar Economy. When you buy a new bottle of vinegar pour half into the old empty bottle, fill up both bottles with cold boiled water and allow to stand three or four days, when the vinegar will be up to strength again.

Tea Economy. You will find that if you crush your tea on a board (not to a dust) you will need to use only half the quantity of tea, in fact a little less than half. This is a great saving in a large family and the particles do not float about in the tea.

If Bread or Cake has become stale, brush it over with a little cold milk and bake in the oven for 20 minutes. It will be crisp and appetising again after this treatment.

Before Boiling Milk, rinse the pan with cold water. The milk is less liable to burn.

Kitchen Sinks. To clear a waste pipe, put a handful of washing soda down the pipe and pour over it half a cupful of vinegar. Leave for some hours, then pour boiling water down the pipe.

To Prevent Paraffin Lamp Smoking

Soak the wick in strong vinegar and dry before using and the flame will then burn clear and bright.

Nailing

Should you experience difficulty in knocking in a nail, thrust the nail or tack through a piece of stiff paper and you will find that it will thus be kept in the correct position for hammering instead of being held by the fingers.

To Remove Glass Stoppers

Apply glycerine freely round the stopper and leave for several hours, when the glycerine will have worked its way down between the stopper and the neck of the bottle. Then gently tap the stopper with another glass stopper.

Another method is to wrap a cloth dipped in boiling water round the bottle up to the neck; the bottle will swell and the stopper can then be easily removed.

LAUNDRY NOTES

GENERAL RULES FOR WASHING DAY

New table linen, sheets, etc., should always be soaked first for some hours in cold water to which a little salt has been added, in order to extract any chemicals that may have been used in manufacture.

Silk goods and artificial silks do not require very hot water.

Nylons should be washed in fairly hot water.

Woollens require warm, soapy water and should never be rubbed but always squeezed and shaken about in the water.

In East Africa it is unwise to dry clothes on grass or bushes, on account of harmful insects which lay their eggs on the clothing. Should clothes require to be bleached they must be boiled after bleaching.

Preparation for Washing Clothes

1. Remove stains.
2. Sort the clothes and divide into heaps according to the method of washing:—
   (a) White clothes.
   (b) Handkerchiefs. Keep separate. If used by any one with a bad cold, salt should be sprinkled on them and they should be left to soak.
   (c) Coloured clothes.
   (d) Woollens.
   (e) Silks, laces and fine things generally.

Washing White Clothes

1. Soak overnight if possible, but always for some hours.
2. Wash by rubbing in hot water with soap.
3. Rinse to remove dirty water.
4. Boil for 20 minutes to $\frac{1}{2}$ hour in water to which a little melted soap or soda has been added. Boiling helps to make clothes a good colour.
5. After boiling, turn out into cold water and rinse.
6. Shake clothes out well and put into blue water.
7. Starch if necessary and hang to dry.

Washing Coloured Clothes

1. Wash articles quickly, one by one, in warm, soapy water, not hot, as colour might run.
2. Rinse well and if colour is coming out add a handful of salt, which helps to fix the colour.
3. Starch and hang to dry in a shady place.

Washing Woollens

1. Avoid extremes of heat and cold.
2. Do not rub on soap.
3. Use no soda.
4. Shake to remove dust.
5. Wash each garment separately, by kneading and squeezing (do not rub) in warm, soapy water. Use soap flakes or melted soap to make the lather. If woollens are very greasy use a little ammonia in the washing water.
6. Rinse in warm water.
7. If desired, white woollens may be blued at this stage in warm, pale-blue water.
8. Shake out well. Hang to dry in a warm, airy place, or if likely to lose its shape, lay the garment out on a clean sheet or towel.

Washing Silk and Fine Articles

1. Wash gently in warm, soapy water to which, for white silk, 1 teaspoon of paraffin may be added to prevent yellowing.

2. Squeeze out. Do not wring, as fine threads are apt to break if twisted.

3. Rinse in warm and then in cold water.

4. White silk may be blued.

5. For silk, if slight stiffness is required, a little melted gum (about 10 g. (⅓ oz.) gum to 5 litres (1 gallon) water) or 1 tablespoon methylated spirit should be put in the last rinsing water. Lace may be stiffened either with gum water or starch. The garment should then be ironed dry.

6. Roll in towel and let towel absorb some of the moisture. Silk should be ironed damp, except tussore silk, which should be hung out of doors and ironed when dry.

IRONING

Hot Water Starched Clothes

1. Dry completely.
2. Damp, sprinkling water evenly.
3. Roll up tightly and leave for some hours.
4. Iron with a hot iron.

Coloured Clothes (unstarched)

1. Half dry and then iron.
2. If dark-coloured material, iron on wrong side.

Woollens

1. When almost dry, press with warm, not hot, iron.
2. Air well.

Silk

Iron wet or very damp.

Lace or Embroidered Articles

1. Iron very damp.
2. Place on a thick flannel pad and iron on wrong side. A piece of muslin may be spread over the article at first, in case the iron sticks.

DRY CLEANING

Dry Cleaning may be done at home with a dry-cleaning preparation, but please follow the instructions carefully. Always hang garment out of doors. Never use spirit near heated iron or flame.

REMOVAL OF STAINS

NOTE:— (a) Always rub towards the centre of a stain.

(b) Try simple remedies before more drastic ones.

(c) Try an enzyme detergent.

251

Animal Stains, *e.g.,* blood, perspiration, etc.
1. Soak in cold water
2. Wash, put into lukewarm water and boil.
3. Bleach in the sun.

Vegetable Stains, *e.g.,* tea, coffee, fruit, etc.
1. Should stain still be wet, put the stained part of the article over a basin or soup plate and pour on boiling water. Try rubbing borax on the stain if necessary.
2. For a firmly fixed stain, use a little chloride of lime, being careful not to burn the material. Dissolve 30 g. (1 oz.) chloride of lime in 300 ml. (½ pint) cold water.

Mineral Stains, *e.g.,* ink, iron, rust, etc.
1. Try milk, sour if posssible, the juice of a lemon, a green tomato or vinegar.
2. If unsuccessful use salts of lemon, which needs care as it is poisonous. Dissolve 1 teaspoon of salts of lemon in ½ cup of boiling water and apply to strain with a small stick, dipped in the liquid. Ammonia may also be tried.

Other Stains
1. COCOA STAINS. Soak the article in a quart of hot water to which has been added a tablespoon of borax. Leave for 1 hour.
2. COFFEE STAINS. Cover the article with glycerine and leave for 1 hour. Then rinse in warm water.
3. GREASE. Use benzine, ammonia or petrol. Eucalyptus oil is very good for removing stains from silk and delicate fabrics. Put a piece of old towel under the stain. Rub in the cleaning agent with another clean cloth till stained part is clean and dry. Always change to a clean place on both cloths as they become soiled.
4. INK. Remove with methylated spirit or milk.
5. MARKING INK. While wet wash in cold water, but if the ink is dry soak in chloride of lime solution and then in ammonia.
6. MILDEW. Rub over with soap and then cover with chalk. Put on soap and chalk from time to time. This stain is difficult to remove but with patience it will come out. Another method is to damp stain with lemon juice, sprinkle with salt and leave for some days.

    MILDEW ON A LARGE SURFACE: Melt 2 teaspoons of salts of lemon in 600 ml. (1 pint) of boiling water in a small basin. Dip the affected parts only in the water till stain disappears.

    As salts of lemon is a deadly poison it must be most carefully used and on no account left lying about.
7. PAINT. Use turpentine, rubbing with a circular movement towards the centre of the stain.

8. SEA WATER STAINS should be treated with a little vinegar and water.

9. TAR. Rub with olive oil or butter; afterwards wash with hot water and soap or clean with benzine.

10. TEA STAINS. Wet and cover thickly with yellow soap. Set aside for about ½ hour, then wash in the ordinary way. Another way is to damp and cover with carbonate of soda and place in the sun for a short while before rinsing.

11. WINE STAINS. These can be removed from light silk by placing over the spots pads of cotton soaked in cold water. Do not rub the mark as this will spread it. If it is obstinate sprinkle on a little salt and continue with the moistened cotton pads. Dry with a warm iron.

To Make Blue Water

Tie a square of blue in a piece of flannel, squeeze in a bath of cold water until the water, lifted in the hand, appears sky-blue.

To Remove Scorch Marks from Linen

1. Rub the place with the juice of a raw lemon and dry in the sun.

2. Damp a cloth and on it put a little chloride of lime. With this, rub over the mark which will disappear. Later finish with an iron, not too hot.

To Wash Chamois Leather

Use same method as for woollens but put soap in the rinsing water (leaving soap in the leather). When hung to dry, rub occasionally to soften.

To Whiten Linen

Bleach on grass in the sun. Spread article wet on the grass, in strong sunlight. When it dries, sprinkle with water. Repeat this process several times. Wash in the usual way, taking care to boil bleached clothes.

Starching Clothes

TO MAKE COLD WATER STARCH:—

2 tablespoons starch	1 breakfast cup water
1 teaspoon borax powdered	1 dessertspoon turpentine
	½ teacup boiling water

1 teaspoon scraped and melted white curd soap or a shred of a wax candle.

Have the articles for starching washed and dried thoroughly and rub them between the hands to ensure that all old starch has been removed.

Put starch in a basin and mix with a little cold water until quite smooth. Put borax and soap into a teacup and fill half full with boiling water. Add the remainder of the cold water to the blended starch, then the melted soap and borax and lastly the turpentine. This starch is just the proper stiffness for collars, cuffs and shirts.

Put each article into this mixture and soak thoroughly. Remove and squeeze fairly dry. Have a large clean towel ready and lay each article side by side on the towel; roll up the towel firmly and set aside for $\frac{1}{2}$ hour, when the starched articles are ready to be ironed with a very hot iron.

HOT WATER STARCH (for table linen, curtains, cotton frocks, etc.)

Use 1 tablespoon of starch to 600 ml. (1 pint) water. Mix to a smooth and stiff paste with cold water. Then pour boiling water slowly over the dissolved starch, stirring all the time until the mixture loses its whiteness and becomes clear like jelly. The starch is now sufficiently cooked. If hard water is used, borax in the proportion of 1 teaspoon to a tablespoon of dry starch should be added. The clear hot starch must be thinned down with cold water to the consistency required.

Water from boiled rice is preferable to starch for fine fabrics such as lawns or muslins.

Sticky Irons. When ironing starched articles and the iron gets sticky with starch rub it on a piece of soap or candle and polish the iron on a piece of brown paper.

Table Linen. It will not be necessary to starch table linen if a tablespoon of methylated spirit is added to the last rinsing water. This makes the linen glossy.

Coat Collars which become soiled long before the rest of the garment requires cleaning, can be freshened by sponging with pure alcohol in which a little salt has been dissolved.

WASHING-MACHINE WISDOM

If you possess a washing machine, always follow the intructions for your particular model. Take care to note the heat of the water, the length of time required for each wash and the quantity of soap powder necessary for the size of the machine.

MEDICINE CUPBOARD

Have a lock-up cupboard in a convenient place out of reach of children.

All prescribed medicines, sedative mixtures, sleeping tablets, antibiotics, etc., should be kept in a separate locked box inside the medicine cupboard if possible.

All tablets, especially those chocolate-coated or brightly coloured, which might be mistaken for sweets, *must* be kept out of reach of children.

Keep **External Applications** separate from Internal Medicines.
Suggestions for External Applications:—

Dettol ⎫
Acriflavine or Iodine ⎬ Antiseptics for cuts
Liniments   for painful joints
Calamine lotion   for rashes and skin irritations
Bicarbonate of soda   ditto, also for first aid treatment for burns
     and scalds.

Methylated spirit
Dusting powder

Suggestions for **Internal Medicines:—**

Aperients, *e.g.* Liver Salts, Epsom Salts, Cascara or Senna.
Aspirin or Disprin for children.
Glucose D.

Keep a **First Aid Box** easily accessible containing:—

Adhesive tape
Bandages of different sizes
Boracic lint
Cotton wool
Dressings, clean pieces of soft linen or cotton
Mild disinfectant, e.g. Dettol, in liquid and solid form
Scissors
Safety pins

HOME REMEDIES

Bruises. If you shut your finger or foot in a door or bruise it in any way, put it in water as hot as you can bear, then in cold water and hot alternately.

Burns. Apply linen rags soaked in soda bicarbonate solution.

Fishbone in throat. If a fishbone sticks in the throat, do not try to remove it with a finger or forceps. Give fresh bread to eat in large pieces. If this is not effective give an emetic when the bone should be ejected with the bread. Should the bone still remain unmoved, try sucking a lemon. The juice gives relief and in time dissolves the bone. It may, however, be necessary to get medical assistance.

Fomentation. Take a bowl, place a towel (to be used as a wringer) across it and put either boracic lint (for an open wound) or flannel (for external use) in the towel. Pour on boiling water. Fold over the sides of the towel, with flannel inside. Take hold of the ends and wring out the water thoroughly. Apply but see that there is no moisture or it will blister the skin. Cover with fine cotton cloth or waterproof material and cotton wool and bandage.

Nairobi Eye (bite from Nairobi Fly). Milk, calamine lotion or soda bicarbonate applied at once will give relief.

Prickly Heat. Apply a thick paste of milk and bicarbonate of soda at night and dust well with powder, or calamine lotion, through the day.

Ringworm. Paint the spot with iodine daily until the ringworm disappears. Ordinary ink has been known to be an equally good cure.

Scalds. Spread scald immediately with dry bicarbonate of soda and cover with cloth, leaving on until heat is entirely extracted. If it is impossible to apply soda immediately, a solution must then be made with bicarbonate of soda and water (1 teaspoon to 1 pint) or salt water and the scalded part of the body immersed in it.

Sea Urchin Spines. Apply sliced pawpaw to the affected part and bandage to keep in place.

Sore Lips. When the lips of a fever patient begin to get cracked and sore, apply equal parts of lemon juice and glycerine with a small piece of cotton cloth. This proves most soothing.

Stings:
ANTS. Some ants sting by injecting formic acid; counteract by applying an alkali, bicarbonate of soda, ammonia, soap or anti-histamine ointment.

BEES. Remove sting if possible, then apply methylated spirit or bicarbonate of soda or blue bag. Treat for shock if necessary.

CATERPILLARS, CENTIPEDES, HORNETS, SPIDERS. Apply ammonia, bicarbonate of soda or anti-histamine ointment.

WASPS. Apply vinegar.

Substitute for Ice. When ice for external use is ordered for a patient and is not obtainable, mix in a basin equal proportions of methylated spirits and milk. Dip a cloth in the lotion and apply. This is the coolest lotion you can make.

Toothache. A pinch of alum, pushed into the cavity, will often give relief, as will a piece of cotton wool dipped in spirits or in oil of cloves.

Wash for coated tongue. An excellent tooth and mouth wash during illness is made by adding 2 teaspoons of lemon juice or $\frac{1}{2}$ teaspoon of soda bicarbonate to a glass of water. This wash will remove tartar and sweeten the breath.

Warts
(a) A quick way to cure warts is to take a piece of washing soda, damp it and rub the wart two or three times a day with it.

(b) Rub wart with a piece of Sodom Apple (little yellow apples which grow wild in the bush). Apply every night for 3 weeks. The wart will disappear.

POISONS

To counteract a poison give an emetic which will cause vomiting. The normal emetic consists of 1 tablespoon salt or 1 tablespoon mustard in 300 ml. (½ pint) water. For young children a third to a half of these quantities will be sufficient.

Alcohol. Administer any quantity of black coffee.

Arsenic (Rat Poison, Paris Green, etc.). Give an emetic and, when this has acted, give plenty of magnesia, lime water, raw egg and milk. Large doses of castor oil afterwards are essential to clear out the system.

Chloral. Give an emetic, then apply friction and warmth to the body, while artificial respiration may be necessary. The patient should be kept awake and stimulated by whisky.

Chloroform and Ether. Render artificial respiration and give free access to fresh air. The patient's head must be kept lower than the hips.

Iodine. Give an emetic and, when this has acted, give starch water, boiled potatoes in milk, or egg and milk drinks.

Lysol. Give olive oil in plenty and egg albumen.

Opium, Morphine or Cocaine. Give an emetic, then very strong coffee or tea. Keep the patient awake by striking the body with wet towels. Artificial respiration may be necessary.

Phosphorus, Matches, etc. Give an emetic of turpentine (1 teaspoon in a tumbler of water) and when this has acted give magnesia or albumen in water but never butter or oil.

Strychnine. Give an emetic, then charcoal or tannin in large quantities. Large doses of alcohol may be tried.

Toadstools or False Mushrooms.—Give an emetic and then whisky or brandy. Apply friction to the body and a mustard plaster over the stomach in severe cases.

Unknown Poisons. Give great draughts of lukewarm water or milk, at once, to dilute the poison, then raw eggs in milk. If the patient collapses, give strong coffee, tea, brandy or whisky as a stimulant.

THE DESTRUCTION OF HOUSEHOLD PESTS

COCKROACHES

These are filthy pests and although they will lay their eggs in cracks and furniture joints and other warm places, e.g. behind cookers, refrigerators and in electrical meter boxes and fittings, they very much prefer living inside drains, particularly the first inspection chamber from the kitchen and from the toilet.

Cockroaches mainly infest kitchens and bathrooms, though in a heavily infested house they will spread to bedrooms, in cupboards, on shelves, etc.

Two or three treatments are recommended in a heavily infested house. Use liquid insecticide which is more effective.

1. Diazinon 60% concentrate is the best liquid insecticide on the market. Powdered insecticides are coming increasingly on to the market, e.g. Baygon cockroach killer. Many Aerosols, particularly those with residual effect, are recommended.

2. Pesticidal varnish. This is applied in small quantities in all places frequented by cockroaches and has a longer life than any other treatment. This could also be mixed with paint when redecorating the house. It will be effective for more than one year.

3. Insecticidal smoke generators have been operative for many years and are still useful. Rooms should be sealed before use and the treatment should be repeated every three months if any sign of re-infestation is noticed.

Last and not least in the control of cockroaches is thorough cleanliness. All preparation tables and dining tables should be scrubbed thoroughly. Pay special attention to the undersides where there may be cracks. Keep your cookers and refrigerators clean, check your electrical fittings occasionally, and, above all, keep all drains clean. Food remains should be disposed of speedily from the kitchen.

FLY CONTROL.

There are many species of flies but the two main kinds of domestic concern are *Musca Domestica* (house fly) and *Crysomia Putoria* (blue fly). The house fly breeds in all decomposing matter both of animal or vegetable origin. Blue fly is mainly found in pit latrines, faeces, animal dung or dead and decomposing flesh of any animal.

Control of breeding sites is vital, and the following should be followed:—

1. House refuse should be buried or burnt or turned into compost.

2. Trenching of refuse heaps or tips should be practised at all times where these are made. Troughs should either be filled with water or sprayed from time to time.

3. Animal manure should either be spread immediately on land to dry or turned into compost.

4. Special attention should be given to refuse storage, and receptacles should always be kept clean and covered.
5. In case of blue fly these could be controlled by regular inspection of latrines and the adjoining ground.
6. Provide light traps in latrines.
7. All food attractive to flies should be covered with screens.
8. Extensive and regular use of insecticides is not recommended as flies easily become resistant to most of the common varieties. However these have to be used occasionally to destroy any flies, mainly in the kitchen.

To-day there are many impregnated strips which can be used in the presence of food. Household aerosols are usually available in the market and all these are safe. They are mainly made of pyrethrum sprays which have a good knock-down effect.

Fly baits have also been found useful. Baygon baits have been used with success in many households.

Formalin Baits can easily be made by mixing 3 teaspoonfuls of Formalin with 2 teaspoonfuls of sugar and 1 teaspoonful of water.

The mixture is normally placed in trays at heights where children cannot reach. In extensive spraying, D.D.T. or B.H.C. should be used.

ANTS.

The common species are sugar ants, brown ants, black ants, and safari ants.
1. Dust the external walls of the house with a D.D.T./Diazinon dusting powder.
2. In the house use a wet cloth dipped into a solution of Dieldrin and wipe all along the edges and window sills. *Dieldrin is poisonous —keep it away from food.*
3. Hunt for breeding nests. Normally they are built in the garden and once found should be dusted with a D.D.T./Diazinon dusting powder.
4. Baits of various varieties are now available in the market. The old Borax bait is still in use today. Residual spraying is not necessary.

BEES.

They are dangerous and should be reported immediately to the nearest Health Office. If only a few are in the house, use a spray of Dieldrin or Lindane.

Survey for nests occasionally and remove them from the living areas.

MOSQUITOES.

Mosquitoes will breed in dirty or clean water, in drains, waste water pits, latrines, septic tanks, rain-water pools, swamps or any other receptacle which is likely to hold water during the rainy seasons.

The most effective method of mosquito control is to reduce the number of breeding places.

All drains should be kept clean and if they have water, it should be running and all obstructions should be removed. Old tins, bottles, etc., should be buried or placed in bins for proper disposal.

Latrines, soakage pits, septic tanks should be checked from time to time. Tanks should be screened from mosquitoes and where a breeding has been discovered it should be dealt with immediately. A solution of Diazinon 60% or Coopers Fluid will kill larvae and stop further breeding.

Long grass and weeds harbour adult mosquitoes. Such vegetation should be cut down. All ground should be well drained.

Pyrethrum sprays could be used in the house in the evening if mosquitoes are discovered. There are also aerosols of different types available and all these could be used.

Residual spraying could be carried out with the following water wettable powders, D.D.T. B.H.C. and Dieldrin.

Many people mistake other insects for mosquitoes. Mosquitoes only bite in the evening or very early in the morning but hide in dark corners, under beds and behind the curtains during the day. All such places should be checked. When you are in doubt specimens should be taken to a Communicable Diseases Control Section for identification. Advice is given free on simple means of control.

BED BUGS.

1. Use a good residual insecticide such as D.D.T., Diazinon, Malathion, etc.

2. Apply liberally by means of a coarse sprayer or by a brush. A flit gun does not apply sufficient liquid to be effective.

3. Treat beds, mattresses, chairs, cupboards and walls of the rooms affected.

4. Insecticidal varnish is effective for a long time if the affected places are kept clean.

This is another pest which can be controlled through good clean habits.

FLEAS.

If you are going away and leaving the house empty, dust floors, carpets, settees, etc., liberally with insect powder before you go. It is not pleasant to come back to a house full of fleas and they are extremely difficult to get rid of once well established.

If you have neglected to take this precaution and find fleas established use a mixture of pyrethrum and D.D.T. powder. Sweep it into cracks in floors and dust it into carpets and chairs. Repeat after a week. Diazinon or Malathion can be used if D.D.T. fails.

Dogs and other animals should always be kept clean and free from fleas.

CARE OF HOUSEHOLD PETS

Pamphlets and advice are available on the care, feeding and treatment of all pets from the K.S.P.C.A., P.O. Box 157, Nairobi.

The K.S.P.C.A. will recommend kennels and catteries in which to leave your pet whilst on holiday or if the bitch or cat is in season.

To control ticks and fleas on dogs the K.S.P.C.A. advises a weekly bath in Dieltox or similar preparation.

To control fleas and ticks on cats the K.S.P.C.A. recommends the use of Gammatox powder.

Puppies should always be de-wormed as soon as possible and once in three months it is beneficial for a dog to have a worm powder.

Dogs are better guards if they are kept inside at night.

CAMPING HINTS

The housewife who finds herself responsible for getting a camping holiday ready will find it best to prepare a list of everything necessary beforehand and to check off the list as the packing proceeds. This list should be kept for future occasions and altered as experience suggests. Careful, well thought out packing makes a difference to the number of boxes required and to the speed with which camp can be struck. It pays to have a special place in each box for each article and to return them to their proper places.

For provisions much depends on the district to which one is going and the tastes of the campers. Each district differs in what it can supply fresh to the camp, but milk, eggs and fowls can usually be obtained, sometimes fresh vegetables and fruit.

Water is an important item for drinking, washing etc.

There are numerous types of water containers available. A canvas water bag known as a "chargul" can be carried on the outside of a car when travelling, and hung in the shade of a tree, is most useful.

Large petrol tins can be filled up with water.

A piece of wood screwed into position across the top of a petrol tin from which the top part has been removed facilitates handling and the tin can then be used for heating water over a camp fire.

Cooking can be done on a piece of sheet iron, 1 metre by $\frac{1}{2}$ metre, in which holes have been cut. Place this on top of a small 3-sided wall built with stones and make a fire underneath.

Baking powder
Bath
Beds and bedding
Bowls (plastic)
Bread
Butter
Cakes
Candles

Cheese
Cups
Cutlery
Dried fruit
Eggs
Flour
Fruit (fresh)
Kettle
Lamps
Lard (or oil)

Mustard
Matches
Panga
Pepper
Petrol and oil
   (spare cans)
Plates
Rice and cereals

Salt
Saucepans or
   sufurias
Soap
Sugar
Soft drinks
Tea and coffee
Teapot
Tinned biscuits
Tinned fruit

Tinned meat
Tinned milk
Tinned vegetables
Toilet paper
Towels
Vegetables, fresh

and never forget

WATER
TIN OPENER
CORKSCREW
FIRST AID BOX

For comfort and convenience the following items may be hired in Nairobi at reasonable rates:—

Camp beds
Camping gas cookers
Camping gas heaters
Camping gas lamps
Canvas bath or wash basin
Canvas bucket
Canvas bottle coolers
Canvas water bags (Charguls)
Chairs, folding

Cooking utensils, cutlery and
   crockery
Cool box
Gas cylinders (spares)
First Aid box
Tables, dining and cooking
Tents
Vacuum Flasks
Water containers.

SWAHILI SECTION

A LIST OF USEFUL WORDS AND PHRASES

HOUSE AND KITCHEN

PLEASE	TAFADHALI	Cork	Kizibo
THANK YOU	ASANTE	Corkscrew	Kitu cha kufungua chupa
Ashes	Majivu	Cup	Kikombe
Bacon	Nyama ya nguruwe	Curry	Mchuzi
Bag	Mfuko	Curtains	Vitambaaa vya dirisha
Bananas	Ndizi		
Basin	Bakuli	Danger	Hatari
Basket	Kikapo	Dates	Tende
Bath	Birika ya kuogea	Dining room	Chumba cha kulia
Beans	Kunde	Dinner	Chakula cha jioni
Bed	Kitanda	Door	Mlango
Bedding	Matandiko	Drawer	Mtota
Bedroom	Chumba cha kulalia	Dressing table	Meza ya kioo
Beef	Nyama ya ng'ombe	Duck	Bata
Bell	Kengele	Dust	Vumbi
Black polish	Rangi nyeusi ya viatu	Duster	Kitambaa cha vumbi
Book	Kitabu		
Bottle	Chupa	Eggs	Mayai
Brains	Ubongo	Fat	Mafuta
Bread	Mkate	Fire	Moto
Breakfast	Chakula cha asubuhi	Firewood	Kuni
		Fish	Samaki
Broom	Ufagio	Floor polish	Rangi kwa chini
Brown polish	Rangi nyekundu ya viatu	Flour	Unga
		Flowers	Maua
Bucket	Ndoo	Food	Chakula
Butter	Siagi	Fork	Uma
		Fruit	Matunda
Cake	Keki	Frying pan	Kango
Candles	Mishumaa		
Carafe	Jagi ya maji	Grapes	Zabibu
Carpet	Zulia	Gravy	Mchuzi
Carrots	Karoti		
Chair	Kiti	House	Nyumba
Charcoal	Makaa	Ice	Barafu
Cheese	Jibini	Iron	Pasi
Chicken	Kuku		
Clock	Saa	Jug	Jagi
Coconut	Nazi	Kettle	Birika
Coffee	Kahawa	Keys	Funguo
Coffee pot	Birika ya kahawa	Kidney	Figo
Comb	Kitana	Kitchen	Jikoni
Cook	Mpishi	Knife	Kisu

263

Lamp	Taa	Room	Chumba
Lettuce	Saladi	Salt	Chumvi
Lemon	Ndimu	Saucer	Kisahani
or Lime		Scissors	Makasi
Liver	Ini	Sheets	Nguo za kitanda
Looking-glass	Kioo	Smoke	Moshi
		Soap	Sabuni
Lunch	Chakula cha mchana	Spoon	Kijiko
		Starch	Wanga
Maize cobs	Mahindi	Step-ladder	Ngazi
Mango	Embe	Stove	Jiko
Mat	Mkeka	String/thread	Uzi
Matches	Kiberiti	Sugar	Sukari
Mattress	Godoro		
Measure	Pima	Table	Meza
Meat	Nyama	Table-cloth	Nguo ya meza
Milk	Maziwa	Taste	Onja
Mirror	Kioo	Teapot	Birika ya chai
Mosquito net	Chandarua	Tin	Mkebe
Mushrooms	Uyoga	Tin-opener	Kisu cha kufungulia mkebe
Mustard	Mastadi		
Mutton	Nyama ya kondoo	Toast	Tosti
		Tongue	Ulimi
Napkin	Kitambaa kidogo cha meza	Towel	Tauli
		Tray	Sinia
Needle	Sindano	Tripe	Matumbo
Newspaper	Gazeti	Tumbler	Bilauri
Oil	Mafuta	Vegetables	Mboga
Onion	Kitunguu		
Orange	Chungwa	Walls	Kuta
Oven	Jiko	Wash (clothes)	Fua
Oxtail	Mkia wa ng'ombe	Wash (dishes)	Safisha
Paper	Karatasi		
Paraffin	Mafuta ya taa	Wash (hands)	Nawa mikono
Paw-paw	Papai		
Pen/Pencil	Kalamu	Water (cold)	Maji ya baridi
Pepper	Pili pili	Water (fresh)	Maji matamu
Picture	Picha	Water (boiling)	Maji ya kuchemk
Pillow	Mto		
Pineapple	Nanasi	Window	Dirisha
Plate	Sahani	Wipe	Pangusa
Pork	Nyama ya nguruwe		
Pot/pan	Sufuria	HEALTH	
Potatoes	Viazi	Accident	Nasibu
		Bandage	Kitambaa
Raisins	Zabibu	Burn	Mchomo
Refuse (waste)	Takataka	Blood	Damu
Rice	Mchele	Cut	Jeraha

264

Cough	Kukohoa	Also	Pia *or* tena
Diarrhoea	Kuhara	Alter	Badili
Dysentery	Kuhara damu	Always	Siku zote
Fever	Homa	Another	Ngine
Headache	Kichwa kibaya	Answer	Jibu
Medicine	Dawa	Angry	Kali
Ointment	Mafuta ya kupaka	Arrange	Panga
Pain	Umivu	Arrive	Fika
Plague	Tauni	Ask	Uliza
Poison	Sumu	Away	Mbali
Quinine	Kwinini	Ayah	Yaya
Rheumatism	Baridi ya bis		
Sickness	Ugonjwa	Bake	Oka
		Ball	Mpira
		Bathe	Oga

PARTS OF THE BODY

		Become	Kuwa
		Beat	Piga
Abdomen	Tumbo	Beat up	Funda
Arm	Mkono	together	
Body	Mwili	Begin	Anza
Brain	Akili	Behind	Nyuma
Chest	Kifua	Bird	Ndege
Ear	Sikio	Boots	Viatu
Elbow	Kisigino	Boil	Chemka
Eye	Jicho	Boil over	Furika
Face	Uso	Break	Vunja
Foot	Mguu	Bring	Leta
Finger	Kidole	Brush	Fagia
Hand	Mkono	Burn	Waka
Head	Kichwa	But	Lakini
Heart	Moyo		
Joint	Ungo	Call	Ita
Knee	Goti	Can (be able)	Kuweza
Leg	Mguu	Car	Motokaa
Lip	Mdomo	Car	Angalia
Mouth	Kanwa	(take care)	
Nail (finger)	Ukucha	Care	Tunza
Rib	Ubavu	(take care of)	
Stomach	Tumbo	Carry	Chukua
Teeth	Meno	Cat	Paka
		Catch	Kamata
		Change	Geuza
		Cheat	Danganya

GENERAL

		Child	Mtoto
Above	Juu	Choose	Chagua
Ache	Uma	Chop	Chanja
Add	Ongeza	Clean	Safisha
Afternoon	Alasiri	Come	Njoo
Afterwards	Halafu	Count	Hesabu
Ago	Tangu	Cover	Funika
Agree	Patana	Cut	Kata
Alone	Peke		

265

Danger	Hatari	Here	Hapa
Day	Siku	Hide	Ficha
Decrease	Pungua	Hit	Piga
Debt	Deni	Hold	Shika
Dig	Lima	How much ?	Bei gani ?
Dish up	Pakua	Hunger	Njaa
Dog	Mbwa	Husband	Bwana
Drive away	Fukuza	Hurry	Upesi
Dry (put	Anika juani	Hut	Kibanda
out to)			
Dry	Kauka	I	Mimi
(become)		If	Kama
		Increase	Ongeza
Easy	Rahisi	Insect	Dudu
Eat	Kula	Interrupt	Dakiza
Empty	Mwaga	Into	Ndani
Enquire	Uliza		
Enter	Ingia	Journey	Safari
Evening	Jioni	Jump	Ruka
Every	Kila		
Except	Ila	Keep	Weka
		Kill	Ua
Fall	Anguka	Know	Jua
Fasten	Funga		
Fault	Kosa	Ladder	Ngazi
Faithful	Aminifu	Large	Kubwa
Falsehood	Uwongo	Last	Mwisho
Far	Mbali	Late	Chelewa
Father	Baba	Lazy person	Mvivu
Fill	Jaza	Learn	Jifunza
Finish	Maliza	Lend	Kopesha
Fold	Kunja	Less	Kasa
Forget	Sahau	Letter	Barua
Fry	Kaanga	Liar	Mwongo
		Lift	Inua
Gather	Kusanya pamoja	Listen	Sikia
Gently	Taratibu	Lock	Funga
Get	Pata	Look	Tazama
Get up	Ondoka	Look for	Tafuta
Gift	Zawadi	Loose	Legea
Go	Kwenda	Lost	Potea
God	Mungu		
Goodbye	Kwa heri	Machine	Mashini
Goodness	Wema	Make	Fanya
Gun	Bunduki	Many	Tele
		Mark	Tia alama
Habit	Mazoezo	Measure	Pima
Half	Nusu	Meet	Kuta
Hat	Kofia	Mend	Tengeza
Hear	Sikia	Minute	Dakika
Heavy	Zito	Mishap	Nasibu
Help	Saidia	Mistake	Kosa

Mix	Changanya	Remove	Ondoa
Money	Fedha	Rest	Pumziko
Month	Mwezi	Retire	Endelea nyuma
Mouse	Panya mdogo	Return	Rudisha
		Reward	Zawadi
Name	Jina	Rub	Sugua
Near	Karibu	Run	Piga mbio
Never	Kamwe	Rust	Kutu
New	Mpya		
News	Habari		
Nice	Zuri	School	Skuli
Noise	Kelele	Search for	Tafuta
Now	Sasa	See	Ona
		Select	Chagua
Obey	Tii	Sell	Uza
Object	Kataa	Separate	Weka mbali
Often	Mara nyingi	Serve	Pukua
Old age	Uzee	Sew	Shona
Omit	Wacha	Shake	Sukasuka
On	Katika	Shame	Haya
Open	Fungua	Sharp	Kali
Overturn	Pindua	Shelf	Ubao
		Sing	Imba
Pass	Pita	Sit	Kaa
Pay	Lipa	Slowly	Pole pole
Peel	Ambua	Smell	Harufu
Place	Weka	Speak out	Sema sana
Pocket	Mfuko	Split	Pasua
Poor	Masikini	Stand	Simama
Pour	Tengeneza	Steal	Iba
Prepare	Weka tayari	Stones	Mawe
Price	Kiasi	Straight	Sawa
Prize	Zawadi	Stupid	Mjinga
Pull	Vuta	Swallow	Meza
Purse	Kifuko	Sweet	Tamu
Put	Weka		
Put out	Toa	Take	Shika
		Take away	Ondoa
Quarrel	Ugomvi	Taste	Onja
Question	Swali	Teach	Fundisha
Quick	Upesi	Tell	Ambia
		There	Huko
Rain	Mvua	Thief	Mwivi
Raise	Inua	Thing	Kitu
Rat	Panya	Throw away	Tupa
Raw	Bichi	Ticket	Tikiti
Ready	Tayari	Tie	Funga
Receive	Pokea	Time	Wakati
Red	Ekundu	Tired	Choka
Refuse	Kataa	Together	Pamoja
Remain	Baki	Tomorrow	Kesho

Under	Chini	
Unfasten	Fungua	
Until	Hata	
Upset	Pindua	
Use	Tumia	
Very	Sana	
Visitor	Mgeni	
Wages	Mshahara	
Wait	Ngoja	
Walk	Tembea	
Want	Taka	
Warm	Pasha moto	
Warn	Onya	
Waste	Haribu	
Weep	Lia	
What?	Nini?	
When?	Lini?	
Who?	Nani?	
Why?	Kwa nini?	
Wind	Upepo	
Work	Kazi	
Workman	Fundi	
Write	Andika	
Year	Mwaka	
Yes	Ndiyo	
Young	Changa	

TIME

Year	Mwaka
Month	Mwezi
Week	Juma
Morning	Asubuhi
Noon	Mchana
Evening	Jioni
Night	Usiku
Day	Siku
Today	Leo
Tomorrow	Kesho
Yesterday	Jana

DAYS OF WEEK

Sunday	Juma pili
Monday	Juma tatu
Tuesday	Juma nne
Wednesday	Juma tano
Thursday	Alhamisi
Friday	Ijumaa
Saturday	Juma mosi

NUMERALS

One	Moja
Two	Mbili
Three	Tatu
Four	Nne
Five	Tano
Six	Sita
Seven	Saba
Eight	Nane
Nine	Tisa
Ten	Kumi
Eleven	Kumi na moja
Twelve	Kumi na mbili
etc.	etc.
Twenty	Ishirini
Twenty-one	Ishirini na moja
etc.	etc.
Thirty	Thelathini
Thirty-one	Thelathini na moja
etc.	etc.
Forty	Arobaini
Fifty	Khamsini
Sixty	Sitini
Seventy	Sabaini
Eighty	Themanini
Ninety	Tisini
Hundred	Mia moja
Two hundred	Mia mbili

TIME OF DAY

7 a.m.	Saa moja
8 a.m.	Saa mbili
9 a.m.	Saa tatu
10. a.m.	Saa nne
11 a.m.	Saa tano
12 noon	Saa sita
1 p.m.	Saa saba
2 p.m.	Saa nane
3 p.m.	Saa tisa
4 p.m.	Saa kumi
5 p.m.	Saa kumi na moja
6 p.m.	Saa kumi na mbili
7 p.m.	Saa moja usiku
8 p.m.	Saa mbili usiku

INDEX

271

273

276

W

Y

Z